What's a Cook to Do?

Also by James Peterson

Essentials of Cooking
Glorious French Food
Sweet Wines
Simply Salmon
Vegetables
Fish and Shellfish
Splendid Soups
Sauces
The Duck Cookbook

What's a Cook to Do?

JAMES PETERSON

Published by Artisan
A Division of Workman Publishing Company, Inc.
225 Varick Street
New York, NY 10014-4381
www.artisanbooks.com

Library of Congress Cataloging-in-Publication Data

Pererson, James.
    What's a Cook to Do?
      p. cm.
    ISBN-13: 978-1-57965-318-7
    ISBN-10: 1-57965-318-9
    1. Cookery. I. Title.

TX651.P484 2006
641.5—dc22

                        2006042904

Design by Nicholas Caruso

Printed in China
First printing, March 2007

10 9 8 7 6 5 4 3 2 1

Contents

Introduction

Like any craft, cooking has its little tricks. It's these observations, short-cuts, and secrets, acquired during forty years in the kitchen, that I offer in *What's a Cook to Do?* I've tried to pass along what I've learned from teaching (students make every mistake there is to make); what I've learned by accident (working in restaurants where you need to think quickly in desperate situations); and what I've learned through the slow perfection of techniques repeated many times (sometimes day after day for years at a time).

If I've learned from my students' mistakes—the time the cherry tomatoes got left in the oven overnight and were the best I'd ever tasted—I've also learned as much from their far-ranging tastes and inquisitive minds. For instance, I am thinking of the student who taught me to use cilantro instead of parsley in the salsa or the one who was fascinated with cooking with organs and things that most of us don't like.

What I try to convey to them—and what I'd like to convey to you—is that most cooking is simple: a chop is sautéed, a fish roasted, a simple sauce whisked together. That you don't ever have to nervously follow recipes step by step if you learn how ingredients behave when exposed to heat, or what really happens when something braises or is poached or sautéed. You can acquire a sense of temperatures and times and know when things are done; that the fish is ready when a skewer slid through the back feels hot on your lip; that the broken mayonnaise can be fixed in a second with a tablespoon of the bottled stuff. You don't need to make a laborious vinaigrette to sauce a salad or labor on complicated sauces. With a few hints you can make a sauce as good as any restaurant in minutes.

This compact but chockful little book is organized with a basics sections up front, which is filled with tips about how to work more efficiently, including seemingly obvious suggestions such as buying an apron that's easy to tie and untie, and a slew of unexpected ones, such as why you can toss out your double boiler and your roasting rack. But the bulk of this book offers answers to all those questions that gave title to this book: from how to keep the butter from burning, how to bread cutlets, and how to store fresh herbs to when the heat should be high and when it should be low.

What's a Cook to Do? also includes a small etiquette section, because I will never forget the look on face of the wife of my French publisher when I mopped up my sauce with bread. When I asked her if that was rude, she said it was done only at home, not in a restaurant. "Oh." I said, "I so love this sauce and there's no other way to get at it." She advised me to tear the bread into minuscule pieces, one at a time, move it around the plate with the tip of my fork, and then eat it with the fork. While such nuances have largely gone the way of the first edition of Emily Post, other little tricks are more useful, such as how to signal the waiter when you're ready to order (stack the menus and put them to one side of the table) or that you've gotten up to go to the restroom and haven't left the table for good (leave your napkin on your chair, not on the table). There are also tips about how to set the table, what glass to use for what wine, and how to order wine in a restaurant.

My sincere hope is that this modest guide makes life easier in the kitchen and at the table. If you think of a tip to add or find something missing, send a note to *What's a Cook to Do?*, care of the publisher and we'll try to answer your concern either by letter, e-mail, or in the next edition.

What's a Cook to Do?

Good cooking is really the result of a collection of little things done well; it gives us pleasure when we perform these tasks quickly and effortlessly. But kitchen chores can be frustrating if we don't have the right tools, our knives are dull, or we don't know the right shortcuts. In this chapter you'll find tips, hints, and advice to get you started and to give you confidence in the kitchen.

Tools, Techniques, and Advice

1 How to clean everything

Despite the variety of sprays and cleaners on the market, virtually anything can be cleaned with four inexpensive products: ammonia, detergent, bleach, or lye. However, none of them should ever be used together.

Ammonia

Because ammonia is a gas, if you buy clear plain ammonia and mix it with hot water and use it for surfaces such as stainless steel and, of course, glass, it leaves no residue or smear.

Detergent

When mixed with hot water, detergent dissolves fats and grease. On its own, detergent is neutralized quickly by fat, such as that on a greasy pot. Rinse off the fat with hot water before washing with detergent.

Bleach

Bleach is the best disinfectant there is; a good splash in a sink or bucket of hot water helps eliminate bacteria from cutting boards, knives, and anything that may have come in contact with raw seafood or meats.

Lye

The cleaner par excellence, lye cuts through the most stubborn baked-on grease and grit better than nearly any store-bought product. You can buy generic lye at a hardware store, but heavy-duty oven cleaner, which is essentially lye, in a spray bottle will also do the trick. Be sure it's heavy duty. Soak anything that's blackened, such as stove inserts, overnight in a sink of hot water mixed with a cup of lye (add the lye to the water, not the other way around). Never touch lye: Use gloves. Don't let lye spatter in your eyes: If it gets in your eyes, immediately flush your eyes with large amounts of cool water. Have a bottle of vinegar on hand in case you get it on your skin—you'll know if you do because your skin will feel slippery and begin to sting. Rub the vinegar on immediately, and you'll feel the slippery feeling go away. Don't use lye to clean anything made of aluminum—lye will eat right through it.

HINT *If you clean the grill rack or grill pan every time you use it, a steel wool pad will usually clean it up again. But for a super-clean grill or pan, over newspaper, spray with heavy-duty oven cleaner. Let sit an hour or two before scrubbing it with steel wool. Remember to wear household or garden gloves.*

2 How to polish copper

Use the age-old professional French chef method—which is actually easier and cheaper than store-bought products—of making a watery paste of coarse (kosher) salt and distilled white vinegar and rubbing it on the copper. As you apply the paste, you'll see the tarnish disappear. Just rinse off the pan and dry.

HINT *Be sure to wear gloves unless you don't mind being made acutely aware of any tiny cuts or scratches on your hands.*

3 Choosing an apron

Choose an apron with long strings that you can tie in front, where you can see what you are doing. Don't buy an apron with strings so short that you have to tie them in back. Whether it is fancy or not, the apron should be long and made of heavy cotton. Have it laundered every once in a while at the cleaners to keep it white or bright. Professionals often wear half aprons that come up only to their waists, but professionals have chefs' jackets to protect their torsos. Unless you have one of those, buy an apron that covers you all the way.

4 Lost your oven mitt?

For those of you who are always in search of misplaced oven mitts, consider wearing a towel. Chefs always keep a kitchen towel tucked into one side of an apron string. Use your towel for handling hot pots and pans and for giving quick wipes to surfaces. Choose a heavy towel that will insulate against high heat. Don't use terrycloth, which can catch fire. Never pick up hot items with a wet towel, which will conduct heat.

5 How to store food

Every food has different qualities and therefore should be stored to preserve those qualities. Don't reflexively wrap everything in plastic wrap.

Vegetables

Uncooked vegetables are best stored in the refrigerator, wrapped in parchment or wax paper, not plastic. Plastic bags trap moisture and can cause mildew. Vegetables that are used for flavor, and when texture is not important (such as that whole bunch of celery you bought for one stalk), can be tightly wrapped in plastic wrap, then in foil, and frozen. They'll lose their texture—they'll be mushy when thawed——but the flavor will all be there.

Seafood

Keep shellfish such as mussels, clams, cockles, and live crabs and lobsters in a bowl, covered with a wet towel, in the refrigerator.

Fish

Whole fish can be kept in a flat container with holes in the bottom, covered with a sheet of wax paper with ice on top. If you don't have something flat with holes, put the fish in a large colander set over a large pan.

Meat

As meats rest in the refrigerator they release liquid. It's in this liquid that bacteria is most likely to grow. Wrapping meat in plastic wrap causes the liquid to accumulate and can hasten the meat's deterioration. A better choice is wrapping the meat in something like butcher paper—ask your butcher for some extra—that absorbs liquid. Alternatively, wrap meat in wax paper with the paper touching the surface of the meat.

6　How to sharpen knives

Dull knives turn otherwise satisfying tasks such as slicing, dicing, and chopping into arduous chores. We try the latest new-fangled knife sharpeners, but they don't work, and when it comes down to it, the idea of a sharpening stone or steel is just too intimidating. Expensive or not, any knife needs to have an edge put on it, preferably, at least at first, by an experienced professional who has the high-powered grinding equipment needed to sharpen rock-hard stainless steel. In the days of carbon steel knives, we could have done this ourselves, but modern steel is just too hard.

If you decide to sharpen your knives yourself, buy a high-quality stone (Japanese-made ones are superior) where tools are sold, not at places that sell gourmet kitchen items. The best stones have two sides, ideally one fine and one very fine, and they need to be soaked in cold water for 15 minutes before you use them.

Using a stone to sharpen a knife

1. Place a folded wet towel on a firm work surface and place the soaked stone on top. The towel holds the stone in place.

2. With the knife at about a 20 degree angle from the stone, start with the tip of the knife against the stone at the end farthest from you.

3. Pull the knife toward you, maintaining the angle, so that the blade of the knife slides along the entire length of the stone and you wind up at the end of the stone nearest you with the base of the knife blade—the end nearest the handle—against the stone.

4. Continue in this way until you feel a "burr"—a rough edge of broken steel along the side of the blade opposite the side you sharpened.

5. Repeat the sharpening process on the other side of the blade, again until you feel a burr on the opposite side.

6. Repeat the process, this time using the finer side of the stone and with the knife at a slightly sharper angle, about 25 degrees. Use very gentle pressure so as not to break off the thin edge you will have formed.

7. Hone the knife by sliding it gently against a sharpening steel. Here we show holding the steel vertically, pinned against the work surface but you can also hold it upward in classic fashion and stroke the knife accordingly.

7 What knives can't I live without?

More-expensive knives, especially some of the popular heavy German knives, are made with such hard steel that they are very difficult to sharpen (see entry 000). Less-expensive knives are usually made from softer steel and can be sharpened quickly. Their blades are also thinner so that when you're slicing a large carrot, for example, the blade doesn't force the slice away and break it. It is possible to find carbon-steel knives from France or Japan, and they are easier to sharpen than stainless steel, but they need to be sharpened more often and honed with a steel every few minutes. They also rust if left in a wet sink and can stain some foods such as hard-boiled eggs or onions. In spite of the drawbacks, many chefs still prefer carbon-steel knives because they're easier to keep sharp.

• **One chef's knife:** Buy the largest chef's knife you can find. A 14-inch knife will chop herbs twice as fast as an 8-inch one.

• **One paring knife:** Buy a knife about 4 inches long and use it for trimming vegetables, boning poultry, or preparing fruit.

• **One flexible knife** (optional): A long, thin flexible knife is handy for filleting fish, and an even longer, thin flexible knife is useful for slicing smoked salmon and prosciutto.

- **One boning knife** (optional): Its narrow medium-long blade is handy for reaching between bones and flesh and into other hard-to-reach places.
- **Bread knife** (recommended): A 10-inch knife with a serrated blade is almost essential.

HINT *Place a cork on the sharp ends of your knives to prevent them from doing damage, especially if you're traveling.*

8 Why you need more than one cutting board

If you're chopping a bunch of parsley or mincing a large amount of anything, you want to chop as much at once as you can. If your cutting board is small, the food will fall off the sides of the board and there won't be enough room to chop. So, your main cutting board should be as large as possible. You should have a medium- to large-size board with a moat around it on at least one side for carving. At the table or in the kitchen, the moat keeps the juices from flowing out onto the tablecloth or work surface. Have a couple of very small boards for tiny chores like cutting lemons or a garlic clove. Wash boards with hot water and bleach after using them to cut up raw meats, seafood, or chicken.

What kind of board should I buy?

Wooden boards are best and won't dull your knives as fast as plastic. The paper-thin plastic "boards" popular now are easy to transport and store, but they tend to move around when you use them.

HINT *To keep the cutting board from sliding around on the surface, put a damp kitchen towel or one or two wet paper towels underneath.*

9 How to use a slicer

Usually called a mandolin, despite looking nothing like the instrument, large and expensive metal vegetable slicers used to be the only ones available. Professional chefs can't live without them, but most home cooks can get by with an inexpensive plastic version for about a fifth the price.

Metal slicers

These are still the best if you do a lot of slicing, and they are great for potatoes. The best brands allow you to take the blades out so you can sharpen them, and they have julienne attachments. These attachments are almost essential if you make french fries with any regularity. But they can be scary because they have lots of sharp little blades that can easily cut you if you're careless.

Benriner plastic slicer   Rotating the nut to adjust the thickness

Plastic slicers

The Benriner brand allows you to adjust the thickness of the slices with a small nut on the back. Other brands use insertable blades that restrict you to only a few thicknesses, none of which seems to be the one you need. Most people lose the safety guard within a few days, so when you're slicing and you're working closer to the blade, hold the food with a towel.

10   Using a food processor

A food processor is a pretty straightforward gadget; it has only one speed and a limited number of attachments. Some newer models have miniature attachments that fit on the motor and make it possible for you to grind or chop smaller amounts of foods, such as parsley, that would otherwise cling to the walls of the processor out of reach of the blade. Some processors also have graters for cheese and vegetables, but don't expect them to do a very neat job. When using a food processor to chop or for delicate operations such as making pie dough, use the pulse mechanism so you don't chop vegetables into purees or over-work doughs.

HINT *When you puree liquids, a blender (immersion or stationery) is usually better than a food processor because the processor often leaks where the blade attaches to the base when filled with liquid.*

11   How to blend hot liquids

An immersion blender, the end held well below the surface, is best for blending hot liquids. If the liquid is too shallow, tilt the pan so the liquid is deep on one end and blend that. Hot liquids blended in a regular blender (see entry 12) have a tendency to shoot out the top.

12   How to use a blender

The blender is often the best device to use for pureeing liquids. The only drawbacks are in having to transfer the liquid from the pot to the blender and the risk of the hot soup or sauce shooting out of the top.

1. When pureeing hot liquids in a regular blender, never fill the blender more than half full.

2. Hold the lid down tightly with your hand wrapped in a towel.

3. Start by pulsing very quickly on the lowest speed. As the air above the hot liquid is heated, the liquid will try to shoot out the top. After several pulses, you should be able to let the blender run.

Immersion blender

An immersion blender, essentially a rod with a blender blade at one end, is designed to be immersed right in the pot. It allows you to puree directly in the pot you use to make a soup or puree, eliminating the need of transferring foods to a regular blender and the dangerous process of pureeing hot foods in a closed blender.

13 How to strain liquids and puree solids and semisolids

Mesh strainer

What's the best way to strain liquids? Ideally, strain through a fine-mesh strainer. Don't use a spoon to work the liquid through, but rather move a small ladle rapidly up and down in quick little movements.

What kind of strainer do I need?

In an ideal kitchen there would be three kinds of strainers.

• **China cap:** This is a large metal cone with holes in it and with a handle. Its sturdy construction makes it handy for straining mixtures containing sharp pieces of shell or bone that might damage a regular strainer. It's also handy for straining large amounts of broth.

• **Mesh strainers:** Coarse-mesh strainers should be as large and wide as possible to make straining more efficient.

Drum sieve

The best fine-mesh strainers for sauces and delicate soups are the classic cone-shape chinois (pictured in the last row on page 166), but round fine-mesh strainers also suit.

• **Drum sieves:** These come in two varieties, small wooden ones with a fine-mesh screen and larger metal ones with removable screens for different finenesses. The wooden ones are finished when the screen wears out, but they are a fourth the price of the metal ones. Drum sieves are the absolute best instruments for making fine silky purees. Semisolid mixtures, like mashed potatoes, can be pureed and strained at the same time through a drum sieve. You can also use a ricer, a gadget that pushes cooked vegetables and fruits through a perforated bowl, or work the mixture through a strainer by pushing it back and forth with a ladle turned downward.

14 What grater to use

Sometimes the old-fashioned inexpensive gadget is the best. A box grater is great for grating most things, but keep in mind that not all box graters are made alike. When selecting one, look for one with very fine teeth that protrude from the sides, not the tiny little punch-outs that turn foods to mush. A rasp grater, essentially a long rulerlike grater with very sharp fine teeth, is perfect for grating hard cheeses and garlic and for zesting citrus fruits.

15 Why do I need a food mill?

A food mill is one of those bizarre-looking kitchen gadgets that you may not have seen since you were rummaging around in your grandmother's kitchen cabinets. Essentially a strainer with a propellerlike set of blades for forcing foods through a metal disk with holes, it is the perfect tool for straining vegetables and making purees at the same time. If you make tomato sauce with any regularity, it's a must.

16 What are "aromatic vegetables"?

The words *aromatic vegetables* describe onions, carrots, celery, and sometimes turnips, celeriac, or fennel that are cooked in broths, stews, or braised dishes to maximize flavor.

17 How to peel onions

Unless you need perfect rounds of onion, such as for onion rings or to garnish a burger, cut the onion in half vertically before peeling—peeling each half is easier than peeling the onion whole.

To peel pearl onions

Plunge them in a pot of boiling water and boil for one minute. Drain them in a colander and immediately rinse them with cold water. Pull away the peel with your thumb, finger, and a small knife.

18 How to chop onions and shallots

To develop your kitchen skills, practice slicing and mincing onions and shallots the way the pros do. By slicing these whole round vegetables in two directions while leaving the slices attached to the base, you can then slice across the vegetable and it will end up finely minced.

1. Notice that the layers of the vegetable attach at one end. Keep this end, called the root end, intact.

2. With the knife on its side, slice the vegetable as thinly as you can as close to the root end as possible—without cutting through it.

3. Next, with the knife in the normal upright position, slice again so the onion is sliced in two directions.

4. Slice the vegetable and it will fall apart into tiny bits. Push the root ends aside and add them to simmering broth or chop them separately.

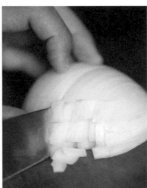

19 Which onions to use for what

The best all-purpose onions are the "yellow" Spanish onions sold at most supermarkets. When serving the onions raw, you may prefer the fresher white onions or red onions, sometimes called Bermuda onions. Very sweet onions, such as Maui onions or Vidalias, are best served raw; when used in recipes, they can make sauces or soups overly sweet. Make a French onion soup, for example, with red or yellow onions.

20 How to get the most flavor out of onions

The secret to getting the flavor out of onions to use in soups or stews is to slice them very finely and then cook them gently in butter until they "melt." Keep in mind that when you slice the onions, what looks like a lot of onions will shrink to about a tenth of their size.

1. Slice onions very thinly and put them in a pan with butter. Cook over medium heat, stirring every minute or so for about 25 minutes.

2. The onions will now have released a lot of liquid. Cook until the liquid evaporates and caramelizes on the bottom and sides of the pan.

3. Deglaze the pan (see entry 36) with a little broth, water, wine, or port, and then caramelize it again. You can repeat this caramelization as many times as you like to magnify the flavor of the onions.

21 How to peel a carrot

You can peel a carrot very quickly by cutting off the root end and holding the carrot diagonally over a cutting board. Cut off the peel in long lengthwise strips, moving a swivel-type peeler (see entry 27) rapidly back and forth.

22 How to slice a carrot

Sometimes you need carrots in perfect rounds so they look their best, but if they're being strained out, such as when making a stew, it's more efficient to cut them into little triangles.

HINT *By turning the knife slightly inward, you'll prevent the slices from rolling all over the work surface.*

To form rounds

Hold the carrot firmly on the cutting board. If you're slicing with your right hand, hold the carrot with your left hand and curl your fingers under. Use the knuckles of your left hand, which should touch the knife, to guide the thickness of the slices.

To form triangles

Many old-fashioned recipes call for chopping carrots into little wedges, because wedges are easy. Cut a peeled carrot in half lengthwise and then each half lengthwise into thirds (maintain a 45-degree angle on each side). A crosswise slice gives you triangles.

23 How to dice carrots

1. Cut peeled carrots into 2- to 3-inch sections and use a vegetable slicer to square off the sides.

2. Use a knife to cut the sections lengthwise at the thickness you want the cubes.

3. Cut the slices lengthwise to the width you want the cubes.

4. Then cut across the sticks to get cubes.

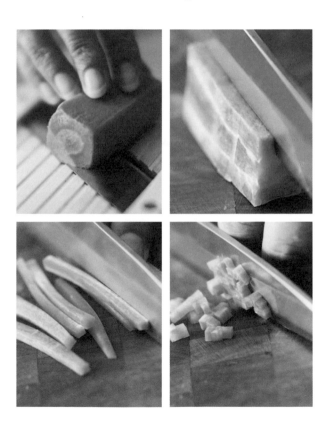

24　How to prepare celery

If you're serving celery sticks you may want to peel the celery to make it less stringy. Cut off the stalk end and wash thoroughly to remove dirt.

Celery (including the leaves) can also be chopped and used in stews and soups.

25　How to peel, mince, and crush garlic

1. Hold a large knife sideways about an inch over the clove. Give the knife a quick whack with your other hand, crushing the clove. Make a thin slice along the root end of the clove to detach the peel and lift it away.

2. Slice the garlic lengthwise, leaving the slices attached at the root end.

3. Make 3 horizontal slices through the garlic, again leaving them attached at the root end.

4. Finely slice the garlic crosswise.

5. To make a garlic paste, crush the minced garlic a tiny bit at a time with the side of a large knife.

26   How to loosen peels

To loosen the peels of fruits and vegetables such as pearl onions, apricots, peaches, garlic, and tomatoes, plunge them in boiling water and drain. Except for pearl onions, the time needed in boiling water depends on the ripeness of the fruit—ripe tomatoes can be plunged for 15 seconds, while underripe tomatoes and harder apricots need 1 minute. After a longer plunging, rinse the fruit or vegetable with cold water or plunge in a pot of cold water, then peel off the skin.

27   How to choose a peeler

There are several kinds of vegetable peelers on the market, and not all are right for all jobs.

Swivel peeler

Nonswivel peeler

Slingshot peeler

Swivel

Most American peelers have a blade that swivels so that it conforms to the surface of whatever is being peeled. Most of us tend to peel away from us, in which case a swivel peeler works best. Use with vegetables that are hard to hold as well as carrots, large potatoes, and zucchini.

Nonswivel

Some peelers have a simple fixed blade. These are best for those of us who peel toward ourselves. For peeling round fruits and vegetables such as turnips and apples, a nonswivel peeler works best.

Slingshot and other shapes

Some shapes, such as slingshot-shaped peelers, are awkward for some tasks (such as peeling potatoes) but fine for others (like curling chocolate). Always buy a peeler that's easy to hold.

28 Choosing pots and pans

Pots and pans are made from a wide variety of materials and come in a wider range of prices. The difference between a pot and a pan is really one of degrees; a pot has sides that are high in relation to the bottom, while pans have low sides. Whatever the size the pot you choose, its bottom should be heavy and thick. Pick it up and get a feel for it—its weight, handle grip, and size. What is important is its being comfortable and manageable in your hands.

Aluminum

If you're buying a very large pot, copper or stainless steel will make it very expensive. Bought at a professional cooking supply store, an aluminum pot is the least expensive and works fine. (Aluminum is rarely a problem, just don't use it to cook egg yolks or artichokes—they will react with the aluminum.) You can also use aluminum for your smaller pots and pans.

Copper

Copper pots are the best conductors of heat and look great in the kitchen. Some of us use copper because of its feel and the incomparable evenness of its cooking. Copper, of course, does tarnish, but it can be easily cleaned (see entry 2). However, there are those of us who don't mind the look of well-used and tarnished pots. For years, copper pots were lined only with tin, but nowadays they are often lined with stainless steel. Unless you're planning to use the pot nonstop for years, tin is the better value—it's cheaper and the copper is thicker and heavier. Copper pots, especially tin-lined ones, are very heavy, so feel them before buying.

Bimetal

Pots of copper clad with stainless steel conduct heat as well as plain copper, but they have the advantage of not tarnishing. These are almost as expensive as copper pots.

tools, techniques, and advice

Cast iron

Cast-iron skillets and pots are cheap, heavy, and easy to find, but they need to be seasoned. To do so, heat oil and salt in them until the oil smokes and then rub them thoroughly with a rag to dry. The cooked oil forms a protective coating that keeps the pan from rusting. Ideally, cast iron should be cleaned only by wiping with a dish towel or paper towel. If you need to wash it with soap and water, you'll need to reseason it. One drawback is that it's hard to see the condition of caramelized juices after sautéing because the pans are dark.

Anodized aluminum

Treated so that it is less reactive, anodized aluminum is dark and, like cast iron, makes it difficult to judge the condition of juices from sautéed meat or fish cooking in the pan.

Enameled iron

Some of the best and least expensive heavy pots and pans are made of cast iron coated with enamel. The enamel prevents the food from touching the cast iron, which can discolor some foods.

Stainless steel

Rugged and durable, stainless steel has the advantage over aluminum, cast iron, and tinned copper of being completely nonreactive so that it doesn't affect the color or flavor of foods. Its main disadvantage is that it's expensive and conducts heat less well than copper or bimetal pans.

Nonstick

Pans that don't stick are a boon for cooking fish, omelets, or anything delicate, and they are now available in a relatively heavy gauge. Because they are nonstick, juices don't adhere to them so in recipes that call for deglazing, there's nothing to deglaze.

29 When do I cover the pot?

There are lots of rules and theories about covering.

Boiling green vegetables for more than 5 minutes with the cover on the pot can cause them to turn gray (volatile acids released by the vegetables are trapped).

When braising something that rises above the surface of the liquid, cover the pot with foil and then press down in the middle. Put on the lid. By suspending the foil over the meat, condensation forms and collects on the underside of the foil and drips over the meat, basting it. Covering the pot allows whatever is above the surface of the liquid to steam; the foil bastes the food from the inside.

If poaching foods in a relatively large amount of liquid (in essence when you make broth), leave the lid off so the liquid can reduce and become more concentrated and to make it easier to skim off fat and scum.

What about partially covering?

If you're braising vegetables, for example, with liquid to come halfway up their sides, you want the part of the vegetable that's above the liquid to steam, hence the need for the cover. But why partially covered? Because sometimes you want the liquid to evaporate and concentrate at the same time the food braises, such as when glazing vegetables.

30 Which sauté pans do I need?

While we have the habit of calling cast-iron pans skillets, a skillet and a sauté pan are really the same thing. A sauté pan has relatively low sides and is used for browning foods, usually over high heat. Sauté pans are available with both straight and sloping sides. Straight sides are good when you're finishing the sautéed food with liquid. Sloping sides are helpful when you want to toss food in the pan. Buy several different-size sauté pans so you're able to cook your food in a pan it fits in, leaving no extra amount of surface on which juices and fats will burn. Buy sauté pans with a shiny surface on the inside so you can see caramelization when it occurs.

- One 10-inch straight-sided sauté pan for sautéing foods and making a pan-deglazed sauce. If you deglaze and reduce a sauce (see entry 36) in a sauté pan with sloping sides, the level of the liquid decreases and liquid burns on the sides. This pan is great for a cut-up chicken. The chicken can be sautéed, the fat poured out, and the chicken put back in the pan to simmer with flavorful liquids such as wine or broth.
- One 12-inch nonstick sauté pan for fish. An oval pan is very handy for whole fish and fish fillets.
- One 8- to 10-inch nonstick sauté pan with sloping sides for omelets (see entry 125).

Why pan size matters

The reason it's necessary to go out and buy a whole collection of different-size sauté pans is to have the pan fit as close as possible to the food you're sautéing. If the pan is too small, you'll have to cram in the ingredients, which can cause them to steam and never brown. If the pan is too big, the juices run over to the part that's uncovered and burn. (If you have to make do with just one, buy a larger pan and when you sauté, fill the empty spaces with trimmings or vegetables.)

31 How to sauté with butter

Butter is great for sautéing because of the flavor it imparts, but it can be tricky to use because it burns easily. Whole butter is perfect for sautéing or panfrying foods such as chicken, potatoes, or pancakes, that require cooking over low to moderate heats. When high temperatures are required, such as when browning thin pieces of meat or fish, sautéing scallops or cultivated mushrooms, or cooking any food that needs to be browned quickly, whole butter can't be used or it will burn. Butter used for sautéing at high temperatures needs to be clarified, which means having the milk-solid proteins that burn removed (see entry 32).

HINT *Despite fears that butter leaves our foods loaded with cholesterol, foods cooked in butter, unless breaded, absorb very little fat and are left coated with proteins from the butter that give them a buttery flavor without the fat; most of the fat is left behind in the pan.*

1. Put butter in a cold sauté pan and gradually heat the pan. (If you add cold butter to a hot pan, the butter will go straight up in smoke.)

2. As you heat the butter, rotate the pan so the butter covers the surface evenly.

3. As the butter gets hot, it will foam; as it gets hotter, the foam will subside. This is the point when food is added to the pan (heated beyond this point with nothing else in the pan, the butter will burn). Make sure that the food completely covers the bottom of the pan or the butter will burn wherever exposed.

Butter, margarine, or shortening?

Margarine and shortening are made by hydrogenating oils into a more saturated form—a row of carbon atoms is surrounded with more atoms of hydrogen—so that it remains solid at room temperature. Margarine and shortening are also emulsions, meaning they contain water dispersed in tiny particles within the fat. Shortening is also a foam, which means that it contains air in tiny particles dispersed in the fat. Because it's an emulsion and a foam and contains just the right combination of hydrogenated fats, shortening works very well in pastries and cakes. Its flavor, however, is ghastly. Margarine and shortening are less expensive than butter, and some brands of margarine no longer contain trans-fats, but when flavor is important, butter is the clear winner.

32 What is clarified butter?

Clarified butter is butter with the milk-solid proteins taken out; these proteins are what cause the butter to burn at low temperatures. If you're sautéing with high heat or for prolonged periods and don't want the butter to burn or flecks of toasted butter adhering to the food, you'll need to use clarified butter.

To clarify large amounts (more than 2 pounds) of butter

1. Melt the butter in a heavy-bottom pot and let it sit for 15 minutes.

2. With a ladle, skim off the froth that has formed on top of the butter and discard.

3. Lift off the melted clear butterfat—the clarified butter—with a ladle, leaving the water contained in the butter, now useless, in the bottom of the pot.

To clarify less than a pound of butter

1. Make what is also called ghee or beurre noisette by cooking unsalted butter in a heavy-bottom saucepan over medium heat until it froths, and the froth begins to settle.

2. As the froth settles, you'll see white specks in the butter; watch these closely. When they turn to brown and adhere to the bottom and sides of the pan, dip the bottom of the pan in a bowl of cold water to stop the cooking.

3. Strain the butter through a paper towel, coffee filter, or fine mesh strainer into a bowl. It is ready to use.

33 Which oil to use for what

Oil is used for sautéing, essentially to prevent food from sticking to the bottom of the pan; for frying; and for dressing salads and flavoring sauces. Unlike butter, which is an emulsion, oil is sometimes emulsified into a mayonnaise or vinaigrette to bring out its flavor. Its high smoking temperature makes it a better medium than butter or animal fats for frying or sautéing. There are many different kinds of oil, each with its own characteristics and uses.

HINT *When using extra virgin olive oil in a vinaigrette or a mayonnaise (see entries 72 and 367), don't beat the mixture hard with a whisk or it will turn bitter. Instead, stir it gently with a wooden spoon. Another hint: Olive oil from Sicily is beginning to appear in fancy grocery stores; it's often a very good value.*

Extra virgin olive oil

It is conceivable for someone to live having only one oil—extra virgin olive oil. This oil results from the first pressing of olives and is best used as a dressing. It's a waste to use this sometimes very expensive oil for frying or sautéing—the high heat destroys its flavor—and there are times, such as when making mayonnaise, when such an assertive flavor isn't appropriate. In an ideal world, we'd have an assortment of extra virgin olive oils from all over the world to use on our salads or on seafood, but most of us can be happy with one. Inexpensive extra virgin olive oil is often comparable to more expensive brands, so unless you're sure of what you're buying, you don't necessarily get more quality for more money. Don't combine extra virgin olive oil with mustard; they don't agree. If you like mustard in your vinaigrette, use "pure" olive oil or vegetable oil.

"Pure" olive oil

In addition to extra virgin olive oil, "pure" olive oil is useful to have on hand. Pure olive oil is the lowest marketable grade of olive oil, which, in processing, has been stripped of most of its flavor components, leaving it with a very neutral taste. This is exactly the point. There are times when we don't want our oil to have any taste. Use pure olive oil for frying and sautéing because it leaves none of the unpleasant fishy taste found in so many vegetable oils. It is also much less expensive than extra virgin oil, whose flavor is destroyed by the heat. Many chefs use it as an all-round oil instead of vegetable oil.

Vegetable oil

Unlike olive or nut oils, which are designed to contribute flavor to a dish, vegetable oils such as canola oil are suited for sautéing and frying and in salads when you don't want the flavor of the oil to be noticeable. Most vegetable oils are relatively benign, but occasionally they take on an odd fishy taste; you may need to experiment with different oils—canola, safflower, peanut—and different brands.

Nut oil

Nut oils have become very popular, but take care with them. Raw nut oils—except for peanut oils—are almost always rancid before you even get them home, and if they're not, they will be soon. The best-known maker of roasted nut oils is Le Blanc. Le Blanc's oils are not cheap in terms of price per volume, but you can use a tenth as much as you'd need of an oil made with raw nuts. Store nut oils in the freezer.

HINT *To avoid rancidity and have an oil with better flavor, buy nut oils made from roasted nuts. Roasting the nuts brings out their flavor and helps preserve them.*

Flavored oil

Some cooks like to flavor their oils with herbs such as thyme or marjoram or with aromatic ingredients such as garlic. Use an inexpensive extra virgin olive oil or pure olive oil, but never toy with the flavor of fine extra virgin oil.

Nut oil varieties

Walnut: most subtly flavored nut oil; goes well with bitter greens such as endive and gives a nutty flavor to mayonnaise

Hazelnut: made from roasted nuts, the most alluring of all nut oils; use in very small amounts since its flavor is very pronounced. Brush vinaigrette made with good vinegar and a little hazelnut oil on fish fillets

Pistachio: hard to find and expensive; adds subtle complexity to delicate greens and is lovely dribbled on roasted or grilled fish

Peanut: supermarket oil doesn't impart a peanut flavor; cold-pressed oils have full peanut flavor; both good for stir-fried and other Asian dishes

Almond: has very little flavor unless made from roasted nuts; delicious on greens, in vinaigrettes, and mayonnaise

Pinoli nut: subtle oil best on grilled fish and shellfish such as shrimp

34 How to intensify the flavor of butter

By using beurre noisette made by caramelizing milk solids in butter (see entry 32), you can give soups and stews, especially those utilizing lentils and beans, a more intensely buttery flavor. Use beurre noisette in recipes that call for melted or clarified butter. Adding a small amount to the egg yolk base for a hollandaise (see entry 384), you can use much less butter but still have buttery flavor. If you're trying to cut down on cholesterol, use half beurre noisette and half neutral oil in emulsified sauces like hollandaise and its derivatives.

35 Does adding oil to butter keep it from burning?

The advice given in many cookbooks to add oil to butter to keep it from burning in a hot pan and allowing it to be heated to a higher temperature is a fallacy. What causes butter to burn is the protein it contains—the milk solids—and unless these proteins are removed, they will burn, regardless of whether or not oil is combined with the butter.

HINT *By starting oil or clarified butter in a cold pan and putting it over high heat, you can judge its temperature by how it looks in the pan. Hot oil begins to form ripples; even hotter oil, necessary for rapid sautéing, begins to smoke.*

36 How to deglaze a pan

Deglaze is just a fancy word for adding liquid to the pan you've used to sauté meat or fish. To properly deglaze, pour any cooked oil or butter out of the pan and add a liquid such as wine or water to dissolve the juices that have caramelized and adhered to the bottom of the pan. Deglazing is often the first step when making a pan sauce.

37 How to make toasts and croutons

If you have slices of bread that won't fit into the toaster, slide them under the broiler—just watch them like a hawk, since they can burn very quickly. Once they are browned on the first side, turn.

Croutons come in various shapes: rounds that can be used as a base for poached eggs and cubes of various sizes for soups, salads, and stuffings. To keep croutons from getting soggy in soups or salads, or when being used to hold poached eggs, cook them gently, in a sauté pan, in butter (ideally, clarified butter) or olive oil until golden brown on both sides. To make tiny croutons for soup, use thin sandwich bread, cut off the crusts, and cut the bread into cubes. Cook these gently in butter or olive oil in a sauté pan over medium heat, tossing often, until golden brown. Bread cubes for stuffings don't need to be cooked, but they will maintain their shape and texture better if cooked in butter or oil first.

HINT *To make garlic bread, toast the bread first, peel a garlic clove for every 6 slices or so, and rub it vigorously over the rough surface of the toast. You can then either butter the bread and put it in the oven a minute to melt the butter, or brush the bread with melted butter.*

38 How to make and use bread crumbs

Cooks often confuse fresh and dried bread crumbs. Dried bread crumbs are sprinkled on something that needs a little texture, an almost imperceptible crunch. For example, dried bread crumbs can be sprinkled over gratins (see entry 145). Fresh bread crumbs are used for covering foods with a delicate soft coating (such as the chicken breasts in entry 300).

To make dried bread crumbs

1. Cut the crusts off white bread and let the bread dry out for a couple of days, or dry it out in a low oven without letting it brown.

2. Process in a food processor and work through a strainer or drum sieve (see entry 13).

3. Sprinkle on baked foods such as tomatoes, cauliflower gratin, or cassoulet to give texture.

To make fresh bread crumbs

1. Cut the crusts off white bread and let the bread sit out for about 12 hours—the bread should be just barely beginning to dry out.

2. Pulverize it in a food processor.

3. Work the crumbs through a drum sieve or strainer.

Panko crumbs

If you like a crusty crunchy coating to your breaded foods, replace the fine bread crumbs with panko crumbs, now available at most supermarkets.

39 Ways to bread

Chicken or veal cutlets, whole fish, or fish fillets can be coated with different ingredients, but the end result is always moister meat.

Coat with flour

Food that has been coated with flour before being sautéed is cooked *meunière* and is usually served with frothy butter and lemon juice.

1. Coat food with flour.

2. Sauté over high heat in clarified butter (see entry 32).

3. Pat off any burned butter and put the food on plates or on a platter.

4. Pour out the cooked butter.

5. Sprinkle the foods generously with lemon juice.

6. Heat fresh whole butter in the pan until it froths and pour it over the food.

7. Serve immediately.

Coat with flour and beaten egg

Flouring and then dipping in a beaten egg make a light coating between meunière and a heavier breading. Prepare as above. The French call this *à la parisienne*.

Coat with flour, beaten egg, and fresh bread crumbs

Coat the food first with flour, dip it in beaten egg, and then dip it in fresh bread crumbs (*à l'anglaise*). Prepare as above.

Coat with flour, beaten egg, and parmigiano-reggiano

Using finely grated parmigiano-reggiano instead of bread crumbs makes this coating *à la milanaise*.

40 What does "to sweat" mean?

Some readers of recipes are confused by directions that say "to sweat" an ingredient, usually a root vegetable such as a carrot or onion. Sweating means to cook in a small amount of fat over low heat, sometimes covered, so the moisture inside the vegetable is extracted to the outside and eventually evaporates, concentrating the vegetable's flavor. The purpose of sweating is to cook the vegetable through and get its juices to caramelize on the vegetable or in the pan only after the vegetable has softened.

41   How to steam

To cook foods with steam, you need to suspend them over boiling liquid in a closed container. Two kinds of steamers are commonly sold. One is a fold-out steamer with perforated leaves, which fits into a small saucepan and holds foods such as vegetables suspended over hot liquid, usually boiling water. The second kind of steamer, sometimes called a couscoussier, has its own pot and an attachment on top with a perforated bottom. Foods such as fish and shellfish can be arranged in the top section while boiling liquid is held in the bottom section.

You can also improvise a steamer by using a round cake rack placed in a pot or wok, to hold foods above boiling liquid.

Foods such as mussels, cockles, or clams can be steamed without a steamer since the shells keep the shellfish for the most part above the liquid.

42   When microwave ovens are a godsend

Microwave ovens are great for those who cook small amounts of food or those who need to cook something quickly. The time needed in the microwave increases with the amount of food—ten potatoes in a microwave might take an hour to cook, while one potato might take 5 minutes. In the conventional oven, one potato can take as long as 20 minutes. As the microwave cooks unevenly, to compensate here are two tips.

1. Reposition root vegetables and tubers every few minutes—turned around, upside down, placed in different parts of the microwave—and allow to rest before each repositioning so the heat can spread evenly throughout the vegetable or starch.

2. Put fish in a flat container with a few tablespoons of liquid such as water or wine and cover the container with tightly sealed plastic wrap. Microwave it until the liquid boils and the plastic wrap puffs up. Reposition the container and let it rest a few minutes, then repeat

the process. In this way the fish is actually braising (after cooking, you can convert the liquid into a sauce in the same way that you could if you had baked the fish or simmered it on the stove).

HINT *If you're cooking for one or two, the microwave often makes sense because small amounts of food cook more quickly in the microwave than in the oven, but to cook for more, the oven or stove are the better bets.*

43 What thermometers do I need?

From left: candy thermometer; alcohol (low-temperature) thermometer; digital instant-read thermometer; fry thermometer with clip; oven thermometer

At least one: an instant-read thermometer for sticking in pieces of meat or fish for an instant read of the internal temperature. These thermometers have made the old-fashioned meat thermometers that are left in the meat as it cooks obsolete. If you like to fry, you'll need a frying thermometer that clips on to the side of the pan and measures the temperature of the oil. A candy thermometer is superfluous if you know how to judge the temperature of sugar by its texture in cold water. If you like working with chocolate, you may be drawn to one of those elegant long mercury thermometers, but if it breaks and the mercury gets loose in your house, there may be dire consequences. Instead, buy an alcohol thermometer or an inelegant digital thermometer that measures in a range between 50° and 200°F.

44 What saucepans are essential?

A saucepan is a small pan used for cooking small amounts of food. Saucepans should have heavy bottoms so foods cook evenly and are less likely to scald. The bottom of the pan should be shiny so you can see if juices or ingredients are caramelizing. Avoid aluminum for egg yolks and artichokes.

• One 3- or 4-quart saucepan for heating and combining liquids and small amounts of food.

• One 3-quart saucepan with sloping sides for hollandaise sauce (see entry 384) or other egg yolk–based sauces. The sloping sides allow you to reach into the corners of the pan with a whisk and prevent curdling.

HINT *The thickness of the sides is unimportant—don't waste money buying saucepans that are heavy all over; it's the bottoms that matter.*

Other useful items

• One Dutch oven, which is about 12 inches in diameter with sides about 8 inches high. It's perfect for making stews—make sure it has a heavy bottom so you can brown the meat in it before you add the liquid.

• One 12-quart pot for boiling pasta or green vegetables. It can be dirt cheap and poorly made as long as you're not cooking vegetables such as onions in oil or butter before adding liquid.

• Small heavy sauté pans with straight sides that will hold one or two steaks.

45 Do I start it in cold water or hot?

If you're trying to decide whether to start a food cooking in cold water or hot, consider whether you want the food to cook quickly or gently and also the size. If you plunge a large object into boiling water, the outside is going to cook before the inside. On the other hand, if you start small pieces of food in cold water, they're likely to overcook by the time the water gets hot.

• **Potatoes, beets, and other large vegetables:** If you want large vegetables such as potatoes to cook evenly, start them in cold water so that the temperature of the inside of the potato has time to heat up at the same rate as the outside. If you plunge a potato in boiling water, the outside will cook while the inside remains uncooked.

• **Eggs:** Plunge eggs into boiling water because you want the outside (the white) to cook faster than the yolk. People like yolks to varying degrees of doneness, but no one likes a runny white.

• **Green vegetables:** Green vegetables or any food that needs to be cooked quickly should be plunged into boiling water—the more the merrier so that vegetables don't cool the water.

• **Meats:** The old axiom regarding meat is that meats should be added to simmering liquids if you want to keep the savor in the meat. If you want the savor to go into the surrounding liquid, the idea goes, start the meat in cold water. I find, though, that if you plunge meat into hot water, it releases proteins that coagulate and cloud the broth. If you start the meat in cold water, the proteins are released more slowly such that they form longer strands that tangle up into froth, scum, and foam, which can then be skimmed off, leaving behind clear broth (see entry 351).

• **Fish:** To poach, start in cold water for very large fish such as whole salmon, and in hot water for small fish. If you poach a large fish in already simmering water, the outside will cook before the heat can reach the center. If you poach a small fish in cold water, it will overcook by the time the water reaches the simmer.

46 Can't find the pot lid?

Unless you're very well organized, you may find yourself spending time looking for the lid that fits a particular pot or saucepan. Don't worry about it: As long as the lid is larger than the pot, without being enormous, it will work. Turn the lid upside down so liquid that condenses on the lid will fall off the convex lid instead of running down the sides of the pot.

HINT *If you are limited to only a few lids, buy larger ones—they'll fit on the small pots, too.*

47 What can be boiled?

Virtually nothing. Boiling meats dries them out; boiling broth turns it cloudy; boiling fish causes it to fall apart; boiling eggs causes the yolks to turn gray. The only foods you can safely boil are green vegetables and pasta (unless stuffed).

48 How to thicken liquids

Often when we deglaze a pan, braise a fish, or simmer down a broth, we want to give the liquid a little more body so it has the consistency of a traditional sauce. Here are some ways to do this.

• **Cream:** Add about a fourth as much cream as there is liquid and boil it down to the consistency you desire.

• **Butter:** Boil down the liquid as much as you plan to—you can't boil it down more once you've added butter—and whisk in a tablespoon or so of cold butter per ¼ cup of liquid.

• **Flour:** If you coat pieces of meat with flour before you brown them for a stew or sprinkle flour over the meat as it's browning, the flour will thicken the stew. You can also work flour and butter to a paste (called a beurre manié) with the back of a fork and whisk it into the stewing liquid at the end. Make sure the liquid is simmering or the flour won't thicken. Flour can be turned into a roux by combining it with butter and cooking it gently for a few mintues. Liquids to be thickened are whisked into the hot roux and gently cooked.

• **Cornstarch or arrowroot:** Make a smooth mixture of equal parts cold water and cornstarch and whisk, a little at a time, into the simmering liquid.

• **Vegetable purees:** Puree some of the vegetables in the stew in a blender and whisk into the stew.

A cornstarch slurry

Beurre manié

Flavoring meat to thicken a stew

49   How to chill broth

At a temperature between 50°F and 140°F, broth can be a medium for bacteria growth. Keep it hot (above 140°F) or chill it as quickly as possible. When above 140°F, broth can be allowed to cool at room temperature—no need to waste ice to cool. Once it's down to 140°F, cool it quickly according to the directions below. Never put a pot of hot broth in the refrigerator because it will warm up the whole refrigerator.

To cool a small or medium amount of broth

1. Let the broth cool at room temperature until it's cool enough that you can comfortably hold your hand against the side of the pot.

(There's no point in wasting ice while the broth is hot enough to be safe from contamination.)

2. Place the pot in a large bowl or pot of ice until cool and then refrigerate.

To cool a large amount of broth

1. Let the broth cool at room temperature until you can comfortably hold your hand against the side of the pot.

2. Thoroughly clean the outside of a pot or bowl that will fit in the pot of broth and fill it with ice. Float the pot in the broth until all the ice has melted.

3. Repeat as often as necessary until the broth is cold. Refrigerate.

50 How to doctor canned soups and broths

Often the slightest hint of a fresh vegetable or herb will give canned broth or soup a little bit of much-needed vitality.

• Try simmering a few sprigs of fresh herbs or a bouquet garni in the soup for 20 minutes.

• If you're more ambitious, sweat some onions (see entry 40) and maybe some carrots in a little butter or oil and stir these into the soup.

• Whisk a little cold butter and/or cream into canned soups just before serving.

• Dice white bread, cook the cubes in butter, and add them to give the soup a buttery crunch.

51 Why avoid a double boiler

A double boiler is a small saucepan with a metal bowl or pan that fits exactly into the top of the saucepan. Food placed in the top of the

double boiler warms in the heat produced by the simmering water in the pan on the bottom without ever directly touching the heat source (burner). The problem with double boilers is that for many preparations, the bowl must be lifted out of the saucepan within a few seconds. Since the edge of the bowl is inside the saucepan, it's hard to get the bowl out quickly enough, and then steam can shoot out and burn you. A better method is to use a bowl that's larger than the saucepan and a saucepan that is smaller than the bowl but large enough that the flame from the stove doesn't climb up the sides of the saucepan and heat the bowl directly. In this way, you can grab the bowl with a towel and take it off the heat in an instant.

52 How to buy and use a roasting pan

A roasting pan should be a good conductor of heat, heavy, and as close in size to what you're roasting as possible.

HINT *Don't use a rack when roasting or, if you do, make sure the bottom of the roasting pan is covered with meat trimmings and/or aromatic vegetables (see entry 16) to keep it at an even and cooler temperature. A roast placed on the rack in an empty roasting pan will release its juices; they will burn because the roasting pan is so hot.*

1. Oval roasting pans are great since most roasts are long rather than square.

2. Copper or enameled iron are excellent choices because they can later be put on the stove for making gravy or jus (see entries 295 and 316). The best bargains are cast-iron skillets, inexpensive and available at the hardware store in all sizes.

3. Attractive roasting pans, such as oval copper or enameled iron gratin dishes, are great and look lovely on the table.

53 Throw out your roasting rack

Using a roasting rack will cause any juices to burn and often stick to the roast and tear the skin. Instead, it's better to keep your roast from sticking by sprinkling the pan with a little chopped onion or a few onion slices and then setting the roast on top.

54 How high to turn the oven

While intuition may tell us that large foods—turkeys, large fish, rib roasts, and the like—require a hotter oven than miniature birds such as quail, the opposite is in fact true. If you put a turkey in a 500°F oven, the outside will burn before the heat penetrates to the center. On the other hand, if you stick a chicken in a 200°F oven, it will over-cook before it even browns. A good rule of thumb is to start out in a hot oven, wait until your food is browned, and then turn the oven down to medium or low—say, about 300° degrees—to finish cooking.

55 Searing on the stove; finishing in the oven

Because small foods such as fish, small birds, or a small roast will take a minimum of 20 minutes to brown in even the hottest oven, this length of time risks overcooking them. It's better to brown them on the stove first, and then finish them in the oven. If you roast a small bird, such as a Cornish hen, in even the hottest oven, it may be dried out by the time it's well browned. Prebrowning on the stove prevents this.

56 How to buy and use a baking sheet

The best pans for sheets are large, made of heavy iron, and come from France. These are expensive and hard to find. However, most recipes for sheet cakes call for half sheet pans, which measure 13 by 17 inches. These pans not as heavy as French pans, but they're deeper, making them suited to most sheet cakes. Sheet pans without sides, or with very low sides, are meant for cookies, not cakes. Obviously, you can adjust the amount of cake batter you make according to the size of the sheet pans you have; just be aware of the size the recipe calls for. Keep in mind that a cake recipe for one 9- to 10-inch cake will make a thin layer cake if the batter is spread out in a 13 by 17-inch sheet pan. To make a sheet cake with the traditional thickness, make a double recipe or the equivalent of two 9- to 10-inch cake layers.

HINT *To emulate a thicker pan, which will cook more evenly, simply double or triple the sheet pans. If you're worried about the bottoms of your cookies burning, for instance, sprinkle water on one sheet pan and put another sheet pan on top of it and bake.*

57 Keeping food hot

One of the greatest challenges to the cook is keeping the food hot from the time it comes out of the oven or off the stove until it gets to the table. Roasts of course are allowed to rest, but in a warm place (the back of the stove is usually good) so they don't cool off. Some foods can be covered with foil or a pot lid, but crusty foods such as steaks and roasts can steam if covered too tightly. Most important is that the plates or bowls be as hot as possible—but not so hot that they'll burn anyone. If you don't have a warming or other oven just for heating plates, use the microwave (make sure your plates are microwave safe—some porcelain will crack, and metal will spark) or one of the latest dishwashers that have a setting just for warming plates. A last method: Put the plates in a bowl or pot of very hot water and dry them quickly as you take them out to serve.

58   Keep the butter cold

Butter is a fragile emulsion of fat in liquid held in place with a small amount of protein. When adding butter to hot foods, the butter must be cold so the emulsion stays intact and the consistency remains silky and smooth instead of oily. Remember this when stirring butter into hot soups, pasta, cooked vegetables, and sauces.

59   How to "shock" green vegetables

Recipes for green vegetables often say to boil the vegetables and then shock them in ice water, meaning filling a bowl full of ice cubes and throwing the cooked vegetables in it to stop the cooking. The problem with this is that it uses up all your ice, and then you're stuck sorting through the ice cubes to pick out the green beans or the spinach leaves. It works just as well to forget about the ice. Drain the vegetables in a colander and immediately rinse them with cold tap water for 30 seconds.

60   How to reheat leftover vegetables

Don't immerse leftover cooked vegetables in boiling water or you'll leach out all their flavor. Don't sauté them in butter either, or they'll get oily. Instead, take a tablespoon or two of cream or water, bring it to the boil; add and toss the vegetables over medium heat, until they're heated through. If you wish, you can then toss them with cold butter.

61 Which salt for what?

There are so many kinds of salt available now that it's become difficult to know which to use for what. Some generalizations can be made, however.

1. A box of inexpensive kosher salt is ideal for salting large amounts of water for boiling vegetables or pasta.

2. Fine salt, either bought fine or ground, is best for seasoning foods in which the crunch of coarse salt would be too much.

3. Sea salt, ideally the rather gray looking sel de Guérande, contains essential minerals and a delicate marine flavor.

4. Fleur de sel is ideal in tiny pinches placed on delicate foods.

What is fleur de sel?

Fleur de sel is a kind of sea salt—salt that is harvested in some parts of France by trapping sea water in lagoons and letting the water dry. As the water evaporates, salt begins to form on the surface of the pond in a characteristic flower pattern. The salt is raked off, allowed to dry slightly more, and marketed as fleur ("flower") de sel. If you look closely at a pinch of fleur de sel, you'll see that it's made of flat crystals that "cleave"; like mica, it has flat crystals that peel away from one another.

HINT *Fleur de sel has a delicate flavor and looks great on top of small servings. It's expensive, so use it at the end.*

Do I need a salt mill?

Admittedly, a salt mill looks classy at the table, but most salt mills work only with salt that's dry. The best sea salts are usually wet.

62   When do I add salt?

It depends. If you have forethought, season fish and meat a couple of hours or more before cooking and then pat them dry before browning. This gives the salt time to penetrate the food. Because salt draws water out of foods, which can interfere with browning, the foods need to be patted dry. If you don't have time to salt ahead of time, salt just before browning (such as for a stew) or just before serving (as for steak). Broths and sauces should be salted just before serving in case you want to boil them down (reduce them) to concentrate them. Boiling down liquids increases the concentration of any salts they contain.

Why is some salt dry and some wet?

Morton Salt made the expression "When it rains, it pours" famous by marketing salt that was always dry. Sea salt is what's called hygroscopic, which means it absorbs moisture from the air and is always somewhat wet. To prevent this, some companies add a magnesium compound to the salt to keep it dry. This also makes it easier to pour.

63   How to grind and use pepper

Freshly grind pepper so that its aroma isn't allowed to evaporate. A small simple pepper mill is best for this—the Peugeot brand is the classic found all over France, both on the table and in the kitchen—and keep it next to the stove. The Peugeot brand is designed so that by turning the mill clockwise, the pepper is ground fine, and by turning it counterclockwise, the pepper is coarse.

When to use pepper

Don't add pepper to foods until just before serving or just before browning; if you do, the flavor of the pepper will cook off and leave a harsh flavor. This is especially true for soups and broths, which should never be peppered before they are served.

64 How to add chile hotness

Chile peppers, especially dried chiles, come in such variety that we often don't know which one to use where. Dried chiles are most flavorful when reconstituted with a 30-minute soaking in warm water. To use them, discard the liquid, seed, and chop into a paste. To help you identify and understand more about fresh and dried chiles, here's a brief rundown.

Fresh

Depending on where you live, a variety of fresh chiles is available at different times of the year. Fresh chiles benefit from being blackened over a flame and then peeled.

• **Anaheim:** These long, thin green chiles are good for stuffing, and like bell peppers, their taste is improved by charring and peeling them (see entry 186) before they are stuffed or added to soups, stews, or salads. Occasionally, you may find red Anaheim chiles, which have a sweeter, less vegetablelike flavor than the green ones.

• **Fresno:** Shaped a little like a stubby jalapeño, these red chiles are, in fact, sometimes mistaken for jalapeños—until they're bitten into. Fresno chiles are considerably hotter and great in salsas.

• **Habanero:** Sometimes described as "lantern-shaped," these roundish chiles come in all colors. Regardless of color, they are very hot; seed them with gloves on to protect your hands from the very hot oil they contain. Use them in salsas or salads containing tropical fruits.

• **Jalapeño:** Usually green, but on occasion red, jalapeños are being bred to be larger and to contain much less heat than they had in the past. They are a good all-round, easy-to-find source of heat, but they don't have much flavor. They are more delicious when they're smoked, and then they're called chipotle chiles and come canned in adobo sauce or dried.

• **New Mexico:** Green or red, as long as nine inches, with medium heat, New Mexico chiles are great used in salsas or, when charred and peeled, in strips in sandwiches and on burgers.

• **Poblano:** One of the most flavorful chiles, poblanos are dark green and more pointed than bell peppers. They range in heat from mild to hot, but they're often good in dishes as a substitute for bell peppers. If you can find red poblanos, which have an even better flavor, scoop them up.

• **Scotch bonnet:** These look like habaneros, small and roundish, and have similar heat: They're very hot. They're used in Caribbean cooking and in jerk rubs.

• **Serrano:** These look like elongated jalapeño chiles and can be used in recipes that call for heat. They tend to be quite hot, although they're not as hot as habaneros or Scotch bonnets. They're usually available green or red.

• **Thai:** These tiny chiles come green or red and are often called for in Southeast Asian cooking. Although they are much hotter than jalapeños, they're also much smaller and can be substituted one for one.

How to peel chiles

Larger chiles can be peeled very easily. Follow the techniques described for peeling bell peppers in entry 186. However, keep in mind that chiles usually have thinner skins than peppers, so it's important not to overcook them, or they'll fall apart.

Dried

When dried, chiles provide us with some of nature's most complex flavors. To bring out their flavor, put them in a skillet over medium heat and stir them around until you smell their fragrance, but be careful not to scorch them. Then soak them for 30 minutes or so in hot water before seeding and stemming them. After soaking, you can puree them in a blender with just enough water to get the mixture to turn around and then transfer the purees to resealable plastic bags and freeze them. When buying dried chiles, look for those that still retain some moisture and have a leathery texture, not brittle.

• **Ancho:** These dark orange chilis are dried red poblanos. They are one of the three chiles called for in mole sauces, but they can also be used in barbecue sauces or, pureed, added to the juices of a pot roast or the liquid in a stew.

• **Chilhuacle negro:** These black bell-pepper-shaped chiles are somewhat rare but have such a distinctive flavor that they're worth searching out. They are used in southern Mexico to make black mole sauces, but they also make a delicious sauce when simply pureed and combined with some heavy cream.

• **Chipotle:** These are smoked jalapeños, but are much hotter. Marvelous in salsas, they add a note of smoky complexity. Canned chipotle chiles usually come surrounded with a tomato sauce called adobo sauce, which can be rinsed off before seeding the chiles, or used in recipes as is.

• **Guajillo:** These long, thin, dark orange chiles are one of the three used for moles. These chiles are also often called for in Mexican-style soups and stews.

• **Mulato:** These almost black, large flat chiles are used to make mole sauces, soups, stews, and braised dishes. Mulatos, like anchos, are a form of dried poblano chiles.

• **New Mexico:** These are simply the dried version of New Mexico fresh chiles; they come in all colors.

• **Pasilla:** These long, thin dark chiles are dried chilaca chiles, chiles we rarely see fresh. The word *pasilla* is sometimes mistakenly used to mean ancho or mulato chiles, or even fresh poblanos.

• **Pasilla de Oaxaca:** These small, very wrinkled, deep orange chiles are hard to find but worth the search. They have a deep smoky flavor and a lot of heat.

• **Pepperoncini:** These long, cone-shaped little red chiles are used in Italy to mildly flavor sauces, pasta dishes, and in antipasti.

RECONSTITUTING DRIED CHILES

Dried chiles have an amazing complex flavor that can be used to flavor all sorts of soups, stews, and sauces. To use them, they must be reconstituted. Their flavor is enhanced if you first stir them around in a skillet over high heat to toast them a little before soaking them in hot water for about 30 minutes to soften them. When they're soft, just remove the stems and seeds and chop the chiles or puree them in a blender. Pureed with a little hot heavy cream, they make any number of interesting sauces for chiles rellenos, enchiladas, seafoods, or chicken.

65 How to marinate

Seafood, meat, poultry, and vegetables are often soaked with flavorful ingredients ahead of cooking so the flavor of these ingredients has time to penetrate the food. What ingredients you put in the marinade depends, of course, on what you're cooking and how. When marinating stew meat, also marinate the vegetables you're going to use in the braise. Combine the vegetables, meat, and herbs and pour over the liquids. If you're marinating steaks or fish that are getting only minimal cooking, don't include wine or other alcohol in the marinade because the alcohol won't get hot enough to cook off.

• **Seafood:** Use chopped herbs such as tarragon for delicate seafood and stronger herbs such as marjoram or oregano for more assertive seafood such as squid. Avoid lemon in seafood marinades, since it can "cook" the seafood and cause it to stick to a grill.

• **Steaks:** Don't use alcohol such as wine because it won't cook off. Keep it simple and try a little soy sauce, thyme, and garlic.

• **Stew meat:** Because stews are cooked long enough to cook off alcohol, include wine in the marinade—use the same wine you're using to stew the meat in—and aromatic vegetables, especially garlic (see entry 16).

• **Vegetables:** Brush vegetables with good olive oil and sprinkle them with chopped fresh herbs. If you're grilling or sautéing more than one vegetable, experiment with different herbs for each one.

66 How to juice a lemon

If you're stuck at the summer rental and have no way to squeeze a lemon, halve the lemons through the equator and poke the inside of each half with a fork a few times. Push the fork into the pulp and twist it while you squeeze the fruit.

If you are in the market for a juicer, here are some suggestions.

• The simplest gadget is a handheld wooden or metal juicer with ridges on it. You insert the juicer into half of the citrus fruit and twist.

• Electric citrus juicers are similar to thr handheld kind with ridges, except that a motor turns the device for you while you press the fruit down on it.

• Don't confuse "juicers" meant for finely pureeing fruits or vegetables with citrus juicers.

• The best juicer is a juicer that you can bolt to your work surface and that has a cuplike receptacle on the base and a squeezer on the top. The whole device looks like an old-fashioned espresso machine.

67 Which vinegar to use

Much underrated, vinegar can have almost as important a role in cooking as wine. Chicken simmered in sherry vinegar is every bit as satisfying as coq au vin. Poor-quality vinegar, in turn, makes less-than-flavorful salad dressings.

Sherry vinegar

At one time this was the best value among vinegars, but the quality of sherry vinegar has slipped, probably because stocks of old sherry have run low as sherry vinegar has become popular. Look for sherry vinegars with the age of the vinegar on the bottle.

Balsamic vinegar

All kinds of vinegar that taste vaguely sweet with a hint of caramel, hide under this name. Cheap balsamic vinegar, boiled down by half, is surprisingly good, but you shouldn't pay much for it to begin with.

Authentic (*autentico*) balsamic vinegar is aged in a succession of barrels made from different woods and is made from grape must, not wine. When authentic, and there are strict laws governing how and where it is made, balsamic vinegar is perhaps the priciest of all liquids, exceeding Bordeaux wine. One doesn't use authentic balsamic vinegar on a salad. Instead, serve it, with an accompanying eye-dropper, with simple pieces of grilled seafood, fruits, or other dishes that benefit from its accent.

Champagne vinegar

While this vinegar tastes nothing like champagne, it offers a clean source of acidity without any bite.

Cider vinegar

Most cider vinegar off the supermarket shelf is harsh, but if you can find a good one, perhaps at the local farmers' market, use it to simmer a chicken and finish the sauce with cream. Use it also to give a note of acidity to cabbage with apples or duck served with fruits.

Fruit vinegars

More often than not, fruit vinegars are indifferent wine vinegar infused with raspberries or other fruit that have been cooked down to concentrate their sweetness. The result is a candylike fruitiness that can ruin a salad. Despite this, it's worth experimenting with infused vinegars at home. The most reliable is tarragon vinegar—just shove sprigs of tarragon in a bottle of white wine vinegar—but other herbs such as marjoram or rosemary work as well.

68 How to make flavored oils and vinegars

The easiest and most straightforward method of flavoring oils or vinegars is simply to push sprigs of fresh herbs into a bottle of favorite oil or vinegar and let sit for a couple of weeks. If you're in a hurry, put the full bottle in a pot of boiling water for 30 minutes to heat it and help extract the flavor of the herb. Alternately, puree the herbs with the oil in a food processor and strain.

69   How to wash lettuce

Many of us brutalize lettuce and cause it to wilt quickly by handling it roughly and by spinning it with too much force in a lettuce spinner. Treat it lovingly, rinse and dry it well (wet lettuce dilutes the sauce so it tastes watery), and don't tear it up into pieces that are too small.

HINT *Wash spinach, Swiss chard, sorrel, and other leafy greens in the same way. Don't run water on the leaves or they'll bruise.*

1. Fill a large bowl with cold water and gently put in the leaves.

2. Stir them around gently and then let them sit a couple of minutes. Transfer them, with splayed fingers, to another bowl.

3. Feel the bottom of the first bowl. If you feel any sand or grit, rinse it out, refill the bowl, and repeat the soaking.

4. Most lettuce requires only one soaking, but some greens, such as arugula or basil, are sandy and require as many as three soakings.

70   How to use a lettuce spinner

A lettuce spinner is one of the great inventions of the twentieth century. Unless you're used to them, don't buy the kind of spinner that allows liquid to come out a hole in the bottom or confused guests will make a mess. When using the lettuce spinner don't become too enthusiastic and spin too fast, crushing the lettuce against the sides of the spinner. It's better to spin gently, take off the top and toss the lettuce in the bas-

ket to redistribute it, spin some more, and repeat until all the water is removed from the greens.

HINT *If you're ever stuck without a lettuce spinner, wrap the lettuce, in batches if necessary, in a kitchen towel or pillowcase, bring up the four corners and hold them together while you walk outside and, with your arm fully extended, make the fastest propellerlike motion you can make with the lettuce. Very effective but you'll be winded.*

71 How to dress a salad

Salad should never come into contact with vinegar before it is served or it will wilt. To prepare a salad ahead of time, put the ingredients for the sauce or a vinaigrette in the bottom of a large salad bowl. Put two long spoons or a salad set in the bowl crisscrossed and put the greens on top. In this way the salad implements keep the salad above the vinegar. You then just toss before serving.

HINT *An emulsified vinaigrette (see entry 72) has more body and is good for spreading on cold or hot foods such as fish, poultry, or veal. If it separates, as it tends to, slowly whisk the broken vinaigrette into a teaspoon of mustard, a tablespoon of heavy cream, or an egg yolk.*

A simple vinaigrette

For salads, just sprinkle over a little vinegar, grind over some salt and pepper, and pour over about 3 times as much oil as vinegar. If doing this by eye makes you nervous, measure out 1 tablespoon vinegar and 3 tablespoons oil for a typical salad for four.

What's the best kind of salad bowl?

Always buy a bowl that's twice the size of the salad you'll be tossing so there's room to toss. The bowl has little to no effect on the flavor of the salad, so wood, porcelain, glass, or even stainless steel will work equally well.

72   How to make an emulsified vinaigrette

A vinaigrette is simply vinegar and oil, and perhaps some additional flavorings, held together in an emulsion with mustard. To flavor a vinaigrette, you can use infused oils or vinegars (see entry 68) and add herbs, shallots, or garlic. The most important thing to remember is to use good-quality vinegar and extra virgin olive oil, each with flavors that both please you and complement each other.

1. To make enough vinaigrette for four, stir together 1 tablespoon good wine vinegar and 2 teaspoons Dijon mustard in a bowl large enough to hold the greens.

2. Add flavorings such as chopped tarragon, basil, marjoram, shallots, or garlic, or none at all. Season with kosher salt and freshly ground black pepper.

3. Whisk in 3 tablespoons extra virgin olive oil in a slow steady stream.

73 How to make your own vinegar

The best and most economical way to get good vinegar is to make your own. With a little luck, you can make vinegar just by letting red wine sit in a warm place in a glass container covered with cheesecloth for a month or so. For more reliable results, use a vinegar "mother"— vinegar with the active vinegar-making bacteria in it—or some home-made vinegar from a friend to get your vinegar going. Better yet, buy a white oak barrel from a wine-making supply store and keep the opening covered with a towel to keep out fruit flies and dust.

1. Combine equal parts mother vinegar and red wine and let sit in a warm place, near a furnace or the water heater perhaps.

2. After 2 weeks, add another cup of wine.

3. Wait another 2 weeks and add another cup of wine; repeat until you have as much vinegar as you want.

4. Wait 6 weeks and then draw out the vinegar, no more than a fourth at a time, and replace it with wine saved from the ends of bottles.

74 How to store fresh herbs

Oily herbs such as thyme are best stored tied loosely together with string and hung in the open air. Delicate watery herbs such as parsley, chives, tarragon, chervil, and basil are best kept with the sprigs submerged in water in a large glass tumbler; the tumbler should be covered with a plastic bag secured to the sides of the glass with a rubber band. Herbs kept this way in the refrigerator will last about 5 days or sometimes as long as two weeks. Change the water every couple of days. If left in plastic bags or wrapped tightly in plastic in the refrigerator, herbs will go bad quickly.

75 How to chop herbs quickly and efficiently

Some cooks, especially novices or those who've never worked in a prep kitchen, will spend the better part of an hour carefully removing the individual leaves from the stems of bunches of herbs. In fact, delicate stems are indistinguishable when chopped with the leaves.

• To chop bunches of parsley, chervil, or cilantro, just cut off the bulk of the stems—particularly those with no leaves on them. Then chop the leaves with the small stems.

• Tarragon and basil have hardier stems, which should be removed before chopping. To take the leaves off tarragon, pull downward along the stem, pinching gently with your thumb and forefinger to pull away the leaves as you slide down the stem. Don't pick off the leaves one by one. This method also works with oily herbs such as thyme, marjoram, rosemary, and oregano.

• Chives require a chopping method all their own. They can't be chopped randomly as you would parsley (see entry 93). Instead, take about 8 chive sprigs at a time, align them carefully with one another, and pinch them together with the thumb and fingers of one hand and use the other to slice. Slice them as thin as you can.

HINT *After you cut off any stems, or if you have any sprigs left over, you can tie them up in little bundles and use in bouquet garnis. Tarragon stems are great infused in poultry broth.*

76 How to grind dry herbs and spices

Herbs that you've dried or that you bought dried and whole are best chopped rather than ground. In fact, a good method is to chop them coarsely a few hours before you need them and then, at the last minute, chop them finely to release their flavor.

Spices are best ground in a clean coffee grinder—preferably one reserved for just this purpose. Cinnamon sticks, however, are too hard and can damage the motor and blade. The only way to deal with cinnamon is to wrap it in a towel and hammer it to break it up. Then grind the pieces in a food processor and then again in the coffee grinder.

How to store herbs by drying

Rather than allow fresh herbs like rosemary, thyme, or oregano to decompose in the refrigerator, tie them in bundles with string and hang to dry. Dried herbs can be kept for a couple of months.

77 How to preserve and dry herbs

Herbs take differently to preserving methods, such as drying or freezing.

HINT *Any herb can be used to make a compound butter (see entry 102), and the butter kept easily for a month in the fridge or longer in the freezer.*

Oily herbs

Oily herbs such as thyme, rosemary, marjoram, hyssop, lavender leaves and flowers, and oregano can simply be tied in small bundles with string and hung up in a dry breezy place. These herbs can also be preserved in oil or vinegar. Sage is an oily herb that doesn't take well to drying but can be preserved easily and well in olive oil.

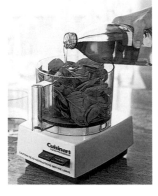

Watery herbs

Watery herbs such as chives, basil, parsley, tarragon, and chervil, don't dry well. Tarragon is delicious in vinegar and keeps its flavor intact (see entry 99), but the others are best made into pestos (see entry 371) by pureeing them with pure olive oil and immediately freezing the mixture in a tightly sealed container.

How much dried herb equals how much fresh?

Herbs all dry differently; some get stronger while others weaken. It's impossible to come up with an equation that will work for all herbs. Dried thyme, for example, is about four times as strong as the same volume of fresh. Dried oregano is about ten times as strong as the same amount of fresh. (Dried parsley, chervil, chives, tarragon, and cilantro are useless in the kitchen because they lose all flavor when dried.)

When making a "fines herbes" mixture, I recommend using 3 times the chervil and parsley to tarragon, since tarragon is much stronger.

78 How do I use basil?

Is any herb more versatile or more seductive than basil? Nowadays, basil is abundantly available from our gardens or local markets in the summer. It's so abundant, in fact, that any large excess can be put in the food processor with some olive oil and frozen into a sort of pesto (minus the garlic, the pine nuts, and cheese), which can whisked into sauces, soups, sautéed vegetables, or pasta to provide a burst of summer in the off months. Chopped or ground with olive oil it is pesto-like; chopped into butter it becomes a bit French and a perfect candidate for finishing a subtle sauce or soup. It's marvelous swirled into a soup of fish or that French edition of minestrone called pistou. Whisk it into a fresh tomato soup or tomato sauce (see entry 374) at the last minute. In fact, basil should always be used at the last minute—its aroma and flavor are short-lived—not simmered as one would thyme.

While it is an herb, basil is also a green, and in the summer months it's great mixed into a salad, not just to flavor it, but to add real substance. Try using equal parts basil leaves and arugula for your summer salads.

79 How do I use bay leaves?

First, buy only imported bay leaves—unless you happen to live in Greece or Turkey. American bay leaves have an aggressive eucalyptus quality that dominates anything they're cooked in. The European bay leaf, sometimes called "laurel," is best in long-simmered stews and braised dishes that contain wine. The flavor of bay leaf (and thyme and aromatic vegetables) merge into the essence of the best braised dishes.

80 How do I use chervil?

Regrettably, chervil is hard to find and not that easy to plant. It is delicate and shade-loving but ever so fussy. This tiny filigreelike sprig has a flavor that's vaguely like tarragon's, but it's much more fleeting. It shares with parsley a subtle freshness that can be used at the last minute for seafood sauces and sauces for chicken, veal, and pork. Unlike parsley, which has become a bit trite, a tiny sprig or two of chervil is a beautiful garniture on a salad or seafood stew. It is also delicious in omelets.

Chervil is often combined with parsley, whose subtlety it matches, chives, and tarragon in the mixture known as fines herbes. While the idea of such a mixture is brilliant, its fault is including tarragon, which is about four times stronger than the three others. The solution, of course, is to cut the tarragon to a fourth as much as the others.

81 What kind of chili powder is best?

Dried chiles have amazingly complex and deep flavors. However, most chili powders are rather uninteresting. The solution is to make your own assortment, using different dried chilies.

1. Seed and stem your favorite chiles and toast them on the stove in an iron skillet.

2. When they're well dried and crisp, grind the chiles in a food processor.

3. Work the ground chiles through a strainer or food mill.

4. Dry what doesn't go through the strainer in the skillet, if necessary. Then grind and strain again.

5. Repeat as often as is practical or necessary.

82 How do I use chives?

Unlike most herbs, which can be chopped haphazardly until fine, chives must be approached with a certain precision or they'll look careless and feel raw in the mouth. Group together tightly as many sprigs as you feel comfortable with and slice them as finely as possible. Don't use scissors, which can't cut them finely enough. Do your best to slice them microscopically thin, using a chef's knife; tiny lengths of chive are unappealing.

Chives are, of course, a member of the onion family and can be used to flavor sauces, in steaming liquids from shellfish, and as a final sprinkle for soups. Combined with parsley, chervil, and tarragon, they create a very subtle combination known as fines herbes.

83   How do I use cilantro?

A few people describe the taste of cilantro—the leaves of the coriander plant—as vaguely soapy. To dispel this impression, and show it off at its best, cilantro is best combined with hot spicy foods—especially Indian and Mexican—and the flavor of hot chiles, both fresh and dried. It's also magnificent with Thai food and other Southeast Asian foods and seems to go perfectly with fish sauce, lemongrass, and kaffir lime leaves. In any dish calling for curry powder (see entry 86), add a little chopped cilantro at the end and watch the flavors of the spices come into focus and gain a new vitality.

Cilantro looks so much like Italian parsley that your best bet is to give it a sniff to make sure you're buying the right one before you get to the checkout counter.

84   How do I use cloves?

Cloves are sometimes called for, ground, in Indian spice mixtures. In European cooking, the classic use is in braised dishes that call for poking a clove into an onion—the subtle presence of clove is essential in a classic white veal stew—or in the classic four spice mixture (quatre épices) used to flavor pâtés. Cloves have been used to ruin many a bottle of red wine in mulled wine.

85 How do I use coriander seeds?

When roasted and ground, these form the base for many Indian curry mixtures. In European cooking, coriander is used to make Greek-style salad (salade grecque) in which vegetables such as baby onions, artichoke bottoms, zucchini, and fennel are cooked together with whole coriander seeds, olive oil, and white wine. Coriander seeds are delicious with fennel and carrots, to which they can be added before pureeing and working through a strainer or food mill. Coriander is also used to make pickles. Coriander leaves are called cilantro.

86 How to use curry powder

Indian cooks never use what we call curry powder, but instead, blend different spices, depending on the recipe. The best cooks roast and grind the spices the day they use them. In order to avoid roasting spices every time they're needed, it's a good idea to roast whole spices in batches (except cinnamon and cloves, which just lose their flavor). After roasting, they should be sealed tightly in small tins or aluminum foil and can be frozen for up to a year.

If you're making your own spice mixture, good spices to start with are cumin and coriander with smaller amounts of cardamom. "Sweet" spices such as cinnamon, cloves, ginger, and nutmeg should be used in very small amounts. To give the blend a more appealing yellow color, include turmeric. For maple flavor, include a generous proportion of fenugreek.

The best curry powders to buy are Garam Masala and Madras blends, which are most sophisticated than the standard "curry" powder. When using curry powder in a recipe, cook it in a pan with a little oil or butter for a minute to bring out its flavor.

87 What do I do with dill?

Dill is delicious incorporated into mayonnaises, which can then be dolloped on cold fish and meats. Chopped dill is also great with cucumbers in a sauce containing cream and lemon. Dill butter is lovely on boiled potatoes. Dill is also the classic flavoring for gravlax and crayfish dishes.

88 How to use fresh ginger

Ginger looks like a knobby root but is actually a rhizome, which is a rootlike stem. If you're infusing the flavor of ginger in a crème anglaise (see entry 465) or in another hot liquid, just slice it thin, add the slices to the sauce for a time, and strain them out. If you're using ginger in a pâté or a cake, it's often more convenient to use powdered ginger. When tasted alone, powdered ginger, of course, has none of the "punch" of fresh ginger, but when baked in a cake it's hard to discern a difference. If you're insistent on using fresh ginger in a cookie recipe, for example, cut off a section of the peel and grate the ginger on the finest side of a box grater or with a rasp grater.

To chop, trim off some of the peel, or cut off a section and chop it. If you're using a large amount, it can be peeled and then be chopped in a food processor.

  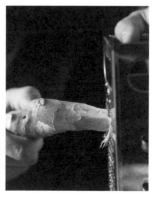

89 How do I use marjoram?

Somewhat hard to find and often confused with oregano, marjoram is worth seeking out. It has a distinctive clean aroma that asserts itself without dominating, which is particularly good on grilled foods. It's better fresh, but drying it doesn't really harm it—it simply weakens the flavor slightly. Chop marjoram with a little olive oil (the oil helps trap its flavor and keep it from turning black) and rub it on fish or meats to be grilled or sautéed. Marjoram is wonderful with lamb— sprinkle it chopped on the meat itself or add it to a sauce. If you have more than you need, you can dry it as you do thyme or infuse it in olive oil; it doesn't do much in vinegar.

90 How do I use mint?

Some varieties of mint are stronger than others and can be chopped or ground and added to a vinaigrette (see entry 72) for a salad. Less aggressive varieties, usually those with larger leaves, can be tossed in the salad along with greens such as basil and arugula. Lightly chopped mint always makes a bit of a surprise on top of fruity summer tomatoes and is a classic addition to cucumber raita, an Indian cucumber salad made with tangy yogurt. Mint can be sneaked into any sauce or salsa that might otherwise call for cilantro; it goes well with the heat of chile peppers in the same way cilantro does.

91 How do I use nutmeg?

Cautiously. Nutmeg, like its close relative mace, is very powerful. It is traditionally used in pork and duck pâtés, in gratins that contain cheese (it's added to the béchamel sauce), and as a final note on top of an eggnog. It also plays a role in several more complicated Indian spice mixtures.

92 What do I do with oregano?

One of the few herbs that becomes stronger as it dries, oregano comes in several varieties that could be confused with marjoram. Dried oregano has a much stronger taste than fresh oregano, whose flavor could almost be described as mild. Use dried oregano on grilled meats—spread it, chopped, on the meat before grilling—and fresh oregano in more delicate dishes such as tomato sauces.

93 Is parsley more than a garnish?

Perhaps it's because it's so available and inexpensive that we take parsley for granted. We don't consider what it adds. A sprig on a plate, in fact, doesn't add much besides a little color. But when parsley is chopped finely at the last minute and added to both seafood and meat sauces, it contributes complexity and nuance. It is often the missing element in a long-cooked sauce that has lost some of its vitality and freshness for having spent long hours on the stove. It's also used in innumerable stuffings, meat loaf, pâté, and salads. And it's the central element in tabouleh salad.

HINT *Stir parsley into meat sauces and stews at the last minute—simmer for 30 seconds or so to give sauces that final note of freshness.*

How to buy and clean

When buying parsley, look for the flat-leaved Italian variety, which has a bit more punch than the curly kind. If you can't find it, the "frizzy" type still has plenty to offer. Cut off the large stems but don't worry about picking off the small stems and separating each leaf. Just hold the bunch of parsley with one hand and cut off the bulk of the large stems with a large chef's knife. Wash the leaves, with the small-

tools, techniques, and advice

67

er stems attached, and dry them in a lettuce spinner. It's important that they be dry before you chop them or their flavor will stay in a puddle of liquid on the cutting board.

How to chop

Chop parsley as you should all herbs—with a razor-sharp knife that will cut rather than crush. When crushed, herbs release their flavors, which end up embedded in the cutting board. Chop the parsley very fine at the last minute. If this isn't practical, chop it three fourths of the way ahead of time and give it a final chop at the last minute in order to release its flavor. Don't chop it entirely ahead of time or it will smell like lawn mower clippings.

94 What do I do with rosemary?

Be careful—rosemary can overpower the taste of what it's supposed to complement. Some cooks automatically think of rosemary when cooking lamb, but rosemary, in fact, can make lamb taste gamy. To use it at its subtle best, shove sprigs on the charcoal fire made for grilling; its smoke is gentle and will contribute a hint of the herb's flavor. Rosemary is good with garlic as long as it is chopped very finely, so that no one is pricked with its sharp needles.

95 How to buy and use saffron

Saffron, which is parts of a small crocus flower call the stigmas, scares a lot of cooks because of its cost and "exotic" nature. Rather than buy saffron in those tiny vials at the supermarket, which cost about as much as good steak, buy it by the ounce (for about $35) online or in shops that sell bulk herbs and spices. An ounce is about 6 tablespoons of threads, and you need only ¼ teaspoon for an average risotto. As the threads dry, you can grind them by pinching them between your thumb and forefinger and moving them back and forth. Saffron ground in this way equals twice as many saffron threads, so adjust your recipes accordingly.

HINT *To release saffron's flavor, crush the threads between your thumb and forefinger and soak them in a tablespoon of water for 30 minutes before adding them, along with the soaking liquid, to soups, sauces, stews, or risottos.*

How to use saffron

Despite the cost and rarity of saffron, its aromatic flavor appears in all manner of dishes all over the world. In addition to risotto (see entry 138), especially risotto Milanese, it is traditionally added to basic rice preparations such as pilafs (see entry 137); couscous; butter and cream sauces for fish; and even cakes, cookies, pies, and custards. It's especially popular seasoning in Spanish seafood or meat dishes such as paella, in bouillabaisse, and in many beef and lamb dishes.

96 How should I use sage?

Sage is lovely with pork and veal. Just lay a few fresh sage leaves on the roast while it's in the oven and they'll perfume it. One of the best ways to use sage is to cook it in butter until the butter froths and lightly browns and then pour this over ravioli that have been stuffed with ricotta. Sage is also good simmered in soups that contain garlic. Sage is best used whole. When it's chopped and added to soups or sauces, it can be aggressive. Dried sage quickly develops a stale dusty flavor. Try cooking chopped sage in a little cream and then tossing the resulting sauce with cooked pasta.

97 What do I do with savory?

Savory comes in a perennial winter variety and an annual summer variety. The winter variety is justifiably preferred by the French, who use it to braise rabbit, wrap goat cheese, and chopped to flavor fava beans. Chopped winter savory adds an exciting note to a green salad.

98 How do I use sorrel?

Sorrel is really less like an herb than it is a green leafy vegetable. It looks vaguely like baby spinach but is greener and shouldn't be cooked, as spinach is, in a pot of boiling water, or it will turn to nothing. When chopped it remains green but the instant it gets hot, it turns a sullen gray. It is divine in fish sauces to which it lends a tangy lemonlike acidity. It can be creamed like spinach and be served as a vegetable to accompany fish and white meats. It makes wonderful soup when added to a basic leek and potato soup and pureed. When pureed in a cream soup thickened with egg yolks and chilled, it becomes one of the world's great soups: potage Germiny. It's hard to find, doesn't dry well, and needs to be used in relatively large amounts to be appreciated. It's a good thing to grow.

99 How do I use tarragon?

Tarragon has an unmistakable flavor that the uninitiated describe as anise- or licoricelike, but when familiar acquires its own identity. Tarragon is so delicious and so perfect with fish. Along with shallots, it defines béarnaise sauce (see Hint, page 322). It goes beautifully with tomatoes, much as basil does, but in a more intricate way, and when cream is included, the aniselike tarragon notes are brought stunningly into relief. Tarragon is delicious with poultry and can be included in a bouquet garni in chicken broth. You can also slide sprigs of tarragon under the skin of a chicken to give it a subtle yet unmistakable flavor.

Once hard to find, tarragon now is sold in such large bunches that we're often stuck with more than we know what to do with. Shoving the extras down the neck of a bottle of vinegar is one obvious solution. Another is chopping it finely with butter to make tarragon butter, which, when tightly wrapped, keeps for months in the freezer and can be used to finish seafood sauces made from the steaming liquids from shellfish or it can be whisked into a deglazed pan used to sauté chicken. It's not bad on grilled corn either. But don't try to dry tarragon, it just turns stale.

HINT *Tarragon dominates the flavor of fines herbs—a pairing with parsley, chives, and chervil—so when used with these other herbs, reduce the amount accordingly.*

100 How do I use thyme?

Thyme may be second only to parsley in usefulness in the kitchen but is used very differently. Thyme can be used in three ways: slowly simmered in liquids to integrate its flavor with that of aromatic vegetables and wine; chopped and added to sauces or liquids just before serving for a sudden burst of direct flavor; or chopped and sprinkled on meats or seafood destined for grilling.

Until not long ago we could find thyme only in jars, but now it's available fresh year-round. You'll rarely need a whole bunch, but since thyme dries easily without loosing its character, drying is an easy solution. Just use as much as you need and tie the rest with string on one end and hang it somewhere in the kitchen to dry. When it's thoroughly dried, just rub the dried bunch while suspending it over a steak or chop and the dried leaves will sprinkle down as seasoning. You may also want to slip sprigs of thyme down the neck of a bottle of olive oil to give a little herbal flavor to your oil. There are several varieties of thyme, including lemon thyme, which isn't a substitute for "regular" thyme. Lemon thyme has a somewhat aggressive lemon flavor that's a little reminiscent of a popular furniture polish.

101 Can I substitute herbs in recipes?

While there's no easy answer as to why an herb works well with one thing and not another, it is possible to divide herbs into two basic kinds: there are those that are oily and whose aroma is contained in the oil, and those that are basically watery (see entry 77). The distinction may seem irrelevant except that the two groups behave in somewhat predictable ways when added to food. Water-based herbs have a relatively fleeting aroma, don't dry well, and grow stale quickly. Oily herbs release their aroma and flavor slowly into surrounding liquids and dry well; in fact it may be that the oil they contain is designed to prevent them from drying out in the hot climates where they like to grow. Oily herbs can be simmered in slow-cooking dishes such as stews—for example, thyme being one of the standard herbs in a bouquet garni—or they can be dried, which intensifies their flavor rather than weakening it, as happens with water-based herbs, and can be sprinkled on meats and seafood before grilling. Watery herbs should be used in ways that capitalize on their color, freshness, and subtlety.

Watery herbs		Oily herbs		
Basil	Cilantro	Bay Leaves	Marjoram	Sage
Chervil	Parsley	Hyssop	Oregano	Savory
Chives	Tarragon	Lavender	Rosemary	Thyme

102 How to make herb butters

Start by chopping fresh herbs with slightly softened but still cold butter. When the herb is well mixed into the butter, form the butter into a rough sausage shape on a sheet of wax paper and roll it up

tightly. Once it's rolled up, twist the paper at the ends of the "sausage" in opposite directions to tighten the shape. Wrap this in aluminum foil to help it hold its shape and to keep the wax paper from coming away from the butter. Freeze for up to a year; refrigerate for up to a month. Cut into slices and use it to top grilled meats and seafood or to whisk into other sauces.

103   What is a bouquet garni?

A bouquet garni is simply a bundle of fresh herbs or a packet of dried herbs used to flavor broths, sauces, and soups. The purpose of tying the herbs together is to make them easier to pull out of the liquid at the end and to keep the herbs from floating up and interfering with the skimming of stocks that release scum and fat. If you put the herbs in the bottom of the pot and cover them with bones, or if the liquid is not being skimmed and is going to be strained, just put the herbs in loose.

HINT *The standard bouquet garni is made of thyme, parsley, and bay leaf, but you can use any herbs you want that release their flavors slowly.*

How to make a bouquet garni with fresh herbs

Wrap your herbs together with string. The size of the bouquet garni depends on the amount of liquid it's flavoring. For 10 quarts of liquid, your bouquet should have the thickness of a wrist. For a very small amount of sauce, the thickness of a finger will suffice. Use parsley, sprigs of fresh thyme, and imported bay leaves.

How to make a bouquet garni with dried herbs

Wrap the dried herbs in a green frond of leek and tie it with string, or wrap the herbs in a packet of cheesecloth held together with string.

104 How to use fish sauce

Fish sauce is the backbone and soul of Thai and Vietnamese cooking. While it might be unpleasant tasting alone, it brings to life all sorts of ingredients. Since fish sauces vary enormously in intensity, it's impossible in a recipe to specify exactly how much is right. The best system for judging is to add the minimum and then continue adding until the dish has the right saltiness.

105 How to use gelatin

Gelatin is a protein that dissolves in hot liquids and sets, or "gels," when cold. It is used to set light custards such as panna cotta (see entry 457) and savory preparations like vegtable gelées.

- The natural gelatin contained in meat and bones is what causes cold broth, consommé, and natural aspic to set.
- Many of us don't like gelatin because when overused, it makes

things rubbery. It's best used in the smallest amount needed to get a liquid to set—about half the amount specified on the package, which says that one packet will set 1 cup liquid. In fact, one packet will barely set (which is ideal) 2 cups liquid.

• When using powdered gelatin, soften it in about 3 tablespoons cold water per packet before adding it to hot or warm liquids.

• Occasionally, recipes will call for sheet gelatin, the preferred form in Europe. When using sheet gelatin, soak it first in cold water until it becomes soft and malleable. It's difficult to arrive at equivalents between sheet gelatin and powdered gelatin because different brands of sheet gelatin contain different amounts of gelatin per sheet.

106 How to roast and store nuts

It's a good habit to roast raw nuts as soon as you get them home from the store, and then to freeze them. Roasted nuts have more taste and will keep longer without turning rancid. This is also the method you use when a recipe calls for roasted nuts.

HINT *Nuts roasted before freezing are always ready to use in recipes that call for nuts, roasted or otherwise.*

1. Spread the nuts in a single layer on a sheet pan.

2. Bake in a 350°F oven for 15 minutes, or until the nuts are golden brown and smell fragrant. If they're not browning evenly, turn the sheet pan around halfway through the roasting.

3. Let cool and store in the freezer in a tightly sealed container. Most nuts will keep in this way for several months.

tools, techniques, and advice

107 Measures and conversions

For a rough equivalent between the metric system and the traditional systems used in the United States to measure weight and volume, a liter is about a quart, 250 milliliters about a cup. A tablespoon is 15 milliliters and a teaspoon 5 milliliters (it helps to remember that a teaspoon is a third of a tablespoon). A cup of flour usually weighs about 160 grams. A liter of water weighs a kilogram, so 250 milliliters of water (and most liquids used in cooking) weigh 250 grams. A kilo is a little more than 2 pounds. A pound is about 450 grams. If you get used to using the metric system in baking, everything is beautifully easy to see in proportions and much easier to remember.

Here are some tables of measurements, as well as some approximate equivalents for commonly used ingredients.

Volume

American	Imperial	Metric
¼ tsp		1.25 ml
½ tsp		2.5 ml
1 tsp		5 ml
½ Tbs (1½ tsp)		7.5 ml
1 Tbs (3 tsp)		15 ml
¼ cup (4 Tbs)	2 fl oz	60 ml
⅓ cup (5 Tbs)	2½ fl oz	75 ml
½ cup (8 Tbs)	4 fl oz	125 ml
⅔ cup (10 Tbs)	5 fl oz	150 ml
¾ cup (12 Tbs)	6 fl oz	175 ml
1 cup (16 Tbs)	8 fl oz (½ pint)	250 ml
1¼ cups	10 fl oz	300 ml
1½ cups	12 fl oz	350 ml
1 pint (2 cups)	16 fl oz (1 pint)	500 ml
1 quart (4 cups)	32 fl oz (2 pints)	1 liter

Weights

US/UK	Metric
¼ oz	7 g
½ oz	15 g
1 oz	30 g
2 oz	60 g
3 oz	90 g
4 oz	115 g
5 oz	150 g
6 oz	175 g
7 oz	200 g
8 oz (½ lb)	225 g
9 oz	250 g
10 oz	300 g
11 oz	325 g
12 oz	350 g
13 oz	375 g
14 oz	400 g
15 oz	425 g
16 oz (1 lb)	450 g

76

Temperatures

	°F	°C
water freezes	32	0
room temperature	68	20
water simmers	205	96
water boils	212	100

Oven Temperatures

	°F	°C	Gas Mark
very cool	250–275	130–140	½–1
cool	300	148	2
warm	325	163	3
moderate	350	177	4
moderately hot	375–400	190–204	5–6
hot	425	218	7
very hot	450–475	232–245	8–9

Butter

1 stick = 4 oz = 115 g
1 tablespoon = ½ oz = 15 g

Eggs

1 large egg = ¼ cup = 2 oz = 60 g
1 egg yolk = 1 Tbs = 15 ml
1 egg white = 2 Tbs = 30 ml

Flour

American all-purpose flour is a mixture
    of hard and soft wheat.
British plain flour is a near equivalent
    to American all-purpose flour.
1 cup all-purpose American flour = 5 oz = 160 g

Sugar

American sugar is finely granulated. British cooks
    should use caster sugar.
1 cup granulated sugar = 7 oz = 200 g
1 cup packed brown sugar = 6 oz = 175 g
1 cup confectioners' (icing) sugar = 4½ oz = 130 g

Garlic

1 large head = 14 cloves = 3 ounces peeled
1 small head = 12 cloves = 1¾ ounces peeled
3 medium cloves = 4 teaspoons coarsely
    chopped = 1 tablespoon finely chopped =
    2 tablespoons thinly sliced = ½ ounce

Onions

1 small onion = 2 ounces = 1 cup sliced
1 medium onion = 5 to 6 ounces = 1 cup
    coarsely chopped raw = ¼ cup cooked
1 large onion = 7 to 8 ounces
1 pound onions = 2 cups sliced

Tomatoes

1 small tomato = 3 to 4 ounces
1 large tomato = 8 to 10 ounces
8 ounces tomatoes, cut into ½-inch dice
    = 1 cup raw
1 small plum tomato = 2 ounces
1 large plum tomato = 5 ounces
2 pounds tomatoes, cut into
    1-inch pieces = 6 cups
1 33.5-ounce can plum tomatoes = 4 cups
    with liquid = 2½ cups drained
1 26.5-ounce container chopped tomatoes = 3 cups

What all these ingredients share is versatility. More often than not, we have all four at arm's reach for

Eggs, Cheese, Pasta, and Rice

making any variety of omelets, soufflés, baked eggs, poached eggs, grilled cheese sandwiches, pasta dishes, risottos, and simple fluffy buttered rice. If you have dried porcini mushrooms and a little cream, you can make a stunning dish with a little dried pasta or risotto. If you have only eggs and a vegetable, turn them into glorious omelets or soufflés. With these ingredients at the ready, a meal is always at hand without going to the market.

108 How to grate cheese

Hard cheese

Grate hard cheeses such as parmigiano-reggiano or aged Gouda in the food processor with the regular blade or with a traditional box grater with the finest teeth (see entry 14). Be sure to use a grater with fine teeth, not punch-outs; they won't really grate the cheese but will shred it. Handheld crank graters are also a nice touch when you want to grate cheese over your pasta at the table.

The relatively new line of rasp graters with surgical-grade stainless steel surfaces, in coarse, medium, fine, and zester grades, work very well for grating cheese of different textures and many other foods.

Soft cheese

For softer cheeses, such as mozzarella or Camembert, use the box grater with the larger punch-outs; the cheese can fall through the holes and not just stick to the grater as you pull it against the holes.

109 How to store cheese

Some soft cheeses such as Camembert or brie, when kept wrapped in the refrigerator, develop unpleasant flavors and never develop that lovely creamy quality. A better method of storing cheeses is to unwrap them as soon as you get them home and put them, unwrapped, on a plate. Cover the plate with a bowl and then store the cheeses at cool room temperature. The cheeses create their own humid environment, which helps their flavor.

Hard cheeses should be tightly wrapped in plastic wrap and stored in a cool place or the refrigerator.

110   How to make the perfect grilled cheese sandwich

There's nothing like a grilled cheese sandwich as a light lunch or afternoon snack. The trick is to use the best cheese you can find, such as aged Gouda or real English cheddar.

For a closed-face sandwich

1. Melt butter in a nonstick pan over low heat.

2. Butter one side of two slices of bread, then add a slice of your favorite cheese. Assemble.

3. Put the sandwich in the bottom of the pan and cover the pan.

4. Cook over very low heat for about 15 minutes. Check every few minutes to make sure the heat isn't too high and causing the underside of the sandwich to burn.

5. When the underside of the sandwich is golden brown and the cheese is melting out the sides, turn over the sandwich and brown the other side over medium heat.

For an open-face sandwich

1. Toast crusty bread slices on one side under the broiler.

2. Turn over the slice and put cheese slices on the untoasted side; slide the bread and cheese under the broiler.

3. Watch closely until the cheese melts, bubbles up, and lightly browns.

111 What's the best cheese for a cheeseburger?

A cheeseburger can be elevated to new heights by using better cheese than the usual sliced American or cheddar from the supermarket. Experiment with good blue cheeses (not Danish blue) such as roquefort, gorgonzola, and stilton, or sharp cheddars from Vermont or England. Aged Gouda is also delicious.

112 Making 10-minute cheese fondue

For some, the idea of cheese fondue seems complicated, but in fact few recipes are easier—essentially you're just melting cheese in wine. This recipe serves four.

1. Grate ½ pound gruyere and ½ pound Swiss emmenthaler cheese. Set aside.

2. Crush 1 garlic clove, pull off the peel, and put the clove in a saucepan with 2 cups dry white wine.

3. Bring the wine to the simmer and simmer for 2 minutes.

4. Fish out the garlic and add the cheese. Stir until the cheese melts.

5. Put the cheese mixture in your ancient fondue pot set over a can of Sterno (to keep the cheese melted and soft), get out your skewers, and serve with chunks of rustic country-style bread.

HINT *You needn't wax nostalgic about the fondue pot. Today, there are several brands of electric pots from which to choose (and, of course, they achieve the same result). You can also rig up your own fondue pot by putting a saucepan on a cake rack held up by two large pots or bricks.*

cheese

113 How to make an emergency instant hot hors d'oeuvre

Make fricos. Fricos are little disks of cheese that heat has made crispy and crusty. To guarantee success, use a nonstick sheet pan.

1. Spread mounds of grated parmigiano-reggiano over the sheet pan.

2. Heat over medium heat until the cheese melts and browns lightly.

3. Peel the cheese off in rounds and let cool.

114 To make savory tuiles

1. Combine ¼ cup flour with 1 teaspoon salt and an extra-large egg white (or more as needed) to make a smooth thick paste.

2. Work in ¼ cup (1 ounce) finely grated parmigiano-reggiano and 4 tablespoons melted butter.

3. Preheat the oven to 325°F.

4. Spread the batter, a teaspoon at a time, in ovals on a silicone non-stick pad. Bake for about 8 minutes, until the rounds are lightly browned around the edges.

5. Lift the rounds off with a spatula and drape them over a rolling pin or bottle to cool.

115   How to make cheese puffs

Cheese puffs (the French call them *gougéres*) are popular as hors d'oeuvres in fine restaurants and at elegant parties. Cheese puffs are made just as cream puffs are (see entry 455); there's just no filling, but cheese is added to the dough.

HINT *Many home cooks become frustrated because their cheese puffs come out heavy, not light and puffy. There are two tricks to avoiding this: Use egg whites instead of whole eggs, and use grated parmigiano-reggiano or another very hard dry cheese instead of the gruyere called for in most recipes.*

1. Cut 7 tablespoons butter into slices and put in a saucepan with 1 cup water. Bring to the simmer.

2. When all the butter has melted, add 1¼ cups (5 ounces) all-purpose flour and stir over medium heat until the dough pulls away from the sides of the pan. Dump the dough into a mixing bowl.

3. Work in 3 eggs, one by one, with a wooden spoon, and then 3 to 4 egg whites. Continue mixing until when you make a deep groove in the dough, it closes in on itself.

4. Work in 4 ounces (about 1 cup) finely grated parmigiano-reggiano. Season with freshly ground black pepper and a pinch of kosher salt.

5. Preheat the oven to 450°F.

6. Pipe the cheese puffs into small mounds of about 1½ tablespoons each, leaving a couple of inches between them. Bake until puffed and golden brown, about 10 minutes. Turn the oven down to 300°F and bake for 15 minutes more.

116   How to break an egg

Tap the side of the egg on a hard surface. Be decisive so the shell cracks with only one tap; further taps will only break up the shell and make it easier for shell to get in your food.

Do I use cold or room-temperature eggs?

Most of the time an egg right out of the refrigerator is fine, and even preferable. For example, a cold egg is better when soft-boiling because it takes longer for the heat to penetrate to the yolk—meaning the white is well cooked before the yolk overcooks. Recipes for cakes occasionally call for room-temperature eggs because they're easier to beat into a foam.

117   How to separate an egg

There are two ways to separate the egg yolk from the egg white—the shell-to-shell method in which you just move the yolk back and forth between the two halves of the broken shell, and the hand method in which you let the white fall between your fingers.

HINT *For preparations calling for beaten egg whites, avoid rupturing the yolk and compromising the whites.*

Shell-to-shell method

1. Crack the shell and open the egg over a bowl.

2. Pass the yolk from shell to shell until all the white falls out of the shells and into the bowl. Slip the egg yolk into another bowl.

Gently pass yolk from shell to shell, allowing the white to escape.

Hand Method

1. This method requires impeccably clean hands. Crack and open the eggs, holding the halves in your hand with your fingers slightly splayed.

2. Let the whites fall through between your fingers into a bowl. If you're separating a lot of eggs, you can work over two small bowls, one for the yolks and one for the whites.

3. Transfer the contents to larger bowls every few eggs. This way, if you break a yolk into the whites, you don't ruin the whole batch.

Crack the egg into your hand.

Let all the whites fall through splayed fingers.

The most important thing to remember when beating egg whites is that they must not contain a trace of yolk or any other fat—even wiping the bowl with a slightly greasy towel can keep them from fluffing up. When beating by hand, you're best off using a copper bowl; it will make the egg whites hold their volume better when baked. Always clean the bowl with salt and vinegar before you do (see below left). Rinse it with hot water and dry it thoroughly with a paper towel. If you don't have a copper bowl, use stainless steel and add a pinch of cream of tartar to the egg whites before you beat them.

If you have a choice, a stand-up electric mixer or a big balloon whisk will make quicker work of beating egg whites. If you use a hand-held mixer, be sure to move it around within the bowl so you beat evenly.

Hand whisk method

When beating with a whisk, do the opposite of what you'd do intuitively. Start beating slowly and then gradually build up speed. Inevitably, this will leave you panting and swearing off baking. However, if you get used to using your less-used hand so you can switch hands when your arm tires, you'll have an easier time of it. If you're right-handed, start by beating with your left hand and switch to your right when tired.

Rinsing copper bowl before use

Breaking up the whites

Start by breaking the whites up a bit by twirling the whisk between both hands, then switch to beating. Beat to desired stiffness.

Electric mixer method

When using a stand-up mixer, start the mixer on slow and gradually increase speed over the next 2 minutes until the mixer is on high. Beat to desired stiffness.

HINT *Buy the largest copper bowl you can find—little ones don't allow enough room to move the whisk and will only frustrate you.*

How to know when the egg whites have been beaten enough

Soft peaks: Peaks are frothy but don't adhere to the mixer or hand whisk.

Medium peaks: Whites stick out from the end of the whisk when it's held sideways, but they sag at the end.

Stiff peaks: Peaks are rigid and adhere to the whisk.

Soft   Medium   Stiff

119 How to beat egg yolks

Many recipes start by beating egg yolks with sugar, occasionally salt, and often sugar syrup. It's best to beat egg yolks in a stand-up mixer. Don't beat or cook egg yolks in aluminum or they'll turn gray.

HINT *The best pan for beating egg yolks with liquids over heat—better than a double boiler—is a saucepan with sloping sides (see entry 28) that allow you to get into the corners with the whisk. You can also use a bowl set over a saucepan of barely simmering water.*

Beating egg yolks with salt

Sometimes you need to make an egg wash to spread in a thin even layer, such as to glaze pastries. To achieve this, add salt to whole eggs or egg yolks. It thins and darkens the egg and makes it easier to spread in a thin layer.

Beating egg yolks with sugar

Many recipes call for beating egg yolks with sugar, usually before combining them with a hot liquid, such as when making crème anglaise (see entry 465). It's important to beat the eggs thoroughly—until they become very pale—in order to stabilize them and prevent them from curdling when heated.

Beating egg yolks with soft-ball syrup

The best buttercream frosting is made by beating soft-ball syrup (see entry 421) into egg yolks. This cooks the egg yolks without curdling them and creates a satiny mixture.

Beating egg yolks with liquids

When beating egg yolks with liquids over heat, use a saucepan with sloping sides (a Windsor pan) or a bowl set over a saucepan of simmering water. Make sure the bowl is larger than the pan so you can pull it off in an instant. When egg yolks fluff up and stiffen after being cooked with liquids, this fluffy mixture is called a sabayon. When clarified butter is added to this sabayon, you create a sauce that is the base for hollandaise and related sauces. Sometimes whole eggs or egg yolks are beaten with sugar and wine over heat to produce sauce sabayon (when white wine is used) or zabaglione (when marsala is used).

120 How to boil an egg

The best way to soft- or hard-boil eggs, both to get consistent results and to keep the shells from sticking to the eggs (making them hard to peel), is to start eggs in boiling water and then to reduce the heat to a gentle simmer. Don't get too hung up on an exact method: Although there is a standard procedure you can follow, remember that the consistency you like is what counts. Keep track of the time it takes to achieve that.

Precise cooking times are impossible to give for eggs because the time depends on the size of the egg, whether it was in the fridge or not before it was boiled (if so, what the temperature of the fridge was), and how hot the stove is. You'll need to experiment a little to get the timing that works for you.

To keep the shell from cracking

Hard- and soft-boiled eggs

1. Bring to a boil enough water to cover the egg(s) by an inch.

2. Using a spoon, gently lower your eggs into the water and begin timing.

3. When the water returns to a boil, turn down the heat to maintain a gentle simmer. Cook the egg(s) according to your taste.

HINT *To keep the shell from cracking while the egg is boiling, poke a hole in the round end of the egg with a pin to allow trapped air to escape.*

Timing guidelines

While you'll need to experiment to arrive at exact cooking times, the following timings provide some guidelines. Note that the timing starts once the egg is put in the boiling water.

Cooking any longer than 10 minutes will dry out the yolk; longer still will leave the yolk black near where it touches the white.

A 4-minute soft-boiled egg is just about right for most people.

An 8-minute egg is usually perfect for a hard-boiled egg—the yolk will still be a little shiny.

121 How to poach an egg

A poached egg can be the perfect light meal for breakfast or at other times in the day. To add excitement, put the eggs on croutons (see entry 37) and spoon over some as hollandaise sauce (see entry 384). You can add slices of cooked Canadian bacon under the egg to make eggs Benedict or experiment with other ingredients such as lightly creamed spinach, cooked tomato slices, smoked salmon, or thin spears of asparagus.

Keep in mind that you can poach eggs that are less than fresh, but they will release a lot of loose protein that forms unpleasant white froth and scum. A skimmer comes in handy for removing this scum and can also be used for taking out the eggs when they're ready.

HINT *Use the freshest eggs you can find—preferably AAA. They will hold together in the simmering water better than older eggs.*

1. Bring about 2 inches of water to a gentle simmer in a skillet large enough to hold the egg(s).

2. Crack the egg into the water, holding it as close to the surface of the water as possible.

3. Maintain the heat at the barest simmer for about 4 minutes, then remove the egg with a skimmer (or a slotted spoon). If the yolks protrude above the surface of the water, baste them until they lose their bright color.

4. With the egg in the skimmer, use a knife to push away the foamy, amorphous part of the white that surrounds the egg.

5. Touch the bottom of the skimmer, with the egg still in it, to a paper towel to absorb any liquid (this prevents it from getting onto the serving plate).

How to poach eggs for a crowd

Poaching eggs for more than a couple of people, and getting them all on the table at the same time, can be daunting. To poach eggs for a crowd, poach them up to a day ahead of time. As you take them out of the water and trim them, slide them into a bowl of ice water. When you're ready to serve, pour off the cold water, pour boiling water over the eggs, and let sit for a minute. Then take them out of the water with a skimmer and put them on a clean towel or directly on croutons (see entry 37) or plates.

Using a skimmer

A skimmer is useful for removing the white froth and scum that eggs throw off during poaching. Don't use a skimmer for removing fat, however—use a ladle instead. It's fine to use the skimmer to take out the finished poached egg.

122 How to make croutons for poached eggs

Specially made rounds of bread, called croutons, work better as a base than the toast often called for in such dishes as eggs Benedict. (When poached eggs are placed on toast, the toast quickly becomes soggy.) To prevent this, cook rounds of thin-sliced white bread in butter (preferably clarified butter) or oil until golden brown. By absorbing the butter, the croutons are protected from absorbing liquid and remain crunchy.

123 How to fry an egg

What Americans call a fried egg isn't really fried (at times the French actually fry eggs by plunging them into a vessel full of hot oil), it is more panfried. Nonstick pans or well-seasoned skillets are best for frying eggs.

HINT *To make fried eggs a bit more luxurious, dribble some heavy cream over the whites when you start frying. This makes the whites more like custard.*

1. Melt butter in a pan over medium heat until it froths; crack in the eggs.

2. Cook over medium heat until the white sets.

3. If you like your eggs "sunny side up" but like the yolk a little more cooked, cover the pan while frying the eggs. You can also add extra butter and baste the egg yolks with the hot butter while they fry. For those who like their yolk a little more cooked, flip the egg over as soon as the white has set and cook it a few seconds or up to a minute, yolk-side down.

124 How to scramble an egg

The French method is more laborious than the American and richer tasting, but you might decide that the result is worth any potential disadvantages.

American method

1. Crack the eggs into a bowl. Beat the eggs with a fork just enough to break them up.

2. If you want extremely tender scrambled eggs, add 1 tablespoon of heavy cream per egg. (Milk, water, or even white wine can be substituted.)

3. Heat as much butter as you dare in a skillet over low to medium heat and pour in the eggs. When the eggs begin to set on the bottom of the skillet, scrape up the congealed egg with a spatula.

4. Continue in this way until the eggs have the desired consistency.

French method

1. Choose a small saucepan and a medium-size metal bowl that will fit on the saucepan without sinking into it. Don't use a double boiler (see entry 51).

2. Beat the eggs thoroughly and strain the eggs to get rid of those little stringy things.

3. Stir in 2 tablespoons of heavy cream per egg and put the eggs in the bowl with 1 tablespoon of butter per 2 eggs.

4. Bring about an inch of water to a simmer in the saucepan and set the bowl on top. Stir the eggs with a whisk over the simmering water until they begin to thicken. Reduce the heat so the water is barely simmering.

5. Continue stirring until the eggs have a consistency slightly thinner than yogurt—they'll continue to thicken off the heat. Serve them in ramekins topped with a dollop of caviar.

Start by accepting the fact that you're going to end up with a few imperfect omelets before you get the knack of it.

Classic French omelet

Firm on the outside, creamy on the inside, made in minutes—omelets are always welcome. Here's the classic method (see photographs above).

1. With a whisk, beat 2 or 3 eggs with kosher salt and freshly ground black pepper to taste.

2. In an 8- or 10-inch nonstick pan with rounded sloping sides, melt

1 tablespoon butter over medium to high heat until the butter froths and the froth recedes.

3. Add the eggs to the pan and stir them with the back of a fork, moving the fork as close to the surface of the pan as possible without actually touching it. Continue in this way until you have scrambled eggs over a thin layer of completely set egg.

4. With the pan tilted away from you, pound on the handle with your fist to get the egg opposite you to fold inward.

5. With the pan still tilted, use a fork to fold the egg nearest you inward. Turn the omelet out onto a plate.

Rolled omelet

Some cooks find it easier to roll an omelet than to follow the classic method (see photographs oppposite).

1. Put beaten eggs into the hot pan in the same way as for the classic omelet.

2. Add beaten eggs and let sit for about 15 seconds over high heat. Pull the pan quickly toward you with a jerking motion so the part of the egg that has set flips inward and exposes more of the pan.

3. Tilt the pan backward so loose egg covers the part of the pan that's been exposed. Let sit again for about 15 seconds and repeat the jerking motion. Continue in this way until there's no loose egg.

4. Turn the omelet out onto a pan.

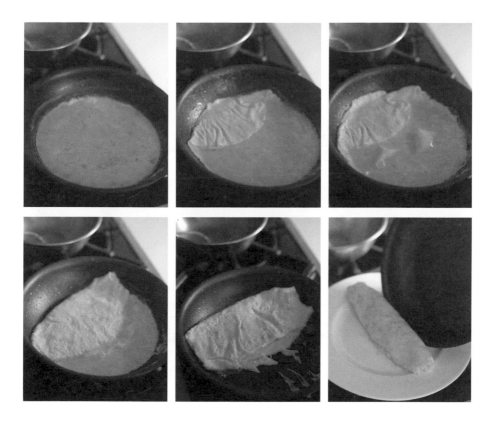

Fluffy omelet

A fluffy omelet is dramatic and soufflélike but it actually requires very little effort (see photographs on next page).

1. Preheat the broiler.

2. Warm 4 eggs in the shell in a bowl of hot tap water.

3. Beat the eggs in a stand-up mixer on high speed until quadrupled in volume, about 4 to 5 minutes.

4. Melt about a half stick of butter in a medium to large nonstick pan and add the eggs. Cook over medium heat, repositioning the pan over the heat every few seconds so the eggs brown evenly on the bottom.

5. After a couple of minutes of browning on the stove, slide the pan under the broiler for a few seconds to set the egg on top.

6. Fold the omelet in half and turn out onto a plate.

Flat omelet (piperade)

Virtually any vegetable can be chopped or diced, cooked in butter or oil, and then have beaten egg poured over to form a flat omelet. Perhaps the most famous of these is the piperade from southwestern France, made with onions, peppers, and ham (see photographs opposite). The peppers have a much better flavor if you char and peel them before cutting them into dice. Potatoes, gently cooked in butter and oil, also make a delicious and substantial base for a flat omelet.

1. Cook chopped onions, diced peppers, and tiny cubes of prosciutto in oil or butter in a large nonstick pan.

2. When the vegetables have softened, pour over beaten egg and cook over low heat until set. Add cheese, if desired. Slide under the broiler to cook the inside.

3. Slide out onto a platter and serve in wedges.

HINT *Don't add butter to a hot pan or the butter will immediately burn. Instead, put the butter in a cold pan and heat the pan. Let the condition of the butter guide you as to the temperature of the pan.*

126 Ways to fill an omelet

There are three ways to fill an omelet, and an almost endless number of things to fill them with. Try them all.

1. You can add ingredients such as chopped herbs (see entry 75), reconstituted dried porcini, or roasted peppers to the beaten eggs.

2. You can add ingredients such as grated cheese or diced ham to the omelet just before you fold or roll it (see entry 125) so they are trapped inside.

3. You can make a basic omelet, cut a long slit along the top, running almost the length of the omelet, and add ingredients such as chopped truffles, caviar, salmon eggs, sautéed wild mushrooms, ratatouille, creamed leeks, or assorted cooked baby vegetables.

127 How to bake eggs for a quick and elegant brunch

If you're in a pinch—friends show up unexpectedly or you're hungry at midnight and the cupboard is bare—try baking an egg or two. For a versatile and delicious breakfast, brunch, or snack, you can add in any number of fillings or ingredients, including creamed spinach or sorrel (entry 200), diced cooked shrimp (entry 262), tomato sauce (entry 374), ricotta cheese, chopped herbs (entry 75), or diced smoked fish. Leftovers are also great.

1. Preheat the oven to 350°F.

2. Put a tablespoon or two of your favorite fillings in the bottom of a 4- or 6-inch ovenproof ramekin.

3. Break an egg over the filling and add a tablespoon or two of heavy cream and a sprinkle of kosher salt, freshly ground black pepper, and grated Parmesan, if you like.

4. Bake in a hot water bath until the egg white is set, about 15 minutes. Serve with buttered toast points or sticks.

Three different fillings: creamed spinach; tomato concassée; duxelles topped with eggs, cream, and (optional) grated cheese

128　How to make a quiche

Since all quiches follow the same general rules—milk is combined with beaten eggs to create a custard mixture that is then baked in a prebaked pie shell—you can easily improvise your own once you get used to working with the basic ingredients. If you don't want to make your own dough and roll it out, you can buy frozen premade pie shells. By prebaking the pie shell (see entry 401), it will stay crisp when you use it to hold the custard. By using the recipe for quiche lorraine as a model, you can see how easy it is to add other ingredients such as cooked vegetables or seafood to the quiche.

To make a classic quiche lorraine

1. Preheat the oven to 300°F or turn it down to 300°F if you've just prebaked the shell (see entry 401) at a higher temperature.

2. Cut 6 ounces bacon crosswise into 1-inch-long strips and cook in a frying pan over medium heat until barely crispy. Drain on paper towels.

3. Sprinkle the bacon strips into the prebaked shell, along with 1 cup (4 ounces) of flavorful cheese such as gruyere, cheddar, or blue cheese.

4. Beat together 2 eggs with 1¼ cups cold milk and season with salt and pepper. Pour this mixture into the shell and bake until set, about 40 minutes.

eggs

129   How to liven up your eggs

Each filling possibility that follows makes enough for about six eggs.

• **Tomatoes:** Peel, seed, and chop 3 medium tomatoes; cook over medium heat until all their liquid evaporates. Flavor with chopped tarragon or basil. Season with kosher salt and freshly ground black pepper.

• **Mushrooms:** Chop a dozen medium mushrooms and cook them in a tablespoon of butter until all the water they release evaporates. Season with kosher salt, freshly ground black pepper, and, if you like, a little thyme.

• **Shrimp:** Sauté 1 large shrimp per serving. Let cool, peel, and dice.

• **Spinach:** Boil the leaves from one bunch of spinach for 30 seconds, drain, and rinse with cold water. Squeeze out the liquid and chop coarsely. Boil down ¼ cup heavy cream in a saucepan until the cream is very thick; stir in the spinach until hot. Season with kosher salt and freshly ground black pepper.

130   How to store and use older eggs

Eggs keep for weeks in the refrigerator, and while it takes them a very long time to actually go bad, there are times when it helps to be able to tell an older egg from a very fresh egg. (Some recipes won't work if the eggs aren't fresh.)

1. An older egg will slosh around when you shake it because some of the liquid it contains will have evaporated and created a large air pocket.

2. Older eggs don't hold together, so that when poaching, for example, the white turns into an amorphous unpleasant foam.

3. When hard-boiling eggs (see entry 120), use an egg that's a little old because it will be easier to peel.

HINT *Eggs are best kept in the refrigerator.*

131 How to cook pasta

The freshest brand of pasta can take 30 seconds to cook in a pot of boiling water, while some dried versions might take 10 minutes to soften to the right degree—the point described as "al dente." This ideal state is when the pasta is completely cooked yet offers a slight resistance when chewed—resistance without rawness. Pasta you make yourself with plenty of egg, or even with just egg yolks, will cook faster than dried pasta. The ideal pasta is fresh pasta you've made with eggs or egg yolks that you then hang and let dry for several hours. The only commercial pasta that can be cooked to the ideal al dente stage is Cippriani (made with eggs), which cooks in about 2 minutes.

HINT *Al dente is the state of cooked pasta when it is completely cooked but its texture is still somewhat firm "to the teeth."*

132 Quick pasta sauces

Pasta dishes are an ingenious way of combining small amounts of proteins and flavorful foods with a basic source of carbohydrates and calories (the pasta). Not only can pasta be sauced with meat sauces (see entry 381), tomato sauces (see entry 315), and mushroom sauces, "filling" ingredients such as sautéed vegetables, sausages, clams, mussels, shrimp, and lobster can be tossed with pasta just before serving.

• Tomato sauces can be simple: Just simmer chopped-up tomatoes until the liquid they release evaporates, then strain the sauce and toss it with pasta. For a more rustic tomato sauce, peel, seed, and chop the tomatoes so they can be left chunky.

• Any stew can be turned into a ragu sauce for pasta. If you make a stew with chunks of beef or veal and plenty of juices, you can then chop up the meat, leave it in the sauce, and use it to sauce pasta.

• A couple of dried porcini mushrooms can be reconstituted (see entry 182), chopped, simmered in cream, and tossed with pasta for an almost instant, elegant dinner or first course.

• Steam shellfish such as clams or mussels and add butter or extra virgin olive oil to the steaming liquid. Take most of the shellfish out of the shells—leave a few in for effect—and toss the rest with the pasta. Serve the pasta in soup plates so the extra shellfish steaming liquid ends up at the bottom, to be mopped up with crusty bread.

• Make lobster or shrimp broth with the shells (see entry 358) and toss the broth with pasta, along with pieces of shrimp or lobster.

• For a carbonara sauce, cut bacon slices, about 2 per serving, cross-wise into strips and cook them in a sauté pan over medium heat, until they just begin to get crispy. Boil spaghetti or fettuccini. Meanwhile, beat 1 egg per serving. Drain the pasta, and immediately toss with the bacon and beaten egg. Serve with grated parmigiano-reggiano.

133 What to do with leftover cooked pasta

Pasta can be made even better the next day, even when you find it stuck together and lumped in the refrigerator.

1. Spread cold cooked pasta in the bottom of a buttered gratin dish or baking dish (in a 1- to 2-inch-thick layer).

2. Sprinkle liberally with grated parmigiano-reggiano or other hard cheese.

3. Season to taste with salt and freshly ground black pepper.

4. Pour over enough cream so that when you press down on the pasta, you see the cream come up.

5. Bake in a 350°F oven until crusty borwn and all the cream is absorbed.

For thin pastas

If you have fine pasta, like vermicelli, left over, put it in buttered 5-ounce ramekins with grated cheese worked in and cream and seasonings added. Bake these individual-size little cakes in a 350°F oven until golden brown, crispy on the outside, and custardlike on the inside. Serve them out of the molds.

134   How to bake lasagna

We're all used to the idea of lasagna—layering cheese and tomato sauce, and sometimes meat sauce, with large flat noodles and baking. We forget that the concept can be used for just about anything. Try sautéing mushrooms and layering them with lasagna and sausage in a casserole or combine chopped spinach with béchamel sauce and layer it in a lasagna. Or take a stew, cut up the meat, and layer it with the stew's liquid in between the flat lasagna noodles; add plenty of grated fresh mozzarella cheese and parmigiano-reggiano and bake.

135   Speed lasagna

Most recipes for lasagna require cooking the noodles before layering them with some kind of tomato sauce and cheese, commonly mozzarella and ricotta cheeses. To speed things up, use no-boil lasagna noodles, which are available at most supermarkets, and make your sauce with more liquid than usual because the noodles will absorb it, just as they absorb water during conventional cooking.

HINT *To make a more "liquidy" sauce, add more tomatoes to your recipe and don't cook down the sauce as much as you might.*

136 How to make fresh pasta

Pasta dough can be made in a food processor in about 2 minutes. It can be kneaded by hand, as you would bread dough, but an easier method is to work it through a pasta machine. A pasta machine is a set of rollers through which you roll dough on successively thinner settings until you reach the thinnest, or next to the thinnest, setting. At the end the pasta is almost translucent. Most pasta machines also come with a second set of rollers that are designed to cut the sheets into thin strips (linguine) or wide strips (fettuccine); for really wide strips (pappardelle), you need to cut the pasta by hand.

1. Combine 3 cups flour, 4 large eggs, 1 tablespoon olive oil, and 1½ tablespoons cold water in a food processor.

2. Process for about 30 seconds, until the mixture is the consistency of coarse sand.

3. Pour the mixture out onto a board and knead it with the heel of your hand until it comes together.

4. Divide the dough into three or four manageable pieces.

5. Set the pasta machine on its thickest setting and roll out the dough one time.

6. Fold the pasta in half over itself once or twice and roll it out again.

7. Repeat this process until the pasta is smooth, doesn't tear, and has the texture of suede.

8. Set the rollers on the machine to progressively thinner settings, rolling out once at each setting.

9. Cut by machine or by hand into the desired width.

HINT *To keep fresh pasta from sticking to itself, sprinkle it liberally with coarse semolina flour while tossing or coiling (shake off before cooking). You can also dry the pasta slightly, making it less sticky, by hanging it over rope or the back of a chair. If you dry it thoroughly, it keeps for months.*

137 How to cook rice

There are three ways to cook rice. And a few suggestions for cooking it perfectly.

• Long-grain rice can be cooked in butter or oil, with sweated onions (see entry 40) and sometimes garlic, before liquid is added and the rice, covered with a round of parchment paper, is finished in the oven or on the stove. This is the method used for rice pilafs.

• Short-grain rice is cooked, for example, in risotto, in a little butter or oil and liquid added while the mixture is stirred constantly. The liquid, often a flavorful broth, is added in small increments while the rice absorbs it.

• Medium-grain rice is the traditional kind used for paella and is cooked in just enough hot liquid so no liquid is left when the rice is cooked. It can also be cooked as you do long-grain rice.

• Long-grain and medium-grain rice can be cooked in an abundance of water and simply boiled like pasta. This prevents any stickiness and keeps each grain separate. The French call this method "Indian style."

Cooking rice like pasta

How to guarantee your rice won't stick

The easiest and surest way to cook rice is to cook long-grain rice as you would pasta in a large amount of boiling water. Boil until done, usually about 15 minutes, and drain in a colander. To know rice is done, bite into a piece. If it is underdone, you will detect firm starchiness in the center of the grain. When the rice is overdone, it will burst open and lose almost all of its texture in your mouth.

How to flavor rice

Use flavorful rice to begin with. Long-grain basmati and jasmine rice, for instance, have a distinctive nutty flavor that makes standard American rice seem bland.

1. In an ovenproof pan over medium heat, cook minced onions or garlic or other flavorful vegetables such as mushrooms and bell peppers in oil or butter until soft.

2. Add the rice and cook it over medium heat, stirring, for 5 minutes. Add 2 cups of broth of your choice or water per 1 cup of rice.

3. Cover the pan loosely with aluminum foil or parchment paper, put it in a 350°F oven, and bake for about 20 minutes, until all the liquid is absorbed.

138   How to make risotto

Risotto is rice that's been slowly cooked in flavorful liquid. Various liquids—including wine, broth, steaming liquids from mussels or clams, broths from reconstituting dried mushrooms, and squid ink—can be used, but the technique is always the same. Use Italian short-grain rice such as arborio, canaroli, or vialone nano.

HINT *Arborio will produce a thicker risotto, while vialone nano, a favorite in the Veneto, results in a looser texture. Canaroli, a more expensive and not as commonly available rice, is preferred by many cooks for its satisfying "bite."*

1. Depending on the recipe, cook finely chopped onion, garlic, or other vegetable in butter or pure olive oil until soft but not browned. Use a wide pan or pot large enough to hold the risotto and its liquid as they cook.

2. Add the rice and stir over low to medium heat for about 2 minutes.

3. Add about a fourth of the liquid called for in the recipe (usually chicken or other kinds of broth) and stir until it's completely absorbed.

4. Continue adding the liquid, a fourth at a time, until the risotto has the consistency you like—risotto can run the gamut from being almost a soup to a very stiff mixture that a spoon will stand straight up in. When you bite into a kernel, there's no feeling of raw starchiness in the center.

5. As the risotto approaches readiness, a finely grated hard cheese such as parmigiano-reggiano or manchego can be added, as well as just-chopped fresh herbs such as parsley, chervil, chives, or tarragon.

139 How to make risotto in advance

Most of us hesitate to make risotto for guests because it requires almost constant stirring for all the liquid to be absorbed and the rice to cook. Fortunately, risotto can be cooked three fourths of the way a couple of hours ahead of time. Just before serving, bring back to a simmer, stir in the usual way, and add liquid as needed.

140 How to make seafood risotto

Venice is famous for its seafood risottos, especially those made with shellfish. Some shellfish (such as shrimp or scallops) can be stirred into a risotto minutes before it is ready, but other shellfish (such as mussels, clams, or cockles) need to be steamed open first and taken out of the shell. The steaming liquid should be used to cook the rice, and the shellfish meats should be stirred into the risotto at the very end, so they don't toughen.

1. Sweat the onions.

2. Lightly cook the rice with the onions.

3. Add the steaming liquid from the shellfish.

4. Add saffron and its soaking liquid.

5. Stir, adding liquid from time to time, until rice has achieved desired consistency.

6. Cook or reheat shellfish in the risotto.

Most vegetables are cooked using one of just a few methods. Green vegetables are quickly boiled or steamed and refreshed or immediately served so they don't loose their color; root vegetables are roasted or glazed. Winter and summer squash are usually baked; the latter can also be grilled, or sautéed. Artichokes, salsify, and cardoons are simmered in water with lemon juice to keep them from darkening. While fruit is usually best raw, its flavor can be intensified by poaching, roasting, or even grilling.

Vegetables and Fruits

141 How to cook green vegetables

The trick to cooking green vegetables is to cook them quickly. Most you can plunge into boiling salted water for a few minutes, and they'll be perfectly cooked. (The salt helps bring out their color and is drained off.) You can also steam them, provided you don't steam them for more than 5 minutes or so since cooking green vegetables covered may turn them gray. Leafy vegetables can also be cooked by swirling them around in a pan with a little hot oil.

How to keep green vegetables green

- Keep green vegetables green by boiling them in a large amount of boiling water so the vegetables don't slow down the cooking when you add them.

- Boil uncovered so volatile acids contained in the vegetables aren't trapped; these could cause wilting.

- Include a large amount of salt in the water to raise the water's boiling point.

- Some cooks add baking soda to the boiling water to neutralize the acids in the vegetables and leave them bright green, but this destroys their texture and makes them mushy.

142 How to cook root vegetables

In the winter we're likely to cook root vegetables such as turnips, celeriac, carrots, onions, parsnips, potatoes, or beets. Other than boiling them to make purees or soups, root vegetables should be roasted (see entry 197) or glazed (see entry 198) for optimum flavor.

143 How to cook green leafy vegetables such as spinach

Cooks continue to debate the merits of steaming versus boiling. The steaming school insists that boiling water leaches out vitamins, while the boiling school feels the vitamins and color are left more intact because the cooking is faster. The first step is to stem and wash the spinach (see entry 69).

To boil

1. Fill a pot with about 3 quarts of water per large bunch of spinach and toss in a small handful of salt.

2. Bring the water to a rapid boil, add the spinach, and wait, about 30 seconds, until the spinach "melts" (goes limp).

3. Drain immediately in a colander and, unless you're serving the spinach immediately, rinse with cold water. Squeeze out water.

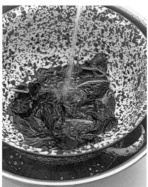

To steam

1. Bring 1 quart of water to a rapid boil in the steamer.

2. Put the spinach in the steamer basket, cover the pot, and steam for 1 minute.

3. Check to see if the spinach has "melted."

4. To serve immediately, drain in a colander and press on the greens to eliminate excess liquid. Otherwise, rinse with cold water if you're preparing it in advance, and squeeze dry.

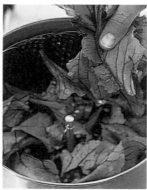

To sauté

1. Heat 1 tablespoon butter or oil in a large frying pan.

2. Add the washed and dried greens. Stir over high heat until the greens "melt."

3. Drain in a colander and press on the greens to eliminate excess liquid.

144 How to grill vegetables

The grill brings out the flavor of vegetables by concentrating their juices and sometimes caramelizing, almost charring their skins.

HINT *To give grilled vegetables a smoky flavor, add some wood chips or sawdust to the coals and cover the grill after the vegetables have been browned. You can also brush grilled vegetables with pesto after they've been grilled and immediately before serving.*

1. Brush the vegetables with extra virgin olive oil and herbs.

2. Grill in pieces large enough not to slip through the grill. Be sure to grill until well browned, almost blackened, for an intense grilled flavor.

145 How to make a gratin

Almost any vegetable or pasta can be turned into a casserole and served as a satisfying side dish to meats and seafood—potatoes au gratin and macaroni and cheese are the best-known examples.

Leftovers, can also be used. A gratin is simply a casserole made by cooking vegetables with béchamel sauce (basically, milk thickened with flour), cream, or a combination, and sometimes tomato sauce. Most gratins also contain grated cheese, such as Gruyère, cheddar, or parmigiano-reggiano.

1. Layer vegetables with liquid, cheese, and seasonings (kosher salt, freshly ground black pepper, a little nutmeg) in a baking dish.

2. Use enough liquid so that when you push down on the vegetables, the liquid comes up to the tops of them. Finish with a layer of cheese.

3. Bake in a 350°F oven until the vegetables or pasta is soft and a brown crust has formed on top.

How to make potatoes au gratin

Unlike many casseroles and gratins, which are made with béchamel sauce, potatoes are already starchy enough and should be baked with cream or half-and-half.

1. Peel and slice waxy potatoes, such as Yukon gold, to about ⅛ inch thick.

2. Layer them in a baking dish with cream or milk or a mixture, grated Gruyére cheese, kosher salt, freshly ground black pepper, and nutmeg, finishing with a layer of cheese.

3. Bake in a 350°F oven until the potatoes are soft and a crust has formed. If all the liquid hasn't been absorbed, it will usually get absorbed if you let the gratin sit for 15 minutes before serving.

How to make a zucchini or summer squash gratin

This gratin is a little unusual in that it uses tomato sauce instead of béchamel or cream.

1. Slice and sauté the squash or zucchini until softened and well browned.

2. Overlap the rounds in a baking dish with pureed tomatoes or basic tomato sauce (see entry 374).

3. Sprinkle with cheese and bake in a moderate oven until crusty.

146 How to butter fresh vegetables

Many cooks love the taste of shell beans, green beans, asparagus, and other fresh green vegetables flavored with butter. But many also make the mistake of sautéing these vegetables in butter, which leaves them tasting oily. A better system is to steam or boil the vegetables, drain them, and, off the heat, toss them with slices of hard butter. In this way, the butter stays creamy and emulsified.

147 How to liven up sautéed vegetables

Crush, peel, and mince a couple of garlic cloves and chop a small bunch of parsley. Combine with 2 or 3 tablespoons extra virgin olive oil or butter and add this mixture, called a persillade, to your sautéed vegetables, just before they're done.

148 How to fry vegetables

Except for potatoes (see entry 189), which need no coating, other vegetables are best sliced thinly and dipped in a batter made with flour and enough water to give it the consistency of heavy cream. Fry the vegetables in 360°F oil until crispy and golden brown, about 2 minutes. Note: You may have to adjust the temperature depending on the thickness of the vegetables (if they're getting brown before they're cooked through, the oil is too hot). Sprinkle with kosher salt before serving.

149　How to cook artichokes

An artichoke is a prickly creature, which is why some recipes instruct you to clip off the ends of the leaves with scissors. Since you're inevitably going to cook the artichokes and soften the spines, this isn't really worth the effort.

1. To cook an artichoke, trim off the stem so the artichoke will stand upright on the plate when served.

2. Put the artichoke in a nonaluminum pot with plenty of water and a tablespoon of olive oil.

3. Cover with a towel. The towel keeps the artichoke covered with liquid.

4. Boil gently until a knife slides easily through the base, about 25 minutes for a large one.

150　How to prepare artichoke bottoms

The bottom is what you get when you trim off the leaves of an artichoke. It's virtually the same as the artichoke heart except that vestiges of the leaves surround the heart. This explains why the bottom is popular as a holder for peas or other vegetables in old-fashioned recipes. Nowadays, artichoke bottoms are best cut into wedges, sautéed, and served as a vegetable.

1. Rotate the artichoke against a sharp knife to trim off the outer leaves.

2. Continue until you see the white flesh of the artichoke bottom.

3. Trim the leaves and green patches off the bottom of the artichokes by rotating the bottom against the knife blade.

4. Cut off the top leaves.

5. Cook the bottoms the same way as you do whole artichokes. When done, scoop out the chokes with a spoon.

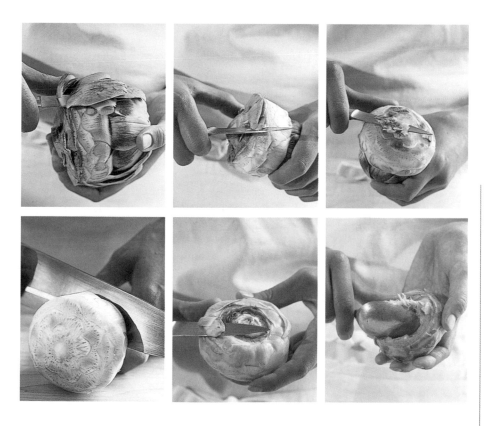

151 How to peel asparagus

The trick to cooking asparagus evenly, so the stems are done at the same time as the flowers, is to peel it first. This is easier if you buy thick asparagus for the simple reason that you'll have fewer to peel. Once it is peeled, just boil or steam asparagus.

1. Cut an inch or so of the woody base off the asparagus stalks.

2. Use a vegetable peeler to peel the whole stalk below the flower.

152 How to cook asparagus

Once peeled, asparagus can be cooked like any green vegetable—in a lot of boiling salted water or by steaming.

1. Bring 3 quarts of water per pound of asparagus to a rapid boil. Add a tablespoon or so of salt.

2. Boil the asparagus over high heat for 2 to 6 minutes, depending on how thick the stalks are.

3. To check doneness, fish out a stalk and bite off a piece or use a sharp knife and insert it in the thick end of a stalk. Either way, asparagus should be tender to the bite.

153   How to serve and eat asparagus

With your fingers. Emily Post says it's all right, even proper, to eat asparagus with your fingers. You can serve it with extra virgin olive oil, melted butter, or hollandaise or maltaise sauce. (Maltaise sauce is hollandaise flavored with boiled-down orange juice and blanched, julienned orange zest.)

154   How to pit and peel an avocado

Look for the avocados with the very rough skin; they're called Hass. They have a richer flavor and a more buttery texture than those with lighter green, smooth skin. When ripe, an avocado should barely give when you press on it with your thumb. If you can only find hard ones, keep them out of the refrigerator for a day or two until they soften up.

HINT *To make perfect avocado wedges without the brownish coating on the outsides, peel the avocado with a paring knife before halving it or cutting into wedges.*

To pit

1. Cut the avocado in half all around the pit.

2. Twist the two halves in opposite directions to detach them.

3. Take a large chefs' knife and give the pit, whichever half it is in, a quick whack so the knife lodges in the pit.

4. Rotate the knife slightly and the pit will pop right out.

To peel

Cut each of the halves lengthwise in half and pull away the peel.

vegetables

155 Secrets to guacamole

- Remember that the essence of guacamole is its texture. Don't mash the avocados, but chop them and leave them in irregularly sized chunks.
- Use chipotle chiles for heat—either reconstitute dried ones or use them out of a can—because they also provide a complex smoky flavor.
- Use poblano chiles (see entry 64), charred, peeled, and chopped for flavor and some heat. Don't use bell peppers.
- Experiment with reconstituting various dried chiles, chopping them fine, and adding them to the guacamole.
- Add chopped tomatoes if you want to stretch the guacamole, but don't overdo it. Their liquid can thin and dilute the sauce.
- Always include fresh chopped cilantro.
- Always add fresh lemon or lime juice to give the sauce some tang.

156 How to boil string beans

Bring 3 quarts of water per pound of string beans to a rapid boil. Toss in a tablespoon or so of salt and boil the beans for 5 to 7 minutes, depending on their thickness and if you like your beans crunchy.

HINT *Many of us can't find or don't want to pay for expensive French haricots verts. You can make your own delicate string beans by cutting thick fresh green beans lengthwise in half with a sharp knife. For even thinner beans, cut the halves lengthwise in half again. Then cook them as you like.*

157 How to braise vegetables

Cabbage, green beans, and broccoli, as well as hardy greens, such as kale, chard, and chicories, are actually most flavorful when cooked slowly in a covered pot. The loss of their color is more than compensated for by their deep, satisfying flavor, especially when they are cooked with ingredients such as garlic, hot chiles, and bacon. Cook at a gentle simmer with enough water or both to come about one quarter of the way up the vegetable—this will be enough so that the vegetable cooks in, and is flavored by, its own juices.

158 Leftover green beans

Never reheat green beans in a lot of boiling water. Use a couple tablespoons of water in a skillet and stir in the green beans, until heated through. If the beans become oily because they were first served with butter, a tablespoon or two of cream heated along with the beans will reemulsify the butter.

159 How to prepare dried beans

While soaking dried beans speeds up the cooking slightly, it isn't necessary; in fact, overnight soaking can make their skin shrivel. A more effective way to speed up the cooking process is to use a pressure cooker, which can have some varieties ready in 20 minutes or so. Dried beans are especially good cooked with pork, especially smoked pork, so consider cooking them with a ham hock, a chunk of bacon, or some diced ham. Duck confit is also tasty.

HINT *Unlike lentils, which are normally very clean, beans may have a little pebble or two in a bag. Before cooking, spread the beans out on a sheet pan and pick out anything suspicious.*

160 To cook fresh shell beans

Fresh shell beans should be shucked and cooked quickly so they keep their fresh flavor and aroma and their color.

To boil

Fresh beans cook relatively quickly—from 1 minute for fava beans to 20 minutes for cranberry beans—in boiling salted water. The best way to know when they're done is to taste one. Once done, drain them in a colander and then toss them with extra virgin olive oil, minced garlic, and herbs and serve. You can also allow them to cool and use them to make salads with other ingredients such as shellfish.

Other preparations

After a preliminary boiling—cooking in water brought to a rolling boil is sometimes called blanching—beans can be cooked alongside braising meats such as pork, and of course they can be cooked with duck confit in cassoulet or cassouletlike casseroles. Cooked beans can also be mashed, flavored with herbs and garlic, and used for dipping sauces or served hot as refried beans.

161 How to roast beets

Beets are best roasted, peels on, in the oven. Trim off the greens, leaving 1-inch stems, and roast at 400°F for 1¼ hours. You can wrap them in foil or put them on a baking dish to prevent them from dripping in the oven.

162 How to peel beets

Beets are easiest to peel after they've been cooked, while they're still hot. Hold them in a towel with one hand and with your thumb and a knife, pull away the peel.

163 How to cook one or two vegetables in the microwave

If you're cooking one or two beets, potatoes, or acorn squash, it may seem wasteful to heat the oven. Following is the trick to microwaving them.

1. Zap them for 5 minutes, and let them rest for 5 minutes so the heat is evenly distributed within the beet.

2. Rotate and reposition them, zap for 5 minutes more, then rest for 5 minutes more.

3. Check for doneness by probing the vegetable with a skewer to see if it's penetrable. If it is, it's done. If not, continue zapping, repositioning, and resting, until done.

164 How to trim and prepare Brussels sprouts

If you get the whole stalk from the farmer's market or fresh from the farm, you can cut the individual sprouts off the stalk with a small knife. Peel off the outermost leaves or any that are wilted. You can cut the sprouts into quarters or halves or leave them whole for sautéing or steaming.

HINT *For a delicious wilted salad, pull away the individual leaves, sauté them with a little bacon, and add a little vinegar.*

165 How to shred cabbage

If you love coleslaw but fear shredding the cabbage needed to make your own, try this and you'll discover it's not so hard after all.

1. Pull off and discard any wilted leaves from the cabbage head.

2. Cut the cabbage in quarters through the core. Cut out and discard the core from each of the quarters.

3. Use a vegetable slicer or a chef's knife to slice the quarters cross-wise into shreds.

How to make the world's best coleslaw

By substituting a flavored mayonnaise (see entry 368)—perhaps containing a little roasted hazelnut oil—and combining it with shredded cabbage, your coleslaw will be the best ever. Try also adding toasted walnut halves for crunch.

166 How to trim cauliflower and broccoli

Before you cut cauliflower and broccoli into manageable pieces, you must trim them.

1. Pull off the greens from the cauliflower.

2. Turn the cauliflower or broccoli upside down on the work surface.

3. Cut around the core of the cauliflower or the base of the broccoli stem so the little bouquets, also called florets, come away.

4. Cut through the bouquets to make them the size you like.

167 How to make cauliflower or broccoli gratin

Once trimmed, cauliflower and broccoli can be boiled and simply served tossed with a little butter or herb butter, or, better, turned into a gratin.

1. Cut either cauliflower or broccoli into little bouquets.

2. Plunge them into a pot of boiling salted water.

3. Boil broccoli for 1 minute, cauliflower for 5. Drain.

4. Layer vegetables pieces with grated Swiss or Gruyére cheese and béchamel sauce and bake in a 350°F oven until a crust forms on top.

168   How to julienne carrots

A Benriner slicer (see entry 9) comes in handy for small tasks, such as cubing carrots or making julienne of them.

1. Peel the carrot and cut it into sections the desired length you want of the julienne.

2. Use a vegetable slicer to slice the sections lengthwise. Slice on each side until you reach the core.

3. Discard the core. If you're a perfectionist, cut away the tapering sides of each of the slices so the slices have the same thickness.

4. Stack 2 or 3 slices and slice into strips as wide as they're thick.

How to chop and dice carrots

The time you take cutting up a carrot depends on how it's to be used. If you're making an elegant stew and want perfect dice, then you need to even the sides of carrot sections, slice the sections into rectangles, and then cut these into perfect dice. Fine dice are called brunoise and larger dice, macedoine. For less finicky preparations, the most efficient way to chop a carrot is to cut it in half lengthwise, cut each of the halves into three wedges, and then slice these strips into little triangles.

169 How to peel celeriac

Many of us are put off by celeriac, a delicately flavored root vegetable, because of its gnarled forbidding appearance. But it is marvelous added to stews or julienned raw and mixed with homemade mustardy mayonnaise in celeriac remoulade. To peel celeriac, use a paring knife. A vegetable peeler doesn't cut in deeply enough to remove the tough outer layer.

170 How to peel chestnuts

Chestnuts have a thick outer layer and a thin membranelike peel that clings to the meat.

Score with an X

Peel while hot

1. To roast and peel them at the same time, preheat the oven to 350°F.

2. With a knife, make an X across the flat side of the chestnuts.

3. Roast the chestnuts for 20 minutes, and while they're still hot, with a towel, rub and pull away the peel. If you're lucky, the inner peel will cling to the outer peel as it comes off. If not, either you can leave the inner peel on (you'll strain it out if you're making puree) or you can boil the already-peeled chestnuts for 2 minutes, drain them, and rub them in a towel.

171 How long to cook corn

If you want your corn to have a grassy flavor, cook it in the husk; if you want it to taste grilled or you just want to make cooking easier (since corn in the husk takes up a lot of room on the grill or in the pot), husk it first.

To boil

1. Pull off the husks and hairy fibers that cling to the kernels.

2. Bring about 2 quarts of water per ear of corn to a rapid boil. Add ears of corn and boil for about 7 minutes.

3. For a little drama, try herb butters (tarragon butter is especially good) or sprinkle grated parmigiano-reggiano over the ears.

To grill

At the height of the season, on the grill with burgers or steaks, grilled cored is sublime. If you grill corn in the green husk, it will actually steam and end up with a slightly grassy flavor. To get a grilled flavor, husk the corn first and grill until lightly browned on all sides. In the husk, corn takes about 30 minutes; out of the husk, about 15.

172 To take the kernels off corn

Many of the best corn dishes—corn salads, succotash, creamed corn—call for fresh corn kernels. Getting the kernels off the corn is easy.

1. Shuck the corn.

2. Hold an ear over a cutting board and slice off the kernels with a knife. Kernels can be taken off the raw corn and cooked afterward or off the cooked ears themselves.

173 How to cream corn

Creamed corn out of a can doesn't hold a candle to homemade creamed corn. To give your corn a smoky flavor, grill the ears with some wood chips on the coals before you take off the kernels. You can also add a smoked chili, such as a chipotle, to the creamed corn.

1. Bring about ⅓ cup cream per cup of raw corn kernels to a boil.

2. Boil the cream briefly until it thickens slightly.

3. Add the corn.

4. Cover the pan and simmer over low heat for 15 minutes. Season to taste with kosher salt and freshly ground black pepper.

174 How to ensure eggplant isn't greasy

Many recipes advise sautéing eggplant in olive oil, but it absorbs too much oil and tastes greasy. Better, peel it and slice as directed, brush the strips with olive oil, and bake them in a 350°F oven until soft and lightly browned. The bright lavender Asian-style eggplants are the least greasy.

175 How to peel fava beans

Fava beans need to be shelled and then individually peeled.

1. To shell the beans, slide your thumb along one side and let the beans fall out.

2. Plunge the shucked beans in boiling water for 30 seconds, drain, and rinse with cold water.

3. Peel the beans with your thumbnail or a small knife.

176 How to prepare fennel

These pale green bulbs often come with long stalks attached. The stalks can be used in broths and braised dishes, and the fuzzy fronds can be used to decorate salads or chopped and added to sauces in the same way as parsley. No matter how you enjoy fennel, it always needs to be trimmed first.

For cooking

1. Cut the stalks off the fennel (they can be dried and used for grilling or, used fresh, put in broths) and peel the outer fiber off the fennel bulb.

2. Cut evenly through the top of the fennel, into the core.

3. Cut the halves into wedges by cutting through the core. Make sure each wedge has some core attached to hold it together.

For braising

1. Prepare the fennel as described above and put the wedges in a pan large enough to hold them in a single layer.

2. Add enough broth, water, or cream to come halfway up their sides. Season to taste with kosher salt and freshly ground black pepper.

3. Bring to the simmer, cover loosely with aluminum foil or parchment paper, and slide into a 300°F oven.

4. When the liquid has thickened, or glazed the fennel, and the fennel is easily penetrated with the tip of a knife, it is ready to serve.

For salads

1. Cut off the stalks, peel away the fibers from the outside of the bulb, and slice the bulb paper thin, crosswise, with a vegetable slicer.

2. Toss at the last minute with extra virgin olive oil and lemon juice.

3. If you like, shave over thin slices of parmigiano-reggiano cheese. Use the little fronds to decorate the salad.

For a gratin

1. Prepare the fennel as described in "For cooking" (page 136) and spread the wedges in a single layer in a pan.

2. Pour over enough water, broth, or cream to come halfway up the sides.

3. Bake in a 350°F oven until the fennel is easily penetrated with a knife.

Use the stalks

Cut off the stalks, which are hard and woody. They can be dried to use on the grill to scent fish, or they can be frozen to add a fresh note to broth. Use the fronds decoratively for salads or sauces, or to stuff fish.

177 How to make roast garlic puree

Great for whisking into sauces or soups, or spreading on toast or baked potatoes, roast garlic puree is worth having in the refrigerator.

1. Cut whole heads of garlic in half crosswise through the equator. Break the halves into cloves.

2. Cover the bottom of a heavy roasting pan with the garlic.

3. Bake in a 300°F oven until completely soft; the cloves completely give when you squeeze one.

4. Process the cloves for 30 seconds in a food processor and transfer to a drum sieve.

5. Work the whole mixture through the drum sieve. If you don't have a drum sieve, use a ladle to work it through a large strainer or a food mill.

HINT *Most of us resort to a garlic press, but it's just one more gadget to lose and it's hard to clean. It's ultimately less work to mince a peeled garlic clove, then crush it with the side of a chef's knife (see entry 25).*

178   How to trim leeks

Many recipes call for only the white of a leek. So when buying leeks, look for those with the greatest length of white. Cut-off greens add to the flavor of homemade broths.

1. Cut off the hairy root just where it joins the white section of the leek.

2. If the outermost membrane of the leek is wilted, pull it off. When cutting off the greens, leave a couple of inches of green attached to the white.

3. Whittle off the outer green leaves to reveal a pale green or white interior. This saves a little leek.

179 How to wash leeks

Leeks, elongated members of the onion family, are grown partly underground so they stay white; because of this they often have sand hidden inside. If you're slicing or julienning leeks, you can slice or julienne first and then wash the slices as you would a green leafy vegetable, but if you're cooking whole leek halves, such as in a gratin, then you'll need to wash the leeks ahead of time.

1. To rinse, cut off the greens of the leek and cut the whites in half lengthwise.

2. Hold the halves of white under cold running water with the root end up so the sand is not driven down into the root end.

3. Flip through the layers with your fingers to get water in between and rinse out any sand.

4. Shake out the excess water.

180 How to julienne leeks

Take two or three layers of leek white and fold them in half, end to end. Slice thinly into lengthwise strips.

181 About wild mushrooms

Most wild mushrooms can be cooked as cultivated mushrooms are—they can be sautéed or grilled. Large-capped mushrooms such as porcini amd portobellos are best lightly coated with olive oil and grilled. Other mushrooms such as morels and chanterelles are best sautéed in olive oil or butter, perhaps with a little parsley and garlic.

• **Morels:** In season in the spring, morels are best cooked whole so they retain their elegant cone shape. While delicious sautéed with garlic and parsley, their flavor is delicate and is best brought out in subtly flavored sauces. They are especially wonderful when added to fish and chicken cream sauces or atop asparagus. They are so special (and expensive) that they are worth serving alone as their own course.

• **Porcini:** Also called cêpes, porcini come in many sizes and can be extremely large. They should not be sliced too thinly or diced too small or their meaty texture, part of their drama, will be lost. Try grilling the caps whole and the stems cut in half lengthwise. They can also be sautéed and served alone or atop grilled poultry or meats.

• **Chanterelles:** These golden mushrooms are great sautéed and make a grand and elegant omelet. They can be used in any recipe calling for mushrooms, but don't chop or cut them into pieces so small that no one recognizes their lovely shape. If the mushrooms are large, cut them following their natural contours so they retain their shape.

• **Shiitake:** These mushrooms can be treated like regular mushrooms except that their stems must be removed because they are leathery (the stems can be added to stocks and soups for flavor).

• **Oyster:** Usually cultivated, oysters are especially vulnerable to mildew, so be sure they are dry and have no wet or soft spots or mildew odor.

HINT *Porcini and morels sometimes have worms burrowed into their interior. If you think you might, to get rid of them, spread out the mushrooms on a sheet pan and bake in a 200°F oven for about 15 minutes. If there are worms, they'll have exited by then. You can also seal the mushrooms in plastic bags for 6 hours, which causes the worms to crawl out of the mushrooms to look for air.*

How to buy cultivated mushrooms

If mushrooms have dried out a little, this is harmless; in fact, you'll get more for your money. Avoid mushrooms that are wet or even moist. When fresh mushrooms with caps are closed, you're unable to see their gills. If the mushrooms have been sitting awhile, the gills will be visible; this is harmless, although the mushrooms may be a little brown.

182 About dried mushrooms

Some mushrooms dry better than others; in fact, some dried mushrooms are even more flavorful than fresh. They're great to have on hand for flavoring sauces, soups, and braised dishes.

To buy dried mushrooms

• Look for large whole mushrooms or thick even slices. Dried porcini should be so aromatic that you can smell them through the bag.

• Dried morels are delicious and add a smoky complexity to sauces. They are especially good in pasta sauces.

• Chanterelles don't dry well.

• Dried shiitakes are usually sold in Asian markets. There are two kinds: those with smooth caps, which are less expensive and less flavorful, and those with fissured caps, which, depending on their size, can be extremely expensive but are correspondingly more delicious.

To reconstitute dried mushrooms

Dried mushrooms must be soaked in some liquid before they can be used. Save the water for adding to whatever dish or sauce is at hand (leave behind any grit in the soaking dish). If the liquid is seriously gritty, strain it through a paper towel or coffee filter before using.

1. Soak the mushrooms in a small amount of water or Madeira. Use as little liquid as possible to avoid leaching out their flavor. This may mean adding only enough liquid to come a quarter of the way up the sides of the mushrooms.

2. Turn the mushrooms around in the liquid every few minutes to get them to soften all over.

3. Some mushrooms soften in a few minutes, while others, such as dried shiitakes, may take several hours.

4. After reconstituting the mushrooms, squeeze any liquid out into the bowl you used for soaking. Use the mushrooms in your favorite recipe.

183   When to wash mushrooms

Many people are afraid to wash mushrooms for fear that they'll absorb too much liquid. In fact, most mushrooms—fresh morels are the exception—absorb virtually no liquid when left in a bowl of water for an afternoon. If you must wash morels, rinse them in a colander while tossing them around. When possible, wash mushrooms just before using.

1. Fill a bowl with cold water, put in the mushrooms, and swirl them around quickly with your fingers.

2. Let sit for 5 minutes and transfer to a colander.

3. Cut off any stubborn patches of soil with a knife.

HINT *If you're not using your mushrooms right away, don't store them in a plastic bag, which will trap in moisture and cause them to mildew. Instead, put them in a paper bag in the refrigerator or in a cool dry place. If they wither and dry a little, no harm is done—in fact, a little aging improves their flavor.*

184   How to slice and chop fresh mushrooms

1. Trim and remove the mushroom stems and slice them crosswise.

2. Slice the caps crosswise.

3. If you want a dice, cut the pieces crosswise in the opposite direction.

4. If you're using the mushrooms for stuffing, chop the pieces finely by hand or in a food processor.

Chopping large-capped mushrooms, stems and all

185 How to sauté mushrooms

Cultivated mushrooms contain a lot of water (buy creminis when you can, they contain less) that is released when they get hot. If you add too many mushrooms to a hot pan, they'll release their liquid faster than the heat can boil it away and they'll end up stewing in their own juices. To avoid this, heat the oil until almost smoking and add a handful of the sliced mushrooms at a time. Wait 30 seconds to a minute, until they sizzle and begin to brown, before adding another handful.

186 How to peel peppers

Roasting peppers until their skin is well charred and their flesh cooked through improves their flavor substantially. Regardless of method, the idea is to completely char the pepper—it should be completely coated in black—but not so much that it turns white, which means you're overdoing it. When it's all charred, pull off as much of the peel as you can, then rinse the pepper and scrape off any stubborn patches of peel with the end of a paring knife. Some recipes call for taking out the seeds to reduce the bitterness and even cutting out the white ribbing on the inside of the peppers.

Note: These techniques can also be used to peel chiles.

Electric stove method

Bend down the ends of a wire coat hanger until they almost touch. Place this directly on the coils of the stove and put the peppers on top. The hanger should keep the peppers about a sixteenth of an inch away from the coils. Turn the peppers every minute or so until evenly blackened.

Gas stove method

Put the peppers, 2 or more at a time, right on the hottest flame. Turn the peppers around in the flame, using tongs, until evenly blackened.

Broiler method

Arrange the peppers on a sheet pan and slide it under the broiler. Turn the peppers as needed to get them to blacken evenly.

How to prepare peeled bell peppers

Strips of grilled bell pepper, flavored with olive oil, a little garlic, and perhaps thyme, make a colorful addition to an antipasto platter or pasta salad.

1. Cut out the stem end off the grilled pepper.

2. Cut the pepper vertically in half and rinse out the seeds.

3. Cut out any white pieces of pulp. The pepper can now be cut into strips, cubes, etc.

187 Which potato do I use for what?

Many of us are perplexed when recipes call for "waxy" potatoes versus, say, Idahos or russets or other "starchy" potatoes. It helps to know the difference—for buying and for cooking, for example, because starchy potatoes such as russets and Yukon golds, will fall apart if simmered in a stew while waxy potatoes will hold their shape. The best Irish stew contains both kinds: a starchy potato that dissolves and gives the stew body and a waxy potato that holds its shape and provides bulk and texture.

vegetables

- **Russets:** In general, russets are the usually large potatoes with dark rough skins. Idahos are a type of russet. Russets are best for French fries and for baking whole.
- **Idahos:** Other than being from Idaho, Idahos are russets that have to meet certain standards. They have an advantage over russets from other places in that they don't turn dark when peeled.
- **Waxy:** These are either pale white or red and have relatively smooth skins. They are best in dishes in which the potato needs to hold its shape—in a gratin (see entry 145), for example, or when sautéing sliced potatoes. Don't make mashed potatoes or soup with waxy potatoes—they can become gluey.
- **Yellow Finn/Yukon gold:** These potatoes have a very fine texture and are best for mashed potatoes and for pureed soups that include potatoes.
- **Fingerlings:** These little pale potatoes (such as La Ratte) do, in fact, look a little like fingers. They are best roasted or sautéed whole.

188   How to bake potatoes

If you like the peel of your baked potato to be soft, wrap the potato in aluminum foil smeared on the inside with a little butter to keep it from sticking. Otherwise, just put the potato in the oven. There's no need to preheat the oven. Set it to 400°F and bake the potato until a knife slides easily through, about 30 minutes. If you're cooking small new potatoes or potato wedges around a roast, you'll still need almost 30 minutes. If you're baking only one or two potatoes, heat them for 10 minutes in the microwave, repositioning the potato on a little plate, and the plate in a different part of the oven, every 2 minutes.

HINT *Make extra baked potatoes for the next day. When they're cold, peel them, slice them about ½ inch thick, and sauté them in butter or olive oil. Or, carefully make a slit along the top of the potato, scoop out the inside, work it through a ricer, and thin it with a little cream. If you like, add some grated parmigiano-reggiano cheese. Put the mixture back in the potato and bake.*

189 How to make French fries

Deep-frying is one of the best ways to cook potatoes, and for that matter, anything. But it requires a few simple things that will safeguard both the fryer and the fried (see entry 302). Russets that have been hanging around for a while are the best to use.

Cut potatoes into slices

With a chef's knife, cut the slices into sticks

First frying

Second frying

The classic French fry

The classic French fry is the size found in fast-food restaurants, between ⅛ and ¼ inch thick. French fries need to be fried in two stages: first, at about 320°F until they soften all the way through, without browning, about 3 minutes (this can be done ahead). Remove the fries from the oil. Then fry for a second time, just before serving, at about 360°F until golden brown, about 1 minute. Sprinkle with salt.

Thick French fries (steak fries)

So-called thick French fries (about ½ inch), like thin fries, should be fried in two stages: first, long enough to soften them through in 320°F oil, about 6 minutes, and second, about 2 minutes in 360°F oil to turn them golden brown.

HINT *If you like to deep fry, buy the largest "spider" you can find. "Spider" is really a bit of a misnomer since the tool looks more like a spiderweb than a spider. The idea is to be able to take foods out of hot oil quickly without taking any oil with it as would a slotted spoon or a skimmer.*

How to know your frying oil is hot enough for French fries

For the lower-temperature oil used for the first stage of frying French fries, drop a potato (close to the surface so it doesn't splash) into the oil. The potato should sink to the bottom and slowly rise, surrounded by bubbles. For the hotter oil, used in the second frying stage, the potato should sink only an inch or two and be immediately surrounded by an abundance of bubbles.

190 How to roast little potatoes

Brown fingerlings and small waxy potatoes in oil in a nonstick pan over high heat. Remove from the pan and pour out the burned oil. Let the pan cool slightly and add a tablespoon or two of butter. Finish in a 350°F oven until the potatoes are easily penetrated with a skewer, about 15 minutes.

191 How to mash potatoes

Boil or steam peeled Yukon gold or yellow Finn potatoes in a small amount of liquid so that the flavor of the potato is concentrated in the liquid, which in turn can be added to the mashed potatoes. Then use one of these devices to finish the potatoes:

• **Ricer:** Vaguely like a giant garlic press, a ricer is one of the best devices for making satin-smooth mashed potatoes. Place one or two cooked potatoes in the ricer, push down the handle, and the potato is forced through the perforations.

• **Masher:** This simple device literally mashes the potatoes; while easy to use, it will not eliminate all the lumps.

• **Food mill:** A large food mill comes in handy for large amounts of mashed potatoes. Use the finest attachment you have.

• **Drum sieve:** This device makes the best mashed potatoes. Use the finest mesh you have and work the potatoes through the drum sieve with a large spoon, plastic pastry scraper, or a small metal bowl.

With a ricer

With a masher

192 How to flavor mashed potatoes

• **Fennel:** Chop 1 fennel bulb per 4 large potatoes and boil with the potatoes. Work the mixture through a drum sieve or ricer.

• **Garlic:** Boil peeled garlic cloves, about 1 per potato, with the potatoes and work the mixture through a ricer or drum sieve.

• **Celeriac:** Boil about half as much celeriac as potatoes with the potatoes before pureeing.

• **Wasabi:** This spicy horseradish, loved by the Japanese, makes a great flavoring for mashed potatoes. Add it carefully "to taste"—it's strong.

193 How to use radishes to make the world's quickest hors d'oeuvre

1. Slice a baguette very thinly and on an angle.

2. If you have time, toast the slices on one side under the broiler.

3. Butter the slices generously. Sprinkle with salt.

4. With a plastic vegetable slicer, slice radishes very thinly and lay the slices on the bread slices.

194 How to section celeriac and turnips

If you're roasting or glazing celeriac or turnips (see entries 197 and 198), cutting them into rounded sections helps them cook more evenly and look more attractive.

1. Cut off each end of the vegetable so it rests flat on the cutting board.

2. Pressing the knife vertically through the vegetable, cut it into wedges—the number depends on the size you want.

3. Round off the sharp edges with a small, sharp knife—a claw-shaped knife is best for this, but a regular paring knife will also work. The best way to approach this is to rotate the knife, against the vegetable, toward you in an arcing pattern.

195 How to dice hard round vegetables

More exacting recipes, especially chefs' recipes, call for vegetables cut into perfect dice. While there are standard sizes for chefs—macedoine (shown below) are ¼ inch on each side and brunoise ⅛ inch—the size may be dictated by the recipe or your own taste. If you decide to take on this challenge, read on.

1. If you're being exact, trim four sides off the vegetable to form a cube.

2. Slice the cube the thickness you want your cubes to be so you'll end up with a small pile of rectangles.

3. Cut these rectangles into strips the same width as the thickness of the slices.

4. Stack these strips and cut across them, again the same thickness as you want the cubes.

196 How to julienne root vegetables

Vegetables cut into thin sticks, about ¹⁄₁₆ inch, are said to be julienned. The most popular julienned vegetable in France is probably celeriac, commonly served in the dish called celery remoulade. Other root vegetables can also be julienned and served either raw with a sauce or cooked along with braised meats. While most vegetable slicers (see entry 9) have julienne attachments, the flesh of most root vegetables is too hard to make using the julienne attachment practical. A better system is to first slice the vegetables with the slicer, then stack the slices three or so at a time and cut across the slices by hand to make the julienne. If you have a soft vegetable, such as a roasted beet (see entry 161), the julienne attachment will, in fact, work.

1. To julienne a round vegetable such as a turnip, cut off the sides, top, and bottom to form a perfect cube.

2. Slice the cube, by hand or with a slicer, into squares about ¹⁄₁₆ inch thick.

3. Stack the slices and slice them again so you get little sticks.

197 How to roast root vegetables

Root vegetables, such as carrots, onions, beets, and turnips, can be roasted whole in their peel or they can be peeled and sectioned, tossed with a little oil or melted butter, and then spread in a roasting pan and roasted on their own or around a piece of meat. Make sure the vegetables are clean, and, in the case of potatoes, use the end of the peeler to cut out any eyes. Roast in a hot oven until evenly browned (stir them around from time to time so they brown evenly) and a skewer slides easily in and out of the vegetable.

How to turn your roast into an elegant one-dish meal

Section a variety of root vegetables, including starchy ones such as parsnips or potatoes, and use them to surround a roast.

198 How to glaze root vegetables

You can glaze root vegetables by simply roasting them (see entry 197) and tossing them with a little butter, or you can cook them with a small amount of liquid, such as water, broth, or cream, until coated with a shiny glaze. Cut carrots, turnips, and celeriac into manageable sections, but leave pearl onions whole.

HINT *The trick to glazing root vegetables is to regulate the heat so the vegetables end up cooked at the same time the liquid evaporates into a glaze. If the vegetables are softening and there's still a lot of liquid in the pan, turn up the heat. If the liquid is almost gone and the vegetables are still hard, add more liquid and turn down the heat.*

1. Spread the root vegetable sections or whole pearl onions in a pan just large enough to hold them in a single layer.

2. Add enough broth or water to come halfway up the sides as well as a tablespoon or two of butter.

3. Cover the pan with a round of parchment paper or aluminium foil.

4. Simmer over medium heat until the vegetables are easily penetrated with a skewer and coated with glaze.

5. If you want the glaze to brown, cook the vegetables until all the liquid evaporates and a brown crust forms on the bottom of the pan. Add ¼ cup of water to the pan to dissolve the crust and form a glaze to coat the vegetables.

199 How to stem spinach

Spinach comes in two varieties: very delicate, smooth leaves for making salads, and larger wrinkled leaves for cooking. These days, you can find spinach in bags already washed, but it's a good idea to wash it again. Spinach bought in loose bunches must always be washed as you would sandy lettuce (see entry 69). The larger wrinkled variety should be stemmed before it is cooked.

1. To pull away the stem, pinch the leaf forward between your thumb and forefinger, the spine of the leaf facing up.

2. Lift and pull back the stem so that the stem attached to the back of the leaf comes away at the same time.

How to make a spinach salad

Use delicate spinach with smooth leaves (packaged or loose), not the thicker wrinkled kind. Wash the spinach as you would lettuce and dress it with a mustardy vinaigrette. Wedges of hard-boiled eggs, crumbled cooked bacon, croutons, and sliced onions or scallions are delicious complements in a spinach salad.

200 How to cream spinach

Creamed spinach can be a smooth and creamy puree or the leaves can be left whole or barely chopped and gently coated with cream.

Whole or coarsely chopped method

1. Squeeze any excess liquid out of the leaves and bring about 2 tablespoons heavy cream per serving to a simmer in a saucepan.

2. Simmer until the cream thickens.

3. Stir in the spinach. Continue to stir until heated through. Season to taste with kosher salt and freshly ground black pepper.

Puree method

1. Prepare the creamed spinach as above but don't cook down the cream as much.

2. Stir the spinach into the hot cream for a minute, then puree it with an immersion blender or transfer it to a regular blender (see entry 12). If it's too stiff to stir around, add a little more cream to get it to the consistency you like.

201 What to do with leftover spinach

Never reheat spinach in boiling water. Instead heat 2 or 3 tablespoons of cream in a sauté pan until the cream thickens. Stir in the spinach over medium heat until it's heated through.

202 Ways with zucchini and summer squash

How to prepare

1. If you want round slices, use a knife or a vegetable slicer (see entry 9).

2. For smaller pieces, cut the squash lengthwise and slice.

3. If you're grilling, slice the squash lengthwise into long strips that won't fall through the grill. A vegetable slicer is good for this.

How to stuff a summer squash

Cut the squash in half and bake in a 350°F oven until the pulp is soft. Scoop out the pulp and chop it. Cook a little chopped onion and garlic in olive oil, flavor with herbs such as thyme, add the chopped pulp and (if you like) some grated cheese. Put this mixture back in the emptied-out squash halves. You can bake them as is or sprinkle with more cheese or bread crumbs to help make a crust. Return to the oven until crusty on top.

How to sauté

1. Heat pure olive oil in a large sauté pan over high heat until it barely begins to smoke.

2. Add the zucchini, at first only enough to make a single layer in the pan, and sauté a minute. Add the same amount of zucchini and continue in the same way. The trick is to avoid adding too much zucchini at once, which will cause it to steam and become watery instead of browning.

3. For added flavor, mix in minced garlic and parsley during the last minute of sautéing.

How to grill

1. Cut zucchini lengthwise into strips between ⅛ and ¹⁄₁₆ inch thick.

2. Brush the slices with olive oil, sprinkle with herbs such as marjoram or thyme, and grill over a fire or in a grill pan, turning until well browned on both sides.

How to stuff and bake

1. Preheat the oven to 350°F.

2. Cut the zucchini lengthwise in half and scoop out most of the pulp from each half.

3. Chop the pulp and cook it with chopped herbs, garlic, tomatoes, or whatever ingredient you like and put it back into the zucchini halves.

4. Sprinkle over cheese or bread crumbs (see entry 38) if you like, and bake until brown, about 30 minutes.

203   How to choose tomatoes

A tomato isn't always better because it's bright red. What's most important is that it be naturally ripened.

1. A perfect tomato should be sticky, drippy, and about to burst. It will have a pronounced aroma.

2. Look for tomatoes that aren't too hard and that have some smell.

3. Avoid tomatoes with wrinkled patches or soft spots.

4. Look for some of the heirloom tomatoes that are beginning to become available—they often taste better than they look.

5. Yellow tomatoes tend to have less acidity than red ones, and when in season, they are often delightful when combined with red or striated tomatoes.

6. Green tomatoes, not to be confused with tomatillos, can be diced in salsa (they're harder and retain their texture) or can be sliced, coated with bread crumbs, and sautéed, traditionally in bacon fat.

7. Out of season, use cherry tomatoes, which often have a good flavor.

8. To ripen tomatoes, keep them at room temperature wrapped in a paper bag.

204   How to peel tomatoes

If you cook whole tomatoes in a sauce, soup, or stew that you're not planning to strain, you need to peel and seed the tomatoes first so you don't have little rolled-up peels and seeds floating around in your dish.

1. Plunge the tomatoes in boiling water for 15 to 30 seconds—the less ripe the tomato, the longer the time.

2. Remove, using a slotted spoon and rinse immediately with cold water in a colander.

vegetables

3. Cut out the stems and peel off the peel with a small knife, your thumb, and your forefinger.

How to peel one tomato

If you have a gas stove and a single tomato, and don't want to bother bringing a pot of water to the boil, put the tomato right on the flame and scald it all around before pulling off the peel.

205 How to cut tomatoes

To section a tomato, cut it in half through the North Pole, and cut each of the halves into wedges the size you like. If you're just squeezing the seeds out, for making soups, sauces, or stews, cut the tomatoes in half through the equator.

206 How to seed tomatoes

Unless you're straining the tomatoes, the seeds and the liquid next to them should be squeezed out. Even if you *are* straining the tomatoes eventually, seeding is still a good idea because you'll also get rid of a fair amount of excess water that will only dilute the tomatoes' flavor.

For chopped tomatoes

If you're chopping or cooking tomatoes in a way that their size isn't important, peel the tomatoes, cut them in half across the equator, and squeeze out the seeds of each half.

For serving tomatoes in wedges

If you're serving the tomatoes in wedges, such as in a salad, push the seeds out of each wedge with a finger.

207 How to chop tomatoes

First, seed the tomatoes by squeezing the seeds out of each half.
Then you can chop the tomatoes to the size you like. If you're making
perfect dice for some elegant dish, peel the tomato and cut away the
pulp that surrounds the interior. Use this, not the inner pulp, to dice.

Chopping simplified

If you have two large knives the same size, you can chop with a rapid
up-and-down movement using both hands. You can also use only one
hand, or you can grip the knife at both ends and chop crosswise in
front of you.

208 How to make salsa

Most salsas are made of more or less coarsely chopped tomatoes
(see entry 207) and/or avocados (see entry 154). Once you have
chopped tomatoes in hand, here are some ways to turn them into
a salsa.

- Add chopped fresh chiles such as jalapeños to provide heat.
- Add reconstituted dried or canned chipotle chiles to provide a
smoky note.

- Add reconstituted, finely chopped dried chiles for complex flavors.
- Add fresh lime juice for a lively, tangy note.
- Add cilantro, which always complements chiles.
- Add avocados for bulk.

209   How to bake tomatoes

Most recipes for baked tomatoes suggest relatively high heat, which softens the tomatoes in about 30 minutes. When you use low heat, say 275°F, and cook the tomatoes until any liquid they release evaporates, about 3 hours, the flavor is much more intense.

1. If the tomatoes are very ripe and soft, peel them; otherwise, leave the peels on.

2. Stem the tomatoes and cut them in half through the equator.

3. Squeeze the seeds out of each half.

4. Dribble extra virgin olive oil and sprinkle fresh herbs into the cavities in the tomatoes.

5. Put the tomatoes flat side up in a baking dish.

6. If you're in a hurry, bake at 400°F until the tomatoes soften, about 30 minutes. If you have the time, slow bake the tomatoes.

210 How to make a basic tomato sauce

Ripe tomatoes make a wonderful sauce all by themselves, but if you want something more complex, sweat aromatic vegetables and dice prosciutto; then add them to the tomatoes.

1. Chop the tomatoes, peel and all, in large chunks.

2. Stew the tomatoes for about 10 minutes, until they soften.

3. Work the softened tomatoes through a food mill.

4. For a perfectly smooth sauce or soup, use a ladle to work the liquid through a fine-mesh strainer. If you like, add cream to the sauce.

211　What are tomato concassée and tomato coulis?

Concassée

Chefs' recipes and menus often refer to these two tomato preparations with no descriptions or explanations. A concassée is simply chopped, peeled, and seeded tomatoes. A coulis, be it tomato or raspberry, is simply a puree that's been strained. When making a coulis, there's no need to peel the tomatoes because they'll get strained anyway. Both concasséed tomatoes and tomato coulis can be made either raw or cooked. A cooked tomato coulis requires roasting, grilling, or sautéing the tomatoes before straining.

212　What is a tomatillo?

Don't confuse tomatillos with green tomatoes. Tomatillos are actually related to gooseberries and have the same papery sheath that must be removed. Once they are ready, the tomatillos can be halved and simmered until they soften into a delicious sauce. For additional flavor, sweat a chopped onion and some garlic, add the tomatillos with a little water, cover the pot, and simmer until the tomatillos soften. If you want a smooth sauce, work the mixture through a food mill.

213 How to buy a truffle

Few of us cook with truffles because they're so expensive and we don't want to waste them by doing something wrong. But you can justify the price of truffles, somewhat, if you think in terms of how much it would cost if you were eating out.

• There are summer truffles and winter truffles. Winter truffles are the more famous, expensive ones. Summer truffles should cost about a tenth of the price and are often a good value.

• Black winter truffles should have a fine white filigree when you slice them; if they're solid black or brown, they're not authentic winter truffles.

• All truffles should be intensely aromatic and smell up the room as soon as you open the lid.

• Truffles should be firm to the touch with no soft spots.

• Truffles are best fresh. Frozen truffles have their aroma intact, but they'll have lost their firm texture, which makes them harder to slice very thin. Truffles in jars rarely have the aroma of fresh or flash-frozen truffles, and canned truffles are not worth bothering with.

How to get the most out of a truffle

Store truffles in the refrigerator in a large jar with unwrapped sticks of butter and some eggs in the shell. The aroma will scent the butter, which you can then use for sauces or mashed potatoes (see entry 191) and will have penetrated the egg shells. You can use the eggs to make a truffle omelet without ever using any of the truffle. Truffles are best added at the last minute and with fats such as egg yolks, cream, and butter.

214 Rescuing flavorless fruits

If you're stuck with less-than-perfect fruit such as hard peaches, plastic out-of-season strawberries, or flavorless apricots, try poaching the fruit in a light sugar syrup.

1. Make enough sugar syrup, with equal parts sugar and water, to come halfway up the sides of the fruit.

2. Add the fruit to the syrup, cover the pan, and simmer gently, until the fruit is soft.

3. Take out the fruit with a slotted spoon.

4. Return the pan to the heat and boil down the poaching liquid until it's lightly syrupy.

5. Let cool and flavor the syrup with a fruit brandy such as kirsch, which is made with cherries; poire William, which is made with pears; Mirabelle, which is made with plums; or framboise, which is made with raspberries.

215 How to make a simple syrup

Simple syrup is useful for brushing on cakes to moisten them, for poaching all manner of fruits, and for lightly candying citrus zests. To make it, combine equal parts sugar and water by volume and stir over medium heat in a saucepan until all the sugar dissolves. Let it cool before adding flavorful spirits.

216 Which nut oils are roasted and why

Most nut oils are made from raw nuts, which makes them extremely perishable and relatively flavorless. Dark Asian sesame oil is made from toasted seeds and has a powerful flavor. Only one maker, Le Blanc, makes nut oils such as hazelnut, pignoli, walnuts, almonds, and pistachio oils from roasted nuts. While these oils are expensive, their flavor is so intense and their shelf life so much longer that they are well worth the cost. In any case, nut oils should be kept in the freezer for longer life.

217 How to peel and core an apple

Wonderful raw or cooked, apples are one of the few fruits that don't release liquid—or at least not very much—when they cook. For this reason, it's easy to use apples in pies and tarts or in turnovers. Like heirloom tomatoes, older and tastier varieties of apples are making a comeback and can usually be found in the fall at a local green market. If you encounter an unfamiliar apple, ask the farmer what to do with it. The choices generally are whether to bake it or eat it raw.

1. Cut out the stem with the end of a swivel peeler and then rotate the apple against the peeler so the peel comes off in a single ribbon.

2. If you need to keep the apples whole, push an apple corer down through the apple, starting at the stem end. Otherwise, cut the apples in half and insert a paring knife a little to the side of center (where the seeds are) and rotate it around the core, forming a cone shape that will come out with the core.

3. If you're coring apple wedges, just cut a little out of the center of each wedge.

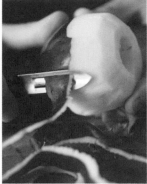

218 How to slice an apple

If you want to slice apple halves and keep the slices together—so that you can fan them out, as in a tart—here's the best way.

1. Slice apple halves with their flat side down on the work surface. To keep the apple slices together neatly, don't cut through—leave a tiny bit of apple attached to each slice.

2. Slice across where they're connected to detach.

Best for cooking		Best for eating raw
Braeburn	Ida Red	Cortland
Cortland	Jonagold	Fuji
Golden Delicious	McIntosh	Granny Smith
Red Delicious	Macoun	Jonagold
Empire	Rome	Macoun

219 How to make the best baked apples

Instead of baking apples whole, cut them into wedges and bake them with sugar and butter. Add a little cream at the end to make a rich, delicious sauce.

1. Preheat the oven to 400°F.

2. To make 4 servings, peel and core (see entry 217) 6 tart baking apples and cut them each into 6 wedges.

3. Put the wedges in a heavy-bottomed ovenproof pan. Pour over ⅔ cup sugar and add 12 tablespoons butter, cut in chunks.

4. Bake until a knife slides easily in and out of the apples, about 25 minutes, and the butter has browned on the bottom of the pan.

5. Put the pan on the stove over high heat and pour in ⅔ cup heavy cream. Boil for 30 seconds. Serve immediately.

220 How to pit an apricot

Grab apricots while you can—the season is so short.

1. Cut all around the apricot, top to bottom, and twist away the two halves.

2. Pull out the pit.

221 How to julienne citrus zests

Since the zest contains most of the fruit's flavor, it's sometimes useful to julienne it, and perhaps lightly candy it, by cooking it in a little sugar syrup (see entry 215), and use it to decorate desserts or savory dishes. Cut the zests off in strips with a small knife. Stack the slices and slice them thinly using the knuckles of your free hand to control the slicing and ensure that the julienne will be very fine.

222   How to zest citrus fruits

The flavor of citrus fruits is less in their juice than in the thin, color-ful, and oily skin called the zest. Many recipes call for scraping the zest off with a grater or shaving it off with a knife. You can also use a zester, which is a little gadget with tiny holes in it that cuts the zest into tiny strips. Or you can cut away the zest with a knife, leaving as little white pulp as possible attached to it. Long flat Microplane zesters, if fine enough—they come in different grades, one made specifically for citrus fruits—make a quick job of it.

Zester

Paring knife

Rasp grater

223   How to get the meat out of a coconut

To ensure your coconut meat is fresh, shred it yourself by grating a shelled coconut.

The liquid inside the coconut, while perfectly drinkable, is not coconut milk and it's not what's typically used in the kitchen. Coconut milk is extracted from shredded coconut with hot water. Coconut cream is that part of the milk that floats to the top and congeals. The best canned unsweetened coconut milk comes from Thailand.

HINT *When buying a coconut, shake it next to your ear; if you don't hear liquid sloshing around inside, don't buy it.*

1. Hammer a screwdriver into two of the soft round spots that appear near one end of the coconut and pour out and discard the liquid.

2. Bake the coconut on a sheet pan in a 350°F oven for 20 minutes.

3. Wrap the coconut in a towel and crack it in half with a hammer. Use a screwdriver to pry the flesh out of each end.

4. If the thin brown membrane adheres to the flesh, peel it off with a vegetable peeler.

How to shred a coconut

Grate the coconut meat by hand or in a food processor and either dry it in the oven or freeze.

How to make coconut milk

1. Place grated coconut in a bowl. Pour over enough boiling water to cover the coconut. Let sit for at least 10 minutes.

2. Strain the mixture.

3. Push on the strainer to extract as much liquid as possible.

4. To get more extract, soak it again and strain again.

224 How to peel a kiwi

Once exotic, then fashionable, and now everyday, kiwi's melonlike flavor is gentle enough that it can be combined with other fruits such as melon, pineapple, mango, and papaya, and with complementary ingredients such as yogurt, lime juice, cilantro, and chiles. Peeling a kiwi with a peeler is next to impossible, and using a knife is a nuisance. Instead, use a spoon.

1. Cut off the ends of the fruit, just deep enough to reveal the flesh.

2. Reach in one end of the kiwi with a tablespoon, sliding it between the peel and the flesh.

3. Move the spoon around the inside of the kiwi with the back of the spoon flush against the skin, until the flesh pulls out.

How to slice a kiwi

Once peeled, kiwis can be sliced into rounds or lengthwise into wedges. If the center white core of the wedges seems tough, cut it out with a knife.

225 How to pit and peel a mango

Mangoes are now available almost year round and are delightful in fruit salads, salsas, or by themselves. You can peel a mango with a vegetable peeler if you need thin, even slices, but for cubes or rough dice, you can take out the pulp with a spoon.

1. Feel the mango and notice that it's thinner in one direction. The pit is flat and lies parallel with the thin side of the mango.

2. Cut through one of the narrow ends until you feel the pit.

3. Holding the knife against the pit, continue cutting through the mango until you detach one half.

4. Cut the pit out of the other half by sliding the knife under it.

5. Make a series of shallow cuts into the pulp, down to the skin but not through it.

6. Make a second series of cuts in the opposite direction.

7. Scoop out the pulp with a spoon.

226 How to pick out a ripe melon

When you want a melon with a smooth skin such as a honeydew, rub the melon gently (ignore the funny looks) and pick out the one that feels the stickiest. The stickiness is from the sugar in the melon. Unfortunately, you can't do this with a cantaloupe because it already has a rough skin. But you can determine ripeness by smell: Sniff the base of the stem—it should smell like suede.

227 How to peel and slice an orange

To make perfect glistening peeled oranges, don't pull away the peel with your fingers; use a sharp knife instead.

1. Cut off the two ends of the orange just deep enough to reveal some of the flesh.

2. Set the orange on one end on a cutting board and cut away the peel, following the contour of the orange as closely as possible.

3. Slice the orange crosswise into rounds.

228 How to cut perfect orange wedges

Here's how to get perfect orange wedges without the white pulpy membrane.

1. Peel the orange (see entry 227).

2. Hold the orange over a bowl and use a paring knife to cut toward the center of the orange, just above one of the membranes that surround the wedges.

3. Cut between the membrane, down toward the center on the other side of the wedge. The wedge should fall out into the bowl.

4. Continue in this way, rotating the orange as you go. When you're done, squeeze the juice out of the core.

229 How to peel and pit a papaya

There are two principal types of papaya available in the United States: the larger Mexican papayas with bright orange flesh, and the smaller, yellow Hawaiian papayas. The Mexican papayas have a somewhat more aggressive flavor and the Hawaiian variety is more floral. Use papaya in fruit salads with other tropical fruits or in savory salads with chiles, other fruits, cilantro, and grilled foods such as chicken or shrimp.

1. Peel a papaya with a vegetable peeler.

2. Or, cut the papaya lengthwise in half, remove the seeds, and scoop out the pulp.

230 How to core a pear

Pears are at their best when they yield to gentle pressure, with no feeling of mushiness when you press on it with your thumb. When you find a juicy ripe one, just slice it lengthwise into wedges and core out each wedge with a paring knife. Sliced pears are delicious with cheese, especially good blue cheese such as Roquefort. Avoid pears with brown soft spots, which are signs of bruising.

How to core a whole pear

To core whole pears, insert an apple corer through the stem end and work it almost all the way through the center of the pear.

To core and seed pear halves

1. To core pear halves, insert a sharp knife to the side of the core and rotate, forming a cone-shaped cutout with the core in it.

2. Cut out the seeds from each half with a paring knife or melon baller.

Because pears are almost always sold underripe, if you want to eat one right away, you have to cook it by poaching or roasting it or by arranging pear halves in a tart shell and baking them.

Roasted pears have much more flavor than poached pears.

To roast

1. Stem, peel, halve, and core (see entry 230) 4 pears.

2. Bake with sugar and butter as you would apples (see entry 219).

3. Use the cream as in the apple recipe and deglaze the pan to create a sauce to serve with the pears.

To poach

1. Stem, peel, halve, and core (see entry 230) the pears.

2. Put them in a pan with enough simple syrup (see entry 215) or red wine to cover.

3. Simmer them gently until they're easily penetrated with a sharp knife, about 15 minutes, depending on ripeness.

4. Remove the pears to a serving plate and return the pan to the heat.

5. Boil down the poaching liquid to about one third its original volume to concentrate the sweetness.

6. Let cool and flavor with poire William (pear brandy).

7. Serve the liquid over the poached pears.

232 How to extract flesh from a persimmon

Those of us who've tasted an underripe persimmon are unlikely to have forgotten the experience of sharp astringency. Persimmons must be very soft to be edible.

HINT *Persimmons are delicious eaten alone, but you can also dice them and combine them with avocado, chiles, cilantro, and lime juice to make a lovely salsa for dolloping on grilled fish or chicken.*

1. To remove the flesh, first cut out the stem.

2. Cut the persimmon in half.

3. Using a tablespoon, scoop out the flesh.

233 How to peel a pineapple

The quality of your pineapple will depend on whether it was allowed to ripen "on the vine" (easy to recognize since such pineapples are golden and not green) and air-freighted to its destination, or it was picked underripe and shipped by sea. The air-freighted pineapples are usually sold as "golden pineapples" or some such thing and usually cost a couple of dollars more per pineapple. The extra cost is worth it. Once you get your hands on a good pineapple, you'll need to peel it.

1. Twist off the greens, cut off the ends, and set the pineapple on end.

2. Slice off the peel deep enough to cut below the little holes that dot the pineapple. If cutting this deep and wasting this much pineapple makes you uneasy, you can extract more pineapple by peeling in the same way, but cutting just deep enough to get off the bulk of the peel.

3. Then, follow the rows of the little holes that encircle the pineapple in a spiral pattern, cutting in a V direction on both sides, so you can cut out the holes in rows.

How to cut a pineapple into wedges

1. Cut a peeled pineapple lengthwise into quarters.

2. Remove the hard woody core from each wedge.

3. If you want smaller wedges, cut these wedges lengthwise in half.

4. Slice the wedges crosswise.

234 How to stem a strawberry

Don't do what most people do and just slice the top off a strawberry. It wastes some of the fruit's sweetness.

1. Cut all around the stem with a paring knife.

2. Remove the cone-shaped piece of flesh with the stem attached.

Most fish can be grilled, poached, braised, or baked, in fillets or steaks or whole. Once you've cooked one fish, you can cook them all. Shellfish are a bit more tricky and

Shellfish and Fish

are cooked according to variety. Mollusks are shellfish such as clams with hard shells, and are usually steamed. Crustaceans such as lobster and shrimp are cooked to extract the flavor from the shell and roe. Last, the cephalopods, such as squid and octopus, are best braised or braised and grilled.

235 What's the difference between farmed and wild shellfish?

Until recently, virtually all shellfish were caught in the wild, except in Europe, where shellfish have been cultivated since antiquity. Today, for example, we're more likely to encounter farmed mussels rather than wild ones. The farmed ones are smaller, contain virtually no sand, and rarely include a bad one. They lack only some of the gamy flavor of their larger wild cousins, but this is still unacceptable to a lot of people anyway. Oysters are now farmed on both the West and East coasts and are no different from wild oysters except that they're all the same size. Scallops are either dredged or harvested by divers—hence "divers'" scallops—and are usually sold out of the shell. If you can find scallops still in the shell, snap them up because they're a rare treat. If you come upon scallops in the shell, the scallop will gape, but it should close, at least slightly, when you press on the top shell.

236 How to spot fresh shellfish

Most shellfish are best bought alive, which guarantees their freshness. Live clams and oysters should be tightly closed, mussels can gape a little but should close when you tap a couple together. Scallops are usually sold already shucked, which is a pity, because they're never as fresh as they should be (see entry 250). Crustaceans such as lobsters, crab, and crayfish should be crawling around and visibly alive.

HINT *If you are in doubt about freshness, smell is a good indicator: Shellfish should smell like the ocean; if they smell like anything else, avoid them.*

shellfish

237 How to get the sand and grit out of mussels and clams

While it's easy to get the grit and sand off shellfish by scraping or brushing them under running water, getting at sand and grit on the inside is a different matter. When you are steaming mussels, hard-shell clams, or cockles, there isn't much you can do except let all the grit and sand settle to the bottom of the steaming pot. Then you can carefully pour the liquid into another container, leaving the grit behind.

Soft-shell clams and razor clams can be soaked overnight in saltwater—throw salt into cold water until it tastes like sea water—so they flush themselves out.

238 How to maximize the flavor of clams, mussels, and cockles

Clams, mussels, and cockles release a briny, flavorful liquid when steamed. One secret to successful steaming is to steam with a small amount of liquid so this flavor isn't diluted.

1. Steam the shellfish in a little wine and minced shallot and drain in a colander over a bowl.

2. Gently pour the steaming liquid from the bowl into a saucepan, leaving any grit behind.

3. Boil down the liquid by a third or even a half—more and you risk making the liquid too salty—and whisk in some good butter or cream. You can also enhance this sauce by whisking in chopped parsley, chives, or chervil.

4. You can leave the shellfish in the shell, shuck them all, shuck half of them, or take off only one shell. Put the shellfish in the sauce and serve.

239 How to clean mussels

Cultivated mussels can get by with a quick toss and rinse with cold water. Wild mussels may need some help:

1. Scrape or brush the shells under cold running water to eliminate encrusted dirt or sand.

2. Pull out the hairy beard with a good yank to detach it. Do this within a few hours of cooking the mussels (see entry 240) because debearding kills them.

3. Small cultivated mussels don't need to have the beards removed.

What should gape and what should not

Many of us are confused about what to do if a mussel, a clam, or cockle shells gape, thinking we should use only those that are tightly closed. In fact, mussels almost always gape and when they do they almost always immediately close when tapped together. (Don't make the mistake of throwing out perfectly fine mussels that are slow to close, only to find them in the trash, firmly closed, later in the evening.) Clams (at least hard-shell clams), cockles, and oysters are a different matter and should never gape when raw. Scallops in the shell almost always gape—tap them together and they should close a little, assuring you they're alive—as do steamers (soft-shell clams), whose spigots prevent them from closing. When cooked, almost everything opens. Mussels that don't should be tossed. Clams that can be easily wedged open with a knife are good.

240　How to cook mussels

The best way to cook mussels is simply to put them in a pot with a little white wine and water and perhaps a minced shallot and steam them for about 5 minutes until they open.

HINT *When the mussels have opened, make sure that they are solidly nestled in one half-shell or the other and not connected to both shells. Otherwise, they will tear when you try to get them out of the shell. A minute or two more steaming fixes this problem.*

1. Simmer about ½ cup of flavorful liquid such as white wine with an equal part of water and a minced shallot. You can also use garlic, chiles, tomatoes, and herbs such as parsley.

2. Add the mussels to the pot, cover the pot, and turn the heat to high.

3. As soon as all the mussels have opened, they're ready. Throw out any that don't open. (Unlike clams that don't open in the pot, if a mussel doesn't open, it's bad.)

4. Serve the mussels with the steaming liquid and plenty of crusty French bread.

How to broil and bake mussels

Many recipes for broiled or baked mussels say to shuck them raw, but this can be labor intensive. It's better to steam them open first. You can save the steaming liquid or use it immediately to make a sauce (see entry 358). Then you can broil or bake the mussels with a sauce such as hollandaise (see entry 384) or a little herb butter (see entry 102).

1. Steam the mussels open.

2. Remove the top shells and nestle the mussels in their bottom shells in a crumpled sheet of aluminum foil on a sheet pan (see Hint, page 196).

3. Put a dollop of herb butter (the parsley and garlic butter used for snails is delicious; see entry 270) or some sauce on the mussels and broil or bake them in a hot oven for 3 to 5 minutes, until the butter froths.

241 How to choose clams

There are basically three kinds of clam: hard-shell clams, soft-shell clams, and razor clams. Hard-shell clams, sometimes called quahogs, come in different sizes.

Hard-shell clams

• **Littlenecks:** These are the smallest clams, and their delicate flavor is best in sauces and refined soups.

• **Cherrystones:** These are slightly larger than littlenecks and are also good for soups and sauces.

• **Chowder clams:** These large clams are usually chopped and used in chowders. They make large amounts of soups and chowders affordable because they're less expensive than other clams, but they lack the flavor of cherrystones and littlenecks.

• **Ocean clams:** Sometimes called mahogany clams, these are about the same size as cherrystone or chowder clams. They can be quite tasty and are well suited for soups.

shellfish

191

Soft-shell clams

Sometimes called steamers, soft-shell clams are easy to recognize because they have a little spigot sticking out the side and their shells are elongated ovals, not round. They are cooked in the same way as hard-shell clams, but they are usually served with just a little melted butter. As you eat the clam, pull away the little leatherlike sheath on the spigot.

Razor clams

So called because they look like old-fashioned straight razors, these need to be cooked a long time to soften them, since they turn rubbery the instant they get hot. They're best in long-simmered soups and seafood stews.

242 How to shuck a clam

Unlike oysters, which are shucked through the hinge, clams are shucked by sliding a thin knife between the two shell halves either on the side or on the opening opposite the hinge.

1. Slide a thin knife between the half-shells, starting on the side opposite the hinge.

2. Once you get between the shells, work the knife toward the hinge and twist.

3. Slide the knife under the top half of the shell to detach it and then along the bottom half-shell to detach the clam.

HINT *If you're cooking the clams, it's easier to lightly steam the clams first to make them easier to open.*

243 How to cook clams

Clams can be simply steamed in water and white wine, seasoned with chopped shallots, chiles, tomatoes, spices, and herbs. Many recipes say to throw out any clams that don't open when they are steamed. More often than not, clams that don't open are perfectly fine and just need a little help. Slide a knife into the gap in the shell and the clam will usually just pop open. If you're in doubt, give it a sniff.

1. Scrub the clams under cold running water. Bring about 1 cup steaming liquid to a boil in a pot large enough to hold the clams with some room left over (there's no need for a steamer).

2. Add the clams to the pot.

3. Cover the pot. Steam for about 12 minutes, until the clams open.

HINT *Make sure the meat clings to one of the shells, but not both, or the meat will tear. If it's clinging to both shells, it's not cooked enough.*

244 How to buy and store oysters

Because of the fragile nature of oysters and because you want to buy the freshest oysters you can find, there are a few things you can do to guarantee the best eating experience you can have.

• When buying oysters, check to see if they are lying flat, which prevents their liquid from draining out. Buy them from a fish store that routinely does this if you can.

• Never buy oysters that are gaping open; they should be closed tightly.

• The old rule about not eating oysters in months not containing an R has some validity, even if not for the original belief that the oysters were likely to be bad during hot months. Instead, it's because during summer months, oysters often have an unpleasant milky consistency, a result of the stage of their reproductive cycle.

shellfish

• Once you've bought them, store oysters flat in the refrigerator. Cover with a wet towel and use within 3 days.

What's in a name?

Most oysters are named after the place where they are harvested. In general, oysters from the colder waters in the East, such as Malpeques (from Prince Edward Island) and Cotuits (from Cape Cod), and oysters from the Pacific Coast, such as Kumamotos, have a brinier flavor than those from warmer waters. Some very lean oysters, such as Belons (from Maine or Washington state), have an almost metallic taste that some love and others don't.

Oysters vary in size. Olympias are the size of quarters, while a large Belon can be the size of a small plate.

245   How to shuck an oyster

If you can have your oysters shucked at the fish store, do so. It's a bit of a chore, especially if you haven't had much practice. If you decide to do it yourself, use an oyster knife with a big rubber or wooden handle you can really grab onto and a semipointed tip that's not too sharp. When handling the oyster, always hold it in a towel, and make sure there's some towel between your hand and the knife—if the knife slips, you want your hand to be protected.

HINT *If shucking the oysters is all just too much, open the oysters by heating them in the oven (see Hint, page 196) or on the grill.*

1. Hold the oyster in a towel with the hinge pointed away from you.

2. Wedge an oyster knife into the hinge and twist until you feel the top shell give.

3. Slide the knife, flush with the bottom of the top shell, along the edge of the top shell to detach the lid without taking any flesh with it.

4. If the oysters are sandy and gritty, rinse them under cold water while you reach your finger around under the oyster where it attaches to the bottom shell. You want to get any sand hiding underneath.

5. Slide the knife along the bottom shell, detaching the oyster. Be sure to leave the little round muscle, the abductor muscle, attached to the oyster, not the shell.

246 Oysters on the half-shell

When you buy oysters, ask the fishmonger to include some of the seaweed the oysters came packed in for delivery. At home, use the seaweed to keep the oysters flat on the plate or serving platter. You can also serve oysters on a big platter of crushed ice. They must be kept very cold. But don't let them sit on the bed of ice long enough for the ice to melt; the water will get into the oysters and ruin them. Also, don't serve them on salt, which inevitably gets into the oysters and affects their taste and draws out liquid.

HINT *In America, we serve our oysters with the bottom muscle cut through so the oyster is no longer attached to the bottom half-shell. In other places (such as France), the oyster is left attached, ensuring the diner that the oyster hasn't been popped out of a can into a saved shell.*

shellfish

195

247   How to cook oysters

For some oyster lovers, cooked oysters are an anathema, but others like oysters in any form, cooked, raw, dead, or alive. The secret to cooking an oyster is to not really cook it at all, but to warm it through, ever so gently. Warm oysters are marvelous served with cream and butter.

HINT *If you plan to serve hot oysters in the shell after shucking, thoroughly wash the bottom half-shells. Place them level on a sheet pan. To keep them level, crumple up aluminum foil, spread it out over the sheet pan, and press the oyster shells into the foil. Heat the shells in the oven before putting in the cooked oysters.*

How to poach

Oysters have enough liquid of their own for you just to shuck them into a pan, put the pan over gentle heat, and as soon as the oysters curl around the edges (after a minute or two), they're done. To give them even more flavor, try this.

1. Simmer ½ cup white wine with a minced shallot until only a table-spoon or two is left in the pot.

2. Shuck the oysters directly into the pot and heat gently.

3. Take the oysters out of the liquid with a slotted spoon and add cream to the poaching liquid. Boil down the poaching liquid and serve it over the oysters.

How to broil

You can't really broil an oyster or it will release its liquid and end up swimming in a pool. But you can poach the oyster, boil down the poaching liquid with cream (see above), and spoon this sauce over the oysters, which have been put back into their half-shells. Then you can quickly broil them, perhaps with a sprinkling of bread crumbs (see entry 38). You can also coat the poached oysters in the half-shells with hollandaise (see entry 384) flavored with curry or saffron and broil them a few seconds until the sauce bubbles up.

How to fry

Use a simple batter, but one that's thick enough to coat the oysters. Fry in hot oil for only a minute or so (see entry 302). Serve immediately.

248   A sauce for cooked oysters

The most famous sauce for oysters is champagne sauce, but to make it, no one uses real champagne—it's a waste, because the bubbles boil off anyway. To get the flavor of champagne without paying for the bubbles, substitute a dry white wine such as muscadet.

1. For a dozen oysters, combine ½ cup white wine and 2 minced shallots in a pot and boil down the liquid to 2 tablespoons.

2. Add shucked oysters to the wine mixture.

3. Meanwhile, heat the empty bottom half-shells in the oven (see Hint, opposite).

4. Gently heat the oysters only until they curl around the edges.

5. Remove the oysters with a slotted spoon and place them on a clean kitchen towel, which will catch any grit that remains.

6. Boil down the poaching liquid to about ¼ cup and whisk in 4 tablespoons butter or more to taste. Season to taste with kosher salt and freshly ground black pepper.

7. Place the oysters in the hot half-shells, spoon over the sauce, and serve immediately.

249 A sauce for raw oysters

The French are famous for using a sauce mignonette, essentially an infusion of shallots and cracked pepper in good white wine vinegar, on their raw oysters. The secret to success is to crack the pepper yourself by crushing the whole peppercorns under a heavy saucepan. Sprinkle the peppercorns on the work surface and rock the saucepan over them, leaning on it with all your weight. Combine 1 tablespoon cracked peppercorns with 2 finely minced shallots and ½ cup white wine vinegar. Let the mixture sit overnight in the refrigerator before serving, with a small serving spoon, with your oysters.

How to eat a raw oyster

First, if you're given the choice, order the smallest you can find—Olympias are the smallest and Kumamotos are usually small too. When confronted with a raw oyster for the first time, you may be easily disconcerted by its appearance. The best approach is to plunge the oyster immediately into your mouth. If you're nervous or queasy, let the oyster slip down your throat while you take a big sip of white wine. As you develop courage, let the oyster sit a moment in your mouth before swallowing; as you grow even more adventurous, bite into it and release even more of its irresistible brine. While many find the flavor of raw osyters impossible to improve upon, some insist on sauce mignonette.

250 How to buy scallops

The ideal way to buy a scallop is like an oyster, in the shell. If you tap it against a hard surface, it will click slightly, which tells you it's alive when you buy it. But scallops in the shell are expensive and hard to find. As an alternative, buy "unsoaked" scallops. Unfortunately, many scallops have been soaked in a phosphate solution to keep them from releasing water after they've been shucked. The problem with this is that these scallops release all their water in the pan or pot. Other than buying them in the shell, the best way to know you're getting scallops that haven't been soaked (and are perfectly fresh) is to look for scallops that appear dry on the surface and have slight variations in color.

HINT *Avoid scallops that are very white and very wet or even sudsy. Scallops should be separate, not in an amorphous mass.*

251 What are bay scallops?

There are three kinds of scallops: sea scallops, which are the large ones; bay scallops, which are about half the size of sea scallops; and calico scallops, which look like miniature marshmallows. If you can find bay scallops in the shell, by all means buy them, take them home and shuck them (see below), and cook them very little. Bay scallops that have been shucked should have color variations and should look distinct from one another. Calico scallops, which are steamed open, are sometimes sold as bay scallops, but they don't have nearly the flavor.

How to shuck scallops

Slide a sharp knife along the underside of the top shell, keeping the knife flush against the shell so as not to damage the meat. Since most Americans eat only the nutty little muscle—the Japanese eat whole bay scallops on the half-shell—cut through the thin membrane that surrounds the scallop and pull away the viscera and eyes. Cut under the "scallop"—that is, the part we eat—to detach it. If you're using European scallops (easy to spot since their shells are striated while ours are not), you can also eat the little tonguelike packet of orange roe that surrounds the scallop.

However you cook your scallops, pull off the little muscle that runs up the side of each one. Discard this, since it turns very tough once cooked.

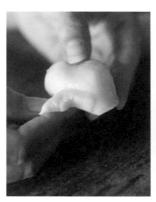 

To sauté

Because scallops often contain a lot of water that gushes out as soon as they are hot, they need a lot of heat applied very quickly.

1. Select a sauté pan just large enough to hold the scallops in a single layer. Add enough clarified butter (see entry 32) or oil to make a thin layer in the pan and heat the pan until the oil begins barely to smoke.

2. Pat the scallops dry, season with salt and pepper, and, over high heat, add 3 or 4 scallops to the pan, each in a different part of the pan. Wait about a minute—if the scallops release water, wait longer—until the scallops are pale brown on the bottom.

3. Add another 3 or 4 scallops and wait again. Continue in this way until you've added all the scallops.

4. Turn the scallops, 3 or 4 at a time, to brown the other side. Wait between each series of turns. Sauté a 1-inch-scallop about 2 minutes on each side.

To poach

Find a sauté pan just large enough to hold the scallops in a single layer. The more tight fitting the pan, the less liquid you need for poaching.

1. In the pan, heat enough vegetable broth or a combination of half wine and half water to a simmer. Add the scallops.

2. Simmer very gently for 2 or 3 minutes. Take out the scallops with tongs or a skimmer.

3. Keep the scallops warm while you reduce the poaching liquid to about ¼ cup per 4 servings.

4. Whisk a little butter or cream into the poaching liquid.

5. Whisk in chopped herbs such as parsley, chives, chervil, or tarragon.

6. Season to taste with salt and pepper and serve over and around the scallops in heated soup plates.

To steam

1. Season the scallops with salt and pepper. If you want to make a sauce with the juices released by the scallops, use very little liquid—a cup or so—to steam them.

2. Bring the liquid to a rapid boil in the steamer and arrange the scallops in the steamer. Cover the steamer and steam for about 4 minutes per inch of thickness.

3. To make a sauce boil down the liquid in the steamer to about a tablespoon per serving. Whisk in ½ tablespoon butter per serving or 1 tablespoon cream per serving. If you like, add minced herbs such as chives, parsley, or chervil to the sauce. Season to taste with salt and pepper. Serve the scallops in soup plates with the sauce around them.

253   How to boil a lobster

First, find a big enough pot. The more water you boil, the quicker will be the lobster's last moments, since the lobster won't cool the water down as much as it would if you were using less water.

1. In a large pot, bring enough water to generously cover the lobsters to a rapid boil and toss in a handful of salt.

2. Preheat the oven to 200°F.

3. Plunge the lobsters into the water and simmer for 5 minutes for a 1½ pound lobster, and another minute per each additional half pound.

4. With tongs, remove the lobsters to sheet pans in the oven. Leave them in the oven for 10 minutes before serving. This method of letting them rest in the oven guarantees they'll be cooked through without being overcooked.

HINT *Arguments about how to most humanely kill a lobster will never be resolved, but certainly the quickest way to kill a lobster is to stick a knife in the center of its head from either the top or the bottom (go from the underside if you want to preserve the head in one piece) and then bring the knife down so the front part of the head is cut in half.*

254   How to cook perfectly tender lobster

Few people use this method but it's the only sure way to guarantee tenderness. The lobsters should take 3 hours to cook. You'll know they're ready when they've turned red all over and you and your guests are on your second bottle of wine (make sure you have an elegant first course over which you can linger if necessary).

1. Rinse the lobster or lobsters and kill them by cutting through the bottom of the head with a chef's knife (see Hint, opposite).

2. Put it in a pot with 1 cup wine and 1 cup water and, if you like, a couple of minced shallots.

3. Cover the pot and put it on the stove on a flame tamer or other heat diffuser with the flame as low as possible. Move the lobster around in the pot every 30 minutes to make sure it is cooking evenly.

How to keep lobster tails from curling

When trying to present sliced lobster tails in even round medallions, it's annoying to find the lobster tail tightly curled. To prevent this, slide a small wooden skewer along the membrane of the underside of the lobster tail. You can also tie the lobsters together with string so they're facing each other.

255 To save on lobster bibs

Lobster tail sliced for serving

You'll do your guests an enormous favor, and save them from expensive cleaning bills, if you take the lobster out of the shell before you serve it. Because extracting the meat from lobsters at the last minute is time consuming, it's possible to cook and shell it in advance and warm the lobster meat in the oven or microwave. However, it's essential that the meat not get too hot.

Oven method

Preheat the oven to 175°F or its lowest setting. Place the cooked meat on a buttered or nonstick sheet pan. Cover the meat with plastic wrap that is touching the surface of the lobster. Heat in the oven for about 10 minutes, until the meat feels distinctly warm to the touch.

Microwave method

Place the lobster meat on microwave-safe plates and cover it with plastic wrap that touches its surface. Microwave it on high for 10 seconds. Move the meat around and feel its temperature. Microwave for 5 seconds more, reposition the meat, and assess its warmth. Continue in this way until all the meat is hot, but *not* superhot.

256 How to get the meat out of a lobster

How you get the meat out of a lobster depends on whether you're in the kitchen or dressed up and sitting in a dining room. In the kitchen, you'll use a knife to crack the claw shells; in the dining room, nutcrackers. If you're serving whole lobsters, do your guests the favor of cracking the claw shells in the kitchen.

1. If you're served a whole lobster or encounter one in the kitchen, first snap off the claws. Gently move the claw pincer from side to side to loosen it and then pull it straight out.

2. In the kitchen, place the claw pincer side up on a cutting board. With a heavy knife, whack the thorny part of the shell, just in front of where the pincer was, embedding the knife about ½ inch into the shell. Turn and twist the knife to crack open the shell and take out the claw meat. Whack at the hinge at the base of the claw and take the meat out of the smaller section. In the dining room, use a nutcracker to break open the shell to get at the claw meat.

3. In the kitchen, use scissors to cut through the remaining sections so that in the dining room, guests can use a small fork or pick to get at the meat.

4. Twist off the tail and snap off the flipper at the back end of the tail. With a cracker or by pushing down on its sides, crack the tail. Pull away the two sides of the lobster tail as the meat pops out. Push the meat out of the shell with a fork.

257 To cut up a raw lobster

Many recipes call for cutting up a lobster before you cook it. A bit grisly, true, but worth knowing how to do so you can enjoy preparing lobster in many more ways.

1. Split the front of the head in half with a chef's knife; this will kill the lobster.

2. Snap off the claws.

3. Twist off the tails. Work over a strainer or colander set over a bowl containing a teaspoon of wine vinegar. The bowl allows you to collect the lobster's flavorful juices and the vinegar keeps it from clotting.

4. Reach into the head and tail and pull out any tomalley and roe into the strainer.

5. Work the lobster tomalley and roe through the strainer with your fingers and transfer the liquid in the bowl to the refrigerator for up to 12 hours. You can use the collected juices for making a sauce (see entry 258).

6. Finish cutting the head in half and remove the gritty grain sac from each side of the head and discard.

When sex matters

If your recipe calls for the dark green, almost black roe that will turn a vivid orange when heated, you'll need a female lobster. To identify her, look at the underside of the lobster to where the tail joins the front "head." The small legs closest to the tail are hard and bony on a male and thin and flexible on the female.

What parts can I eat?

Except for the shell, virtually all the lobster is edible, including the green tomalley and roe—the latter is the most delicious part of all! When the lobster has been properly cooked, the roe is still undercooked and dark green; however, when the lobster is overcooked, it hardens and turns bright orange.

The only part you should discard is the grain sac, which you cut in two when you split the head. It's easy to feel—it's rough and gritty—and easy to pull out.

258 How to make the best lobster sauce

Most of a lobster's flavor is in the shell, roe, and tomalley. By cutting up the lobster alive (see entry 257) and saving the strained roe and tomalley, you can make magnificent sauces.

Using the shells

If you're taking the meat out of the lobster in advance, once you've done so you can use the shells to make a sauce. Discard the large claw shells; they are so hard that they can damage a food processor.

1. In a food processor, grind the tail shells and small claw shells for 1 minute.

2. In a pan over medium-high heat, sweat onions and carrots (see entry 40) and add the shells, some chopped tomatoes, and some cream.

3. Simmer for 30 minutes, adding water as needed to keep the cream from breaking. When thoroughly combined, remove the sauce from the stove and strain first through a coarse strainer, then through a fine strainer (see also entry 13).

Using the roe and tomalley

1. Start with a basic sauce such as one made by using the shells (see above), or, if you've steamed the lobster with a little white wine, the liquid left in the pot.

2. Combine the sauce or liquid with the strained roe and tomalley and gently reheat the mixture, whisking all the while. Don't let the liquid boil or the roe will curdle. If the sauce contains enough roe, it will turn from dull green to bright orange as you heat it.

259 How to buy shrimp

Shrimp are sold in two ways. One is used more often within the industry; the other is encountered more often at the retail level.

HINT *A good rule of thumb is to buy 4 ounces of headless shell-on shrimp per serving for an appetizer portion and 7 ounces per main-course serving.*

By the number

Within the industry, shrimp are sold by the number of shrimp per pound, usually expressed in a range such as 18/22, meaning there are 18 to 22 shrimp per pound. The smaller the number, the larger the shrimp. Note that the number of shrimp per pound varies according to whether the shrimp have their heads on.

By size

In stores, shrimp are usually sold according to size, such as baby, small, medium, large, extra large, and jumbo, terms that are very imprecise: someone's extra large can very well be another's jumbo. The size of the shrimp is up to you, but if you're buying extra large or jumbo shrimp, you may want to have them counted out so that you have the same number for each serving.

A recommendation

Buy wild shrimp when you can, as they usually have much more flavor; and if you can find them, buy shrimp with their heads on.

260 How to peel and devein shrimp

Some shrimp have a "vein," actually the intestine, that's full of grit and has to be removed. If you're serving shrimp in the shell, removing this vein is obviously up to the guests, some of whom won't bother. But if you're serving shrimp out of the shell, you may want to slide a knife along the back of one or two to reveal the vein and see if it's black and gritty; if so, you'll want to devein the shrimp.

1. Pull the shells away from the sides of the tail and, depending on how you're serving the shrimp, leave or pull off the tiny tail shell.

2. Slide a small knife along the outer curve of the shrimp, cutting in about ¼ inch to reveal the vein.

3. Pinch the vein with your fingers or separate it with a knife, and pull it out. Discard.

261   For plump and juicy shrimp

Many shrimp nowadays lack the rich juiciness of the wild shrimp that used to be the only kind we could get. There is a way to help make your shrimp plumper and juicier, however.

1. Dissolve ¼ cup kosher salt and ¼ cup sugar in 2 quarts water.

2. Most shrimp should be soaked, in their shells, in this brine for 30 minutes at room temperature, but you may have to experiment. Changes in the temperature of the brine affect the process (colder is slower), as does the size of the shrimp. You can speed up the process by peeling the shrimp before brining.

262 How to cook shrimp

It depends. If you want to make eating the shrimp easy and neat for your guests, you'll want to peel the shrimp first; but if you're more concerned about the flavor of the shrimp, cook the shrimp in the shell so their flavor stays sealed in. In an ideal world cook wild Gulf shrimp with their heads on and encourage guests to twist off the heads and suck out the juices.

Shrimp can be sautéed, grilled, steamed, stewed, or fried. The important trick when cooking shrimp is to cook them just until they turn orange, 1 or 2 minutes. Serve them the instant they're ready.

HINT *If you can find shrimp with the heads, you can grind the heads in a food processor and simmer them as the base for soups, sauces, or stews.*

263 For the best shrimp stews and sauces

The fact is that most of a shrimp's flavor is in its head. To overcome this, don't throw away the heads. Ask your fishmonger to get you wild Gulf shrimp with the heads on (generally from Mexico or the United States), or if he or she will save the heads for you. If you're not going to make a soup, stew, or sauce right away, save the heads in the freezer until you are. When the time comes, crush or process them and simmer them with aromatic vegetables (see entry 16) and cream to extract their flavor and have a fabulous base for sauces and soups.

264 Freezing shrimp for quick dinners

Shrimp are good to have on hand in the freezer for impromptu sautés, salads, and pasta dishes. The cat, too, loves it when you can whip up a few shrimp for an occasional treat. However, if you freeze shrimp in a clump in a bag, they stick together. Then, when you go to use them, you have to thaw them all in order to get at only those you need. There is an alternative.

1. Because virtually all shrimp sold in the United States has been frozen and then thawed at the fish market or supermarket, to get the "freshest" possible shrimp, buy a frozen 5-pound block of shrimp.

2. When you get it home, put the block in a bowl of barely warm water.

3. As the block starts to thaw, break off individual shrimp before they thaw completely, pat them dry with a towel, and place them on a sheet pan in the freezer. Don't allow any to touch each other.

4. When the shrimp on the sheet pan are solidly refrozen, transfer them to plastic bags. Stored in this way they don't stick together and you can reach in and take out only as many as you need.

265 What kind of crab is this?

It wasn't so many years ago that crabs were regional specialties: blue crabs in Baltimore, Dungeness crabs in San Francisco, and king crab in Alaska. Now, you can find them everywhere.

Blue crabs

These little crabs live all along the East Coast as far north as Rhode Island and are the source of most of the commercial crabmeat sold in the United States. Because of their size—usually that of a woman's hand—they take patience and experience to eat.

Soft-shell crabs

These are blue crabs that have shed their shells. When you buy them, make sure they're alive. After you've cleaned and cooked them (see entry 269), they can be eaten whole.

Jonah crabs

These crabs come from Maine and are much like Dungeness crabs, but they are not quite as large. They are cleaned and eaten in the same way.

Peekytoe crabs

Fashionable menus have made these once lowly sand crabs very desirable. They are very perishable, so, unless you live in Maine, it's likely that you'll be able to find this crabmeat only frozen.

Dungeness crabs

The main West Coast crab, a Dungeness crab is meaty and delicious. It's best to buy these crabs live and boil them yourself (see entry 267). Short of that, get them freshly cooked from a reliable fishmonger. A favorite way to serve them is cold with homemade mayonnaise (see entry 367).

King crabs

Normally, you'll see only the giant legs of these creatures from Alaska, and they are sold frozen. You can access the meat in king crab legs by buying legs that have been split lengthwise or by buying whole legs and cutting through the shell with scissors. The whole meat can be used in salads (it's already been cooked on the boat) or gently reheated. The split legs are best quickly broiled or baked in a hot oven with plenty of butter.

Snow crabs

Like king crabs, snow crabs are from Alaska, but unlike king crabs, they have thin legs and hence provide less meat.

shellfish

There are two basic considerations in buying crabmeat: the form the meat comes in and the grade.

Form

• **Fresh:** The traditional wisdom is that "fresh" crabmeat is the best. This is crab that has been lightly steamed or boiled and its meat extracted. It's usually sold in plastic containers, always on ice, and tends to be the most expensive.

• **Frozen:** Frozen crabmeat is often better than fresh because it actually stays "fresher." It doesn't have the flavor and moistness of crabmeat that's never been frozen, however.

• **Canned:** Canned crabmeat is usually made from crab imported from outside the United States. It often lacks flavor.

• **Pasteurized:** "Fresh" crabmeat—that is, crabmeat extracted on the premises—is sometimes heated to kill bacteria so that it stays fresh longer. While not as delicious as truly fresh crabmeat, because of its shelf life, it's often fresher tasting than so-called fresh crabmeat.

Grade

• **Jumbo lump back fin:** This meat contains the largest chunks of crab and is considered the best. Do as little as possible to it to appreciate its full flavor and texture.

• **Back fin:** Much like jumbo back fin, this grade may contain smaller chunks of meat and is likely to contain a bit of shell (see Hint).

• **Special:** This meat is sometimes called "flaked" because it comes from all over the crab and hence is made of smaller pieces. Its flavor, however, is fine.

• **Claw meat:** This meat is delicious, but because of its brown color many people eschew it in favor of more expensive grades.

HINT *To get pieces of shell out of fresh crabmeat, spread the crabmeat on a sheet pan and pass it under a broiler for a few seconds to barely cook the edges of the meat. The shells will turn red and will be easy to recognize.*

267 How to cook a crab

Hard-shell crabs can be cooked in a pan of boiling water, as described below. Soft-shell crabs are best sautéed.

While blue crabs are usually sold alive, Dungeness crabs are usually sold already cooked. However, you can guarantee freshness by buying your Dungeness crab alive and cooking it—as you would blue crabs—in a big pot of boiling water.

1. Fill a pot with enough water to cover the crabs abundantly and bring to a boil.

2. Brush the bottom of the crabs with a stiff brush under running water. Be especially attentive to the area under the shell near where the legs attach.

3. Boil blue crabs for 5 minutes and Dungeness crabs for 10 minutes; drain.

268 How to get the meat out of a crab

Blue crabs

Blue crabs, unlike their meaty Dungeness cousins, take patience if you are going to get to their meat.

1. Turn the cooked crab upside down, unfold the "apron" or tail, and twist it off.

2. Grab the top shell with one hand and the inside of the crab with the other and yank off the shell. Discard.

3. Pull off the spongy gills that cling to the shell and discard; do the same with any remaining viscera clinging to the crab. Don't discard the yellow "mustard" (roe), which is good to eat.

4. Break or cut the crab in half and snap off the legs and claws. Each leg contains a small piece of flesh. Pick out the meat of the body

where the legs connected. Pick the meat out of the legs and crack the claws. With a knife or a pick, extract the meat.

Dungeness crabs

The process is essentially the same as getting the meat out of a blue crab, but it's much more satisfying because there is much more meat.

1. Turn the cooked crab over and unfold the apron. Break it off.

2. With the crab upside down, pull away its top shell. The shell will contain the "mustard," which is delicious. Don't discard the mustard. Discard the shell or save it for shellfish broth (see entry 358).

3. Pull off the gills clinging to the crab and discard.

4. Break the crab in half down the middle.

5. Use nutcrackers to break the claws. With a knife or pick, remove the meat there.

269 Handling soft-shell crabs

Soft-shell crabs should always be purchased alive. Although they are best cooked the day they're bought, they can be held, refrigerated and covered with a moist kitchen towel, for a day.

To clean

1. Rinse off the crabs.

2. Use scissors to cut off the front of the crab, including the eyes.

3. Open and pull off the "apron" on the bottom of the crab.

4. Fold up one side of the top shell, which will reveal the gills clinging to the bottom of the crab. Pull the gills off on both sides.

To cook

1. Heat olive oil over medium-high heat in a nonstick pan.

2. Sauté top side down until brown and crispy, about 4 minutes. Sauté the other side for 2 minutes.

270 How to eat snails

The eating of snails (escargots) is a peculiar luxury: They're expensive, have little flavor, and have a rubbery texture. The pleasure of eating a snail comes from holding the shell in special tongs, fishing out the snail with a two-tined fork—dangling it about for other diners to see—but most of all, mopping up the snail butter (essentially butter worked with chopped parsley and garlic) with crusty French bread. Since snails in cans are fully cooked, when we "cook" snails we are just reheating them.

HINT *You can find seafood utensils, such as snail or mussel plates, two-pronged forks for "fetching" creatures from their shells, and snail tongs, online at kitchen and restaurant supply sites and at kitchen or gourmet specialty stores.*

1. Ideally, you should have those specially made plates with shallow indentations that hold the snail shells upright and collect any melting butter. If you don't have the plates, nestle the snail shells together on soup plates, making sure the shell opening is facing up so as not to release the butter.

2. If you don't have tongs made for holding the shells while you dig in to extract the creature with an oyster fork, you can always hold the shell wrapped in a cocktail napkin while you spear the snail with a fork or toothpick.

271 How to cook crayfish

To anyone born north of New Orleans, eating a crayfish (there called a crawfish) is somewhat exotic, even if they look suspiciously like a miniature lobster. While picked crayfish-tail meat is sold much as crabmeat is and can be used in salads or in dishes as you do crabmeat, aficionados insist crayfish must be bought alive, like lobster. If you find yourself confronted with live crayfish, spread them out on a sheet pan and separate out any dead ones—be careful, the live ones pinch. Once you've verified they're all alive, just plunge them in a pot of boiling water for 2 minutes and they're done. To get the meat out, twist off the tails, pull off the tiny flippers, and pinch the tail on both sides until you feel the shells crack. The tail meat will pop out when you pull apart the sides. You can use or freeze the heads for making shellfish broths and sauces (see entry 358).

272 How to cook squid

Squid, newly popular, are now served grilled, braised, and fried as appetizers, in pasta, or as main courses. The secret to tender squid is to barely cook it by frying, grilling, or sautéing or to cook it to death by braising—nothing in between.

HINT *Buy squid already cleaned; doing it yourself is a chore.*

To sauté

The secret to success is to make sure your pan is very hot and to add only a couple of squid at a time; otherwise, the squid release their water and you end up boiling them.

1. Toss the squid with flour and pat off the excess.

2. Heat pure olive oil or clarified butter (see entry 32) in a sauté pan over high heat.

3. Start by adding a small amount of squid and waiting until the squid starts to brown before adding more. Sauté for about 3 minutes. Turn, and sauté for about 2 minutes more, until done.

To fry

The secret to good fried squid is to fry it for only 1 minute. Use a light batter of flour and water, or just flour (see entry 39).

1. Heat the oil to 360°F.

2. Toss the squid with batter or flour and pat off the excess.

3. Fry in batches not so large that they'll cool the oil or cause it to overflow. Fry about 30 seconds to a minute per batch.

To braise

Cooking with a little liquid for an hour or so makes squid very tender.

HINT *Use braised squid for grilling and you don't have to worry about it being tough.*

1. Gently cook aromatic vegetables in butter or olive oil, add the squid, and stir over high heat until the liquid released evaporates.

2. Pour over enough red wine to cover the squid and add a bouquet garni. Simmer for an hour. Strain and reserve liquid. Reduce the braising liquid until you have ¼ cup per serving.

3. Whisk in 1 tablespoon butter per serving or 1 tablespoon beurre manié (see entry 48) per cup of braising liquid. Reheat the squid in the sauce. Serve with aïoli (see entry 369) and crusty bread or toast.

273 What are cuttlefish?

Until recently, we never saw cuttlefish in the United States because they are found mostly on the other side of the Atlantic and in the Adriatic. Cuttlefish look very much like squid and have a flavor to match. However, they are meatier and need to be braised or simmered for a long time to tenderize them.

HINT *What really makes cuttlefish special is their ink, called sepia. It's found in a sac, which is a small pouch with a black pastelike filling—the ink—that can be used to color pasta, risotto, soups, and stews.*

274 What to do with an octopus

It used to be that most of us would never have considered getting near an octopus, much less eating one. But now we're so well traveled and cosmopolitan that we're up for eating (or at least trying) almost anything. Much is made of tenderizing octopus—we see the pictures of Greek fisherman pounding it on rocks—and cookbooks are filled with various techniques, but if octopus is braised in the same way as stew meat, it inevitably becomes meltingly tender. Once braised, it can subsequently be grilled, sautéed, or sliced and served cold in a salad with good olive oil. Most octopus you buy have been frozen and already cleaned. Freezing actually helps tenderize the meat.

1. Thoroughly rinse the cleaned octopus.

2. Cut the tentacles into 2-inch-long pieces and cut the top into wedges.

3. In a wide sauté pan with straight sides, heat pure olive oil and cook a chopped carrot, chopped onion, and 3 cloves garlic, chopped, until soft.

4. Add the octopus with enough red wine to come halfway up the sides of the pan. Nestle in a bouquet garni.

5. Cover the pan and simmer very gently for 45 minutes. Turn over the octopus pieces so that the bottom is on top. Simmer for 45 minutes more.

6. Remove the octopus and use it for other dishes or simmer down the braising liquid and thicken it with a paste of flour and butter and reheat the octopus in it. You can also finish the sauce with chopped parsley. Serve with aïoli (see entry 369) and crusty bread.

To grill

1. First braise the octopus for 2 hours (see entry 272).

2. Toss the sections of octopus with olive oil and herbs such as thyme or marjoram.

shellfish

221

3. Place the octopus on a grill and cook just long enough to heat the octopus through.

4. Save the leftover braising liquid from the octopus stew so that if you have leftover grilled octopus, you can dice the pieces, melt the braising liquid (which will have gelled), and layer them together in a terrine (see entry 331). Serve the terrine in thin slices as a first course.

275   How to buy fish from a fish market

It's easier to judge the freshness of fish when the fish is whole. In fact, if you're interested in buying fillets, buy the whole fish and ask the fishmonger to fillet it, or fillet it yourself when you get it home. To determine if a whole fish is fresh, check the following.

• **Eyes:** Whole fish should have shiny bright eyes that look a little indignant—they should still have personality.

• **Scales:** The scales should be shiny and bright. The fish should look wet.

• **Firmness and stiffness:** If you can touch the fish, or have the fishmonger hold one, the fish should be stiff and not sag when held sideways by the head. Again, the fish should look wet.

• **Smell:** If you can smell the fish, lift the cartilage at the base of the head and sniff the gills—they should smell like the ocean, not fish.

How to buy fish fillets and steaks

Again, try to buy a whole fish and have it filleted. This obviously isn't possible if you're buying a chunk of swordfish or tuna steak.

• **Color:** When buying fillets or steaks, notice the coloration on white fillets or steaks such as swordfish. It should be pink or red, with no hint of brown (which is a sign of oxidation). The steaks and fillets should look moist. Red fish, such as tuna, should be bright pink or red, again with no hint of brown.

276 How to know when fish is done

If you're cooking whole fish, insert an instant-read thermometer in the back of the fish, along the spinal bones, until you reach the main spine bone. The temperature should read 130°F, and you should be able to just barely pull the fish away from the bone.

Fillets and steaks

If you're cooking fillets or steaks, you can sometimes tell by texture—the fish bounces back to the touch when done—but you can also insert a thermometer into the center of the fish, if it is large. Again, it should read 130°F. If you're cooking tuna steaks, you may want to leave it rare or even virtually raw in the center. To pull this off, monitor the temperature with a thermometer as you would a steak (see entry 317).

277 How to stuff a fish

The old way to stuff a fish was simply to put the stuffing in the stomach opening, but fish stuffed this way is a mess to eat, and the rib bones come loose and get into the stuffing. A better system is to partially bone the fish and create an opening for the stuffing. If the fish hasn't been gutted, bone it through the back; if it has been gutted, bone it through the stomach. Bake the stuffed fish and serve it sliced crosswise in boneless slices.

HINT *You can stuff the inside of the fish with something as simple as chopped tarragon or as substantial as cooked-down chopped mushrooms.*

Boning through the back

1. Scale the fish but don't cut it. Slide a knife along the back of the fish as though you're going to fillet it, and continue following along the bones, including the ribs.

2. Turn the fish around and repeat on the other side of the spinal bones.

3. Cut out the spine by snipping it with scissors where it joins the head and tail.

4. Pull out any remaining bones and the viscera and rinse out the opening.

Boning through the stomach

1. Slide a long flexible knife under the ribs of each fillet.

2. Pull the backbone away. With scissors, cut it where it joins the head and tail and remove it.

3. Remove any remaining bones with shears or needle-nose pliers.

278 How to poach a whole fish

Many people forget that the most flavorful way to eat fish is to eat the whole fish—fish cooked on the bone and in its skin just holds in more taste. If you want to guarantee that your fish is perfectly cooked, poach it in 135°F liquid. It will take longer, but it will be impossible to overcook the fish. Don't confuse poaching with boiling. When you poach something, it's cooked in barely simmering liquid. You can poach fish in any liquid—as simple as saltwater with perhaps a few herbs simmered in or more complex, such as a vegetable broth (see entry 356).

• Poach small fish in a frying pan or any other pan you can put on the stove and that has sides high enough that you can add liquid to cover the fish.

• You can wrap large or small fish in cheesecloth so you can more easily lift them out of the poaching liquid: Grab the end of the cheesecloth or use a long spatula.

• Start poaching small fish in hot liquid—if you start in cold, you're likely to overcook the fish by the time the liquid gets hot.

• For large fish, you'll need a fish poacher, which has a rack that makes it easy to pull the fish out of the hot liquid.

• In the case of large fish, start poaching in cold liquid and gradually add heat. If you were to start in hot liquid, the outside of the fish would overcook and dry out by the time the heat penetrated to the inside.

HINT *Don't serve poached fish with the skin, which is rubbery. Peel it off while the fish is still hot.*

What is cooking *à la nage?*

A fish poached in vegetable broth (also called court bouillon), served in a soup plate, and surrounded by the poaching liquid and the vegetables used to make the poaching liquid, is said to be *à la nage.*

279 How to fry a fish

Tiny whole fish, sometimes called whitebait, are delicious coated with a light flour-and-water batter and fried for a few seconds. To fry larger fillets, cut them into ½-inch-thick strips on a bias, toss them in flour, and fry for about 5 seconds.

HINT *An electric frying pan makes a great fish fryer, especially for small fish.*

280 How to braise a fish

To braise a whole fish, put the trimmed fish in an oven-proof pan, preferably one that conforms as closely as possible to the fish's shape, with enough liquid such as fish broth (see entry 357), white wine and water, or vegetable broth (see entry 356) to come halfway up its sides. Bring the liquid to the boil on the stove, cover the fish loosely with aluminum foil, and slide the pan into a 350°F oven. Bake until the fish is done (see entry 285) and then boil down the braising liquid and finish it with herbs, a little cream, and a little butter.

281 How to steam a fish

If you have a steamer, just bring some water and/or wine to a boil in the bottom of the steamer and steam the fish whole. Leave the scales on so the fish won't stick to the steamer surface. Peel off the skin along with the scales before serving.

282 How to sauté a whole fish

Unless the fish is very large, you can sauté it in a (preferably oval) frying pan. If you have a nonstick pan, use it; if not, move the pan back and forth while the fish is sautéing to keep the fish moving, not giving it time to attach to the pan. If the fish weighs more than a pound, you may want to brown it in a pan on the stove and finish cooking it in a low to medium oven. This prevents overbrowning the skin and gives the fish time to cook through.

283 How to grill a fish

While straightforward, grilling fish has one drawback: the fish can stick. The easiest way to avoid this is to leave the scales on, and then when you serve the fish, just peel off the skin, scales and all. But if you like the skin, try flouring the fish (see entry 39), spraying the clean grill (before heating) with nonstick cooking spray or using a fish basket. Whatever you do, don't scrape under the fish with a spatula to try to turn it. Instead, take a long-pronged fork or two metal skewers and slide them under the bars of the grill and lift up the fish, gently detaching it where it may have stuck.

HINT *A fish basket is about the same size as the fish and encloses it. It has a long handle so you can turn the fish over without having to touch the fish.*

284 How to grill using a grill pan

Some people are so enamored of the taste of grilled food that they want to have it all year round—and even indoors. To give foods the look of the grill and a mild grilled flavor, use a grill pan—a skillet with a ribbed surface. To retain the most heat, buy the heaviest pan you can find.

1. Rub the pan with oil.

2. Place the pan over high heat until the oil smokes.

3. Open the windows (you don't want to set off any home fire alarms) and grill away.

285 How to bake a whole fish

The easiest—and, I think, best—way to cook a fish is to just stick it in the oven on an oiled nonstick sheet pan or a regular sheet pan topped with a silicone pad. The smaller the fish, the hotter the oven should be. You don't even need to scale the fish, since you can peel the skin and scales off together when it's done.

1. Rub the fish all over with pure olive oil, season to taste with kosher salt and pepper.

2. Bake according to the size of the fish—350°F for large fish 2 pounds or more, 400°F for fish less than 2 pounds but more than 1, and 450°F for small fish of a pound or less—so the skin ends up crispy.

3. Whole fish usually take about 10 minutes per inch of thickness at their thickest part. To be safe, check the inside temperature by sliding an instant-read thermometer into the back of the fish along the spinal bones. When the temperature reaches 130°F, the fish is ready.

How to scale a fish without making a mess

Hold the fish inside a large clear plastic bag so the scales don't fly around. A fish scaler is a worthwhile investment, but you can also scrape the fish with the back of a knife.

HINT *If you don't have a thermometer, slide a knife into the back of the fish and look at the flesh where it is attached to the spinal column. It should be just slightly shiny but not raw.*

286 How to carve a whole fish

Fish come in two basic shapes: flat and round. Flatfish such as sole, flounder, fluke, and halibut are, well, flat and usually diamond-shaped or elongated ovals. They have a dark side and a white side and eyes on top, on the dark side. They swim dark side down, both eyes up. Round fish have eyes on both sides and swim stomach down.

Round fish

Many of us don't know what to do when we are served a whole cooked fish. At the table, you can fillet it with a fish knife—the kind with an offset wedge-shaped blade—and a fork or a couple of spoons.

1. Cut along the base of the head all the way down to the bone, and slide the knife along the back of the fish to remove the tiny bones that run along the back.

2. Divide the top fillet in half by sliding the knife along the ribs. Cut the fillet into 4 sections and lift off the sections.

3. Pull off the bone structure and vertebrae. Push the bones to the side.

4. Inspect the bottom fillet for bones, especially ribs, and pull these away. Cut the bottom fillet into 4 sections and serve.

Flatfish

Eating a whole flatfish such as sole, flounder, or fluke requires a slightly different approach from that of a round fish.

1. Slide a knife all around the edge of the fish, pushing away small bones.

2. Slide the knife down the center line of the fish.

3. Slide the knife under one of the fillets and lift it away.

4. Repeat with the other side.

5. Remove the bone structure and vertebrae.

6. Remove any bones from the bottom fillets.

7. Stack the fillets, reconstructing the fish, on a heated platter.

287   Should I eat fish skin?

It depends on the fish and how you're cooking it. If you're poaching or braising a whole fish, pull the skin off when the fish is cooked—you won't want to eat the skin because it will be rubbery. If you're sautéing fillets of fish such as bass, snapper, pompano, or salmon, make sure the skin is well scaled. Sauté skin side down first, and hold the fish down with a spatula to cook the skin and prevent curling. Sautéed, roasted, or grilled skin is crispy and good.

Press down to brown the skin and stop curling

How to remove skin from fillets

If you are poaching, braising, or steaming fillets, it's easier to take the skin off first.

1. With the end of the fillet toward you, make a cut between the end of the skin and the end of the flesh.

2. When you've detached a little flap of skin, grip the fillet—use a towel if slippery—and slide a flat flexible knife between the skin and the flesh.

3. Pull on the skin, moving from right to left, while pressing down with the side of the knife. Most of the movement should be the skin, not the knife.

288   Quick braised fish fillets

Here's a great way to cook fish fillets and end up with a fantastic sauce. The trick is to cook the fillets with a little tasty liquid, and when they're done, convert the liquid into the sauce.

HINT *This kind of simple sauce can be flavored with finely chopped herbs such as parsley, tarragon, or chervil, or with spices such as curry powder or saffron.*

1. Preheat the oven to 400°F.

2. Season the fillets with kosher salt and freshly ground black pepper and put them in a metal pan just large enough to hold them in a single layer.

3. Pour over enough dry white wine or sherry to come halfway up the sides of the fillets.

4. Put the pan on the stove over high heat until the liquid comes to the simmer. Slide the pan into the oven.

5. Bake until the tops of the fillets lose their sheen. Transfer the fillets to heated plates.

6. Put the pan with the wine in it on the stove and boil down the wine to about ¼ cup per 4 servings.

7. Add a tablespoon of heavy cream per serving and simmer a minute until lightly syrupy. Season again and spoon the sauce over the fillets.

289 To make a fish soup or stew

The world's repertoire is filled with recipes for fish soups and stews. The only difference between a stew and a soup is the amount of solid to liquid. Traditional bouillabaisse is an example of a fish soup/stew made with whole fish. The broth is served first, followed by the fish.

HINT *To modernize soups and stews made with whole fish and to make them easier to eat, get the fish filleted and make a broth with the heads and bones (see entry 357). Cut the fillets into manageable pieces and poach them in the broth just before serving.*

1. Gently cook aromatic vegetables such as onions and carrots in oil or butter.

2. Add fish bones and heads, along with liquids such as water or wine and a bouquet garni. Simmer for 30 minutes, then strain.

3. Some fish soups and stews are enriched at this point with cream, coconut milk, even peanut butter.

4. Finish the stew by adding the fish shortly before serving. Simmer about 9 minutes per inch at the fish's thickest part with a flavorful sauce such as aïoli (see entry 369) or rouille—a sauce made from peppers and often used to flavor bouillabaisse. Neither aïoli nor rouille (if made with egg yolks) should be allowed to boil.

5. You may also finish the stew.

Precooking fish for soups and stews

Here's a way to organize serving fish soup or stew for a crowd.

1. Cut the fish into manageable and attractive pieces.

2. Heat pure olive oil in a nonstick pan until it just begins to smoke. Place the fillets one or two at a time skin side down in the oil. Immediately press on the fish with the back of a spatula to prevent the skin from contracting and causing the fillet to curl.

3. Sauté for about 30 seconds, remove from the heat, and transfer to a sheet pan. If it's hot in the kitchen, put an ice-filled sheet pan with sides under the first fish to immediately chill it.

4. When all the fillets have been seared, sort them according to thickness on different sheet pans.

5. Minutes before it's time to serve, bake the fish—put the thicker fillets in the oven first—skin side up and heat up the broth.

6. To serve, arrange the fish in the bowls and ladle over the broth.

290 How to bone fish steaks

To make fish steaks easier to cook and eat, cut out the bones that run through the center of the steak while leaving the skin intact. Pull out any pinbones with needle-nose pliers and fold the flaps inside. Tie into a neat round with string.

HINT *If you have large halibut steaks, notice how they are divided into four almost equal size pieces. By cutting along the bones, you can separate these and cook one or two per serving.*

291 How to get the best anchovies

The tastiest preserved anchovies are salted and come in blue cans from Sicily. Although you can buy anchovies from already opened cans, it's better to buy your own can—they come in different sizes. Soak the anchovies in cold water long enough to dissolve most of the salt and then fillet them. Repack in small jars, covered with extra virgin olive oil.

Poultry and Meat

Most of the time we cook meat and poultry using one of six basic techniques: grilling, sautéing, braising, roasting, poaching, or frying. Each of these techniques has its rules and caveats, but fundamental to virtually all cooking is the notion of adjusting the temperature of our cooking medium—the oven, hot oil, a grill—according to the thickness of what it is we are cooking. Pay attention to how foods cook when they're exposed to heat and you'll soon master the art of cooking.

292 How to butterfly birds for grilling and roasting

To speed up roasting and grilling of whole birds (see entries 293, 308, and 314), butterfly them by cutting out the backbone. Birds prepared this way can be baked in a hot oven—they'll cook faster than if whole—or they can be grilled.

1. From the inside of the cavity, use a knife or kitchen shears to cut along each side of the backbone.

2. Remove the backbone and open up the bird.

3. Tuck the legs into and under the skin.

293 How to roast a chicken

Very few things are easier to make than roast chicken. If it's undercooked, you just put it back in the oven; if it's a little overcooked, the breast meat will be a little dry, but you'll have plenty of juices with which to make gravy (see entry 295), since the longer it cooks, the more juices are released.

1. Preheat the oven to 500°F. If you wish, truss the chicken to help it cook evenly and look neater at the table. Roast the chicken until well browned, about 20 minutes. Turn the oven down to 300°F and continue roasting about 30 minutes more.

HINT *Make a double sheet of aluminum foil shaped like a trapezoid—a triangle with the top cut off—and butter it on one side. Put the buttered side down on top of the chicken, covering just the breast but not the thighs. Take the foil off about 15 minutes into the cooking. This slows down the cooking of the breast meat so it doesn't overcook by the time the thighs are ready.*

poultry

How to know when chicken is done

Judge doneness by tilting the chicken in the pan and looking at the juices that come out of the cavity. They should be clear and streaked with red, not perfectly clear, which means the chicken is overdone. If the juices are pink and cloudy, the chicken isn't ready. An instant-read thermometer stuck between the thigh and breast should read 140°F when the chicken is done—more cooking dries it out. Properly cooked chicken is pale pink where the thigh joins the breast.

How to make roast chicken a one-dish meal

Remember that most root vegetables, peeled and sectioned, are delicious roasted with poultry or meat (see entry 197) because they get coated with the fat and juices from the meat. Surround your chicken with carrots, turnips, or celeriac, and baby potatoes. Turn the vegetables once or twice during the roasting so they brown evenly.

294 How to truss a chicken

Most of us don't bother to truss a chicken, but a bird that's been trussed cooks more evenly and looks nicer. If you decide to try, here's an easy way.

1. Slide the center of a 2½-foot length of string under the tail end of the chicken about 1 inch in.

2. Cross the ends of the string over the drumsticks, making sure that each of the drumsticks is caught by the string.

3. Tuck the left end of the string under the right drumstick and the right end under the left drumstick, making an X.

4. Pull the ends of the string tight so the drumsticks come together.

5. Pull the string back along the breast and over the wings.

6. Stand the chicken neck side up so the string hooks on top of the wings.

7. Turn the chicken over, pull the string tight over the wings, and tie a knot. Fold under the end of each wing so that it hooks under the back of the chicken and stays in place.

295 How to make chicken "jus" or gravy

The longer you roast a chicken, the more it will release juices into the bottom of the pan. If the chicken is overcooked, you'll be compensated by having enough jus or gravy to spoon over the meat, which may need it because the breast meat, at least, will be a bit dry. One way of producing more jus without having to overcook your bird is to put trimmings such as wing tips, neck, and giblets in the pan to contribute to the roasting juices.

1. When the chicken is done, tilt the pan as you remove the bird so any juices in the cavity drain out into the pan.

2. Put the roasting pan on the stove and boil down any juices until they caramelize into a brown crust on the bottom of the pan. Pour off any fat.

3. If you're making gravy—jus thickened with flour—put 1 tablespoon butter and 1 tablespoon flour in the roasting pan and stir until the mixture smells "toasty."

4. Deglaze the pan: Add ½ cup chicken broth (see entry 351) or water to the pan and simmer gently while scraping the bottom of the pan with a wooden spoon. Pour the gravy into a sauceboat and pass at the table.

HINT *You can intensify the flavor of the jus by deglazing the pan (see entry 36) with more broth—boiling it down a second time once you've added the broth, then caramelizing it again. You can repeat this caramelization as many times as you want; each time will make the jus tastier. Consider adding a little fresh tarragon to the jus; it's marvelous. If the jus seems thin or there's not enough of it, add a little heavy cream or swirl in some butter to finish.*

296 To separate tiny amounts of poultry juice and fat

If you roast chicken, you'll often end up with a few tablespoons of juices and about twice that amount of liquid fat in the roasting pan. Separating so little liquid is next to impossible. The solution is to put the roasting pan on the stove and boil down the juices with the fat until the fat is clear and the juices dry and form a crust on the bottom of the pan. (This is one argument for avoiding nonstick roasting pans.) Pour out the fat, deglaze the pan (see entry 36) with a few tablespoons of broth, wine, or water, and you'll have a delicious light gravy. For larger amounts of juices, such as those given off by a roast turkey (see entry 308), just skim off the fat with a ladle into a glass pitcher or with a degreasing cup.

297 How to carve a chicken

Carving a chicken at the table creates an elegant rite that elevates something simple to something rather special. Start practicing carving with friends and family until you get the knack.

1. With a long fork inserted in the cavity, hold the chicken steady on a cutting board (ideally, one with a moat to catch juices) or a platter.

2. Slide the carving knife through the skin that separates the thigh from the breast and cut as far down as you can.

3. Push the thigh away from the breast with the side of the knife. This should reveal the joint where the thigh joins the backbone of the chicken. Cut through this joint and pull the thigh away. If you wish, cut away the drumstick so the leg is a separate piece.

4. Find and cut into the joint where the wing is attached to the backbone. Separate the wing.

5. Slide the knife along the side of the breastbone on the same side. Keeping the knife as close as possible against the bone, cut down until you separate the breast. Repeat carving on the other side.

298 How to use leftover chicken

It's a good idea to always make more chicken than you need, or to roast or sauté a second chicken at the same time. Serve cold chicken with homemade mayonnaise or wonderfully flavored mayonnaises (see entries 367 and 368). You can also pull the meat away from the bone in strips and combine it with briefly cooked green vegetables such as peas, asparagus tips, or green beans. Toss it all in your favorite vinaigrette, mayonnaise, or yogurt. It's also great in a tropical fruit salad spiced up with chiles (see entry 64) and cilantro, or added to hot pasta or rice salads.

299 How to avoid dry boneless chicken breasts

Chicken breasts are sometimes pounded so thin that they overcook almost immediately once they hit the pan. To prevent this, pound on the chicken breasts only a little on the thicker side, so they're of even thickness, and then bread them with fine bread crumbs (see entry 38). By breading the breasts, they can be cooked to a golden brown over gentle heat while not drying out.

300 How to sauté chicken

The secret to perfect sautéed chicken parts is to use a fair amount of butter and not to overcook the chicken. The chicken ends up "low fat" because the fat in the skin is rendered out and discarded. The butter leaves flavorful milk solids—proteins—attached to the skin to give it flavor, but leaves no fat in the chicken.

1. Sauté one cut-up chicken in 4 tablespoons butter, skin side down, in a nonstick pan over medium heat until the skin is golden brown, about 12 minutes.

2. Turn over the chicken pieces and cook until the meat bounces back to the touch, about 10 minutes more.

3. Remove the chicken pieces from the pan. Pour the fat out of the pan and notice how much more you're pouring out than you put in.

How to sauté bone-in breasts and thighs so they're done at the same time.

When sautéing chicken thighs with the drumsticks attached, take out the thigh bone. Thighs partially boned in this way will cook at the same time as bone-in breasts.

How to sauté boneless chicken breasts

To make boneless breasts more flavorful, bread them by lightly flouring them, dipping them in beaten eggs, and then patting them with fresh bread crumbs. Sauté them gently—breaded foods need to be cooked at lower temperatures than uncoated foods because the breading browns relatively quickly—in clarified butter. Clarified butter won't coat the chicken with dark specks as will whole butter; by using fine bread crumbs (work them through a sieve), they'll absorb a minimum of butter so the chicken won't seem greasy. Cook on both sides until golden brown and firm to the touch.

The secret to the juiciest chicken breasts

Cook the breasts with the bone attached until the meat just bounces back to the touch of a finger, about 12 minutes. Cut off and pull away the bones and cartilage while the breast is still hot—use a towel when you do this, if you need to—and serve the meat immediately. The bones will have sealed-in juices and flavor and imparted them to the breast meat.

301 How to improvise easy chicken dishes

Chicken is infinitely versatile. One of the easiest ways to improvise is to simply sauté a cut-up chicken in butter and then make a sauce in the pan.

1. Sauté cut-up chicken pieces (see entry 300) and pour out all but 2 tablespoons of the cooked fat in the pan.

2. Add ingredients such as minced shallots or onions, minced garlic, sliced mushrooms, carrots, or ginger and stir around in the cooked fat over medium heat for about 5 minutes.

3. Add 2 to 3 cups liquid or liquid-containing ingredients such as chopped, peeled, and seeded tomatoes, wine, vinegar, or broth of your choice and simmer down to about a third the original volume.

4. Add about ½ cup heavy cream, some chopped herbs such as parsley, tarragon, or chives, and simmer down to the consistency you prefer. Season to taste with kosher salt and freshly ground black pepper. Pour over the chicken.

302 How to fry chicken

Many of us avoid fried chicken because we think it's greasy. To avoid greasiness, don't use a batter with eggs, which will absorb too much fat. Flour the chicken and pat off the excess, or make a thin batter the consistency of heavy cream, using only flour and water. Dip the chicken in the batter just before frying at 350°F. An electric frying pan makes the job easier. For more flavor, marinate the chicken with wine, onion, and thyme for a few hours before frying. Here are some things to keep in mind when you are frying chicken or other food.

- **The fryer:** A fryer or electric frying pan automatically controls the temperature of the frying oil. If you don't have either, use a heavy-bottom pot large enough that you don't need to fill it more than half full with oil to avoid splashing. Heat the oil to 350°F. Test the oil with a small amount of the food you're frying.
- **Safety:** Place the pan, pot, or fryer and the oil on the back of the stove. Turn any handle to face the wall so no one can bump it. Have a supply of salt on hand for dousing fire should it occur.
- **Judging the temperature:** You can judge the temperature by how quickly the food floats to the surface and is surrounded by bubbles. This should happen immediately.
- **Fry basket:** Use a fry basket or "spider," which, predictably, looks like a spiderweb with a long handle on it. It allows you to quickly remove foods from the oil without bringing along much oil. Skimmers or slotted spoons are good second choices.

303   How to poach a chicken

Poaching is a great way to cook and serve chicken, especially if you want to avoid fat. You can serve the poaching liquid, a rich chicken broth, as a first course, and then carve the chicken as you would a roast chicken (peel off the skin and discard) as a main course. When you include vegetables in the poaching liquid, a poached chicken becomes a one-pot meal.

HINT *If you poach chicken on a regular basis, don't serve the poaching liquid, but save it for the next time. Keep using it and it will become more and more concentrated so that at some point you can serve it as a rich clear broth or use it as the base for a sauce.*

1. Truss the chicken (see entry 294). Submerge it in a pot of barely simmering broth. If you like, add vegetables such as carrot sections, small peeled onions, leeks, wedges of fennel, etc., that can surround the chicken when you serve it.

2. When the chicken is done—the temperature on the instant-read thermometer inserted between the thigh and breast is 140°F—lift it out of the liquid, peel off the skin, and carve it as you would roast chicken (see entry 297). Serve in heated soup plates surrounded with the broth and vegetables.

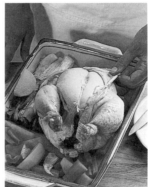

304 To "stuff" chicken under the skin

Rather than stuff the cavity of a chicken or other bird, stuff the bird under the skin. Stuffings can be simple things like sprigs of tarragon, thin slices of either fresh or reconstituted dried porcini mushrooms (see entry 182), or slices of truffles. They also can be made more substantial by using cooked chopped mushrooms, a layer of ricotta cheese, chopped steamed or boiled spinach (see entry 143), roast garlic puree (see entry 177), thin slices of prosciutto, and so on. By covering the breast meat with a layer of stuffing, you slow down the cooking so the breast won't dry out while the thigh is cooking through.

305 How to make the best truffled chicken

Especially around the holidays, some of us can't resist the indulgence of a truffle or two. Unfortunately, many dishes that call for truffles—and they seem ubiquitous these days—don't use them at their best and the wonderful truffle flavor is lost. For example, roasting a chicken with sliced truffles under its skin will only cause the aroma of the truffle to dissipate. However, there is another, if less elegant, method of roasting the chicken with truffles under the skin, and that is to wrap the chicken in aluminum foil.

HINT *Despite the tradition of never cooking white truffles, this dish is especially good with sliced white truffles, although it also works well with black truffles.*

1. Slice the truffles thinly and slide the slices under the skin of the chicken (see entry 304).

2. Wrap the whole chicken tightly in aluminum foil. Let it sit in a cool spot for a few hours if you have the time.

3. Preheat the oven to 400°F.

4. Roast the chicken for 50 minutes to 1 hour, until a thermometer inserted between the thigh and the breast reads 145°F. The juices in the cavity should be clear, with streaks of red.

5. At the table, unwrap the chicken over a deep plate to catch the juices that run out of the foil. The whole room will smell of truffles. Serve the juice in a sauceboat or over each slice.

306 What does brining do?

Brining allows meat and fish to remain moist as they cook. Turkey, chicken, pork, whole fish, and fish steaks take well to brining.

Turkey can be brined overnight, chicken for 4 hours, meat and fish steaks need only 30 minutes.

For a simple brine, use ½ cup kosher salt and ¼ cup sugar per 6 cups water.

307 Why not stuff turkey or chicken?

Most of us expect a savory stuffing to be served with a roast turkey (see entry 308) or chicken (see entry 293), but roasting stuffed birds can cause some problems. First and foremost is that in the bird, stuffing sits a long time in the cavity at a temperature favorable to bacterial growth. In conventional roasting, the heat works from the outside in, so the stuffing is the last part of the chicken to get hot enough to kill most bacteria, 140°F. You have to overcook the bird if you are to heat the stuffing to that temperature. The other disadvantage is that when inside the cavity, the stuffing absorbs a lot of the juices that you would otherwise use for jus or gravy. To avoid these problems, stuff the chicken under the skin, or cook the stuffing outside of the chicken or turkey in the roasting pan.

308 How to roast a turkey

Start the roasting process by taking the turkey out of the refrigerator for several hours before roasting to let it come to room temperature. It will roast more quickly and evenly. Don't use a roasting rack, which can cause the turkey to stick to the rack and tear the skin. It also allows the juices to drip down on the burning hot roasting pan and burn rather than caramelize.

1. Rest the turkey on the neck and giblets in a roasting pan to keep the turkey from sticking. Let the turkey come to room temperature for 4 hours before roasting.

2. Tie the drumsticks together to keep the turkey looking neat.

3. Preheat the oven to 375°F.

4. Fold a triple-thick triangular sheet of aluminum foil just large enough to cover the turkey breast without covering the thighs. Smear one side of the foil with butter and set it on the turkey breast butter side down.

5. Roast until the thighs are well browned, about an hour, and remove the foil. Start checking the internal temperature by inserting an instant-read thermometer between the thigh and the breast. If the temperature is above 100°F and the breast is not yet brown, turn up the oven to 425°F.

6. Roast until the temperature reads 135°F. Remove it from the oven and let rest loosely covered with aluminum foil for 25 minutes.

 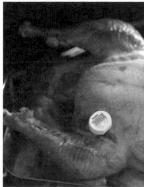

HINT *Cover the breast with a buttered sheet of aluminum foil for the first 40 minutes of roasting to slow the cooking so it is done at the same time as the thighs.*

309 How to make turkey gravy

Make the gravy as soon as the turkey is ready.

1. Put the pan over the flames and continually move it around.

2. Reposition until the juices caramelize and the cover the pan with a brown glaze.

3. Pour out and discard the fat.

4. Add flour to the pan and return the pan to the heat.

5. Pour broth into the hot pan and scrape the bottom with a wooden spoon.

6. Strain the gravy.

7. Chop the giblets and add them to the strained gravy. If needed for desired thickness, cook a little longer.

8. Pour the gravy over the sliced turkey.

310 How to extend turkey gravy

Everyone likes turkey gravy, but sometimes, especially if the turkey hasn't been overcooked, there aren't enough drippings. To stretch the gravy, make a broth with extra turkey necks and giblets or chicken necks and giblets.

1. While the turkey is roasting, make giblet broth. Simmer the giblets, including the liver, for 2 hours in just enough water or broth to cover. Save the broth for adding to the juices.

2. When the turkey's done (see entry 308), strain the drippings into a degreasing cup or a glass pitcher and separate or skim off the fat that soon rises to the top.

3. Calculate how much gravy you'll need—about ¼ cup per serving—and add giblet broth as needed to the juices.

4. Combine 2 teaspoons flour and 2 teaspoons butter per cup of the combined juices and broth. Add the liquid to the flour mixture and bring to the simmer.

5. Chop the giblets, not too fine, by hand or in a food processor. Add the chopped giblets to the gravy.

HINT *If you don't stuff your turkey or bake stuffing in the roasting pan, you'll have more juices and thus more gravy.*

311 How to carve a turkey

Part of the drama of roasting a big turkey is presenting it and carving it at the table.

1. Set up a cutting board—preferably one with a trough to trap juices—in the dining room with the platter next to it.

2. Cut through the piece of crispy skin that joins the thigh and breast.

3. Continue cutting down, pulling the thigh away from the turkey with a fork, until you reach the joint where the thigh meets the breast. Cut through the joint and remove the leg.

4. Place the leg on the cutting board and cut apart the thigh and drumstick. (The joint is farther into the drumstick than you might think.)

5. Slice the "second joint" dark meat off the thigh and transfer it to the platter. This meat is juicier than the "first joint" meat on the drumstick.

6. Slice the meat off the drumstick.

7. Make a slight diagonal cut just above the wing. This will allow the breast meat slices to come away as you carve the breast.

8. Slice the breast meat. Use the carving fork to aid slicing.

9. Continue slicing until you see the wing joint. Insert a knife into the joint and remove the wing. If the wing is large, the meat on the wing can be sliced.

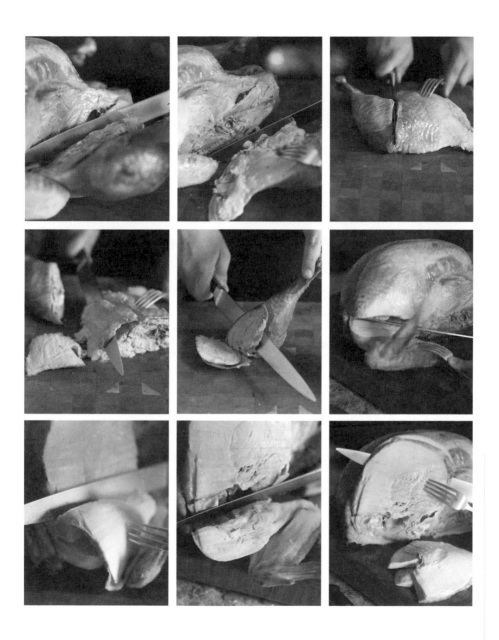

312 What to do with leftover turkey

- Don't try to reheat white meat; it will dry out. Dark meat can be reheated.
- Cold turkey makes delicious salads. Try tossing it in a green salad or combining it with cooked green vegetables such as peas, asparagus, or green beans or with tropical fruits enlivened with chiles and cilantro.
- Make a little turkey curry: Combine 2 tablespoons flour, 2 tablespoons curry powder, and 4 tablespoons butter in a small saucepan over low to medium heat until you smell the curry, a minute or so. Add ½ cup dry sherry or white wine, ¾ cup milk, and ¾ cup broth and simmer until the sauce has the consistency you like. If desired, add 2 tablespoons finely chopped cilantro and ½ cup or so heavy cream. Just before serving, heat cut-up pieces of turkey in the sauce.
- Make a delicious broth by simmering the turkey carcass for about 3 hours, and then use the broth to make French onion soup.

313 How to cook a duck

Most American ducks, and certainly those we find frozen at the supermarket, have gotten much meatier in recent years. They have a lot of fat in the skin, making it impossible to roast the duck as you would a chicken and have crispy skin and rare to medium-rare meat. If you roast a duck rare, it will be covered with a layer of flabby raw fat; if you cook it long enough to crisp up the skin and render out the fat, the meat is overcooked. The way around this is to cut the duck into boneless breasts and thighs and cook each using different methods, or to try the method given here if you want to roast a whole duck.

Whole duck

1. Make a series of thin slashes in two directions (see photograph) on the breasts, without cutting all the way down to the meat, to expose a maximum of fat.

2. Wrap the duck in aluminum foil (which keeps it from drying out), put it in a roasting pan, and roast it for 3 hours in a 300°F oven to render the fat and soften the meat.

3. Unwrap the duck and return it to the roasting pan. Increase the oven temperature to 400°F and put the duck back in the oven. Roast the duck until crispy brown, about 20 minutes.

Duck breasts

1. Make a series of thin slashes in two directions on the skin, without cutting all the way down to the meat, to expose a maximum of fat.

2. Season the duck breast to taste with kosher salt and freshly ground black pepper and cook it skin side down in a nonstick pan—there's no need for oil— over medium heat until the skin turns crispy and brown, about 12 minutes for Pekin duck breasts and 17 minutes for mullard duck breasts.

Duck thighs

There are several ways to cook duck thighs, all involving slow, gentle cooking. The easiest method is to put the thighs in a medium oven and roast them for a couple of hours until they soften. At that point vegetables such as cabbage (either fresh or sauerkraut) can be added to the thighs and cooked, covered, another 30 minutes or so. You can also braise the duck thighs in a little broth or red or white wine. The braising liquid can then be simmered down, finished with a little butter, and used as the sauce for both the thighs and the breasts.

SLOW ROASTING

1. Season the thighs to taste with kosher salt and freshly ground black pepper and arrange them skin side up in a roasting pan.

2. Bake in a 300°F oven for 2 hours for Pekin duck thighs, 3 hours for mullard thighs. The skin should be brown and crispy, and the meat meltingly tender.

BRAISING

1. Brown the thighs on both sides in a little oil on the stovetop over medium heat.

2. In a pan just large enough to hold the duck thighs in a single layer, cook onions, carrots, and garlic in a little butter until soft.

3. Put in the thighs and pour in enough liquid such as wine, wine vinegar, broth, or water to come halfway up the thighs. Nestle in a bouquet garni.

4. Cover the pan and simmer gently—1 hour for Pekin duck thighs, 2 hours for mullard duck thighs—over low heat or in a 300°F oven.

5. Strain, degrease, and reduce the braising liquid slightly. Put the thighs in a clean pan and pour the liquid over the meat.

6. Turn the oven up to 400°F. Put the thighs in the oven and baste them, uncovered, until they're coated with a shiny glaze.

What's the difference between mullard and Pekin ducks?

The standard duck you're most likely to see at the supermarket is called Pekin duck. In recent years we've begun to see oversize duck breasts from giant ducks called mullards, a cross between mallards and Muscovy ducks. Besides being much larger and meatier than Pekin ducks, mullards have better-tasting fat. Both mullards and Pekins can be cooked the same way—thighs slow-roasted or braised, breasts sautéed or grilled.

314 How to "roast" small and medium birds

Tiny birds such as quail are impossible to roast and brown at the same time because our ovens aren't hot enough to brown the birds before overcooking them. The better method is to brown small birds in a sauté pan and finish in a 500°F oven. Birds such as pheasants and quails have white meat and so should be cooked to the same degree of doneness as chicken; squab has red meat and should be roasted rare or medium rare.

Another good way to cook small birds

If you're serving squab, quail, or other small birds, you can avoid last-minute carving by cutting off the two breasts and the thighs and sautéing them at the last minute. Over high heat, cook on the skin side in olive oil until brown, about 3 minutes, and on the meat side for 1 minute. Serve squab rare to medium rare.

If you separate the breasts, thighs, giblets, and carcass ahead of time, you'll have the wherewithal to make a sauce.

A quick carving method for small birds

You can carve small birds in the same way as a chicken (see entry 297), but a simpler method is to slide a large knife into the cavity slightly to one side and press down firmly so you cut through the back. Then repeat, holding the knife to the other side so that you cut out the back. Turn over the bird and cut straight down the middle, separating the two halves. Serve one or two halves per person.

315 How to buy beef

For anyone confused when it comes to going to the supermarket and choosing or asking for a piece of meat for dinner, here is a little primer.

Roasts

The most expensive roasts are from the rib section of the steer—what would be the equivalent of a rack on a lamb—and the loin section, a little lower down the back, from which are cut strip steaks, sometimes called New York cuts, or, if the whole loin is sliced into cross sections, you'll have T-bones or porterhouses.

Prime rib   Tenderloin

• **Prime rib:** Count on one rib per two servings, but for a legitimate roast, you'll need at least three ribs. Order the ribs from the loin end, which will be more compact and less fatty. Ask the butcher to cut off the chine bone (the spinal column) so you can carve through and separate the ribs.

• **Strip (New York cut):** Ask for a section from the rib end—where the strip meets the ribs—and count on about ¾ inch of thickness per serving.

• **Eye of the round:** This and other cuts from the leg can be somewhat tough and are best served thinly sliced, not as you would prime rib.

- **Tenderloin:** You can buy a whole trimmed tenderloin and roast it in a hot oven or you can slice it into steaks as shown here.
- **Sirloin:** Usually sold in steaks, the sirloin also makes an excellent roast and is often a good value.
- **Top round or chuck:** This roast tends to be tough, so it needs to be served sliced thin; it is good for sandwiches.

Steaks

Most steaks are simply slices of what would otherwise be roasts. Rib steaks come from the rib section, strip steaks from the loin, fillets from the tenderloin, and so on. Depending on how the loin is butchered, it may have been sliced into porterhouses or separated into New York strip and tenderloin, both of which can be roasted whole.

Strip

Porterhouse

- **Strip and shell (New York cuts):** These are the large tenderloin muscle from lower down the animal along the back, after the last ribs. A strip is boneless; a shell steak has the bone attached. These are not quite as tender as the tenderloin, but they can be much tastier.
- **Rib steak:** This is a tender, expensive steak much like shell steak, except that it has a chunk of fat—easily circumvented—in the middle of each steak.
- **Tenderloin:** The most tender steak of all, that taken from the thinner end of the long, tapering tenderloin, is the filet mignon. The larger round is sometimes called tournedos.

meat

261

- **Porterhouse and T-bone:** These are cross sections of the back of the animal. The T-shaped bone separates the larger loin muscle (the New York cut) and the tenderloin. T-bones include only a small piece of the tenderloin, as well as the loin (the strip). A porterhouse, the most luxurious of steaks, includes both.
- **Sirloin:** Unless the label says "sirloin strip," which refers to the more expensive strip steak, the sirloin is cut from further down the back of the animal from the strip. Sirloin is often a good value because it's tender and can be well marbled and very flavorful; it is considerably less expensive than the strip.
- **Eye of the round:** This looks like a tenderloin, but it can be quite tough. It's best to serve this steak thinly sliced (see Hint, page 266).
- **London broil:** The original London broil was a flank steak—the flaps that hang from the sides of the animal—but nowadays it is usually a chuck steak, and rather tough. Be sure to serve it thinly sliced across the grain to diminish the impression of toughness.
- **Flank steak:** Once a very good value, flank steak has gotten a bit pricey. But it's very flavorful. Serve it sliced thinly across the grain, which on flank steak is very easy to see.
- **Hanger steak:** Once a cut the butchers took home because no one wanted it, this has become a popular steak. It looks a little like a knotted rope—not very pretty to look at, but very tasty—and has a strip of sinew down the middle that should be cut out.

Pot roasts

Pot roasts aren't really roasted, but braised, and are made from tough cuts of meat well marbled with fat. Large pieces of chuck, especially the blade roast, are best for braising (pot roasting).

316 How to get more jus from roast meats

A jus is simply a gravy that hasn't been thickened. The jus is released by the roast. But when a roast is cooked only until rare, it releases very few juices, something cookbooks never mention. The solution is to cut about a pound of inexpensive stew meat into strips and put them, along with any trimmings from the roast (take off any fat) and the bones, in the pan you're using for the roast. This meat caramelizes and contributes its own juices to those of the roast.

1. In a hot oven, roast the stew meat and defatted trimmings with a few garlic cloves and a couple of quartered shallots for 30 minutes.

2. Put the roast on top and adjust the temperature to suit the roast.

3. When the roast is done, remove it from the pan and add 1 cup water or broth and boil it down on the stovetop while scraping the bottom with a wooden spoon until it caramelizes.

4. Add an additional ⅓ cup broth or water per serving and simmer for about 3 minutes while scraping the bottom of the pan. Strain.

317 How to test for doneness

Before you start cooking the meat, especially rare steaks, make sure it's at room temperature or even warm before you sauté (otherwise a steak cooked rare will still be cold inside when you serve it).

• **For the rarest steak:** Brown it as fast as you can on both sides and serve.

• **For rare steak:** Wait until you see a little blood forming on the raw surface of the steak before you turn it, and then sauté it just enough to brown it on the other side.

• **For medium-rare steak:** When the blood becomes more abundant (but not brown), sauté for a couple of minutes on the other side.

• **For medium steak:** Turn when the surface is covered with blood. Cook it until it's completely firm to the touch.

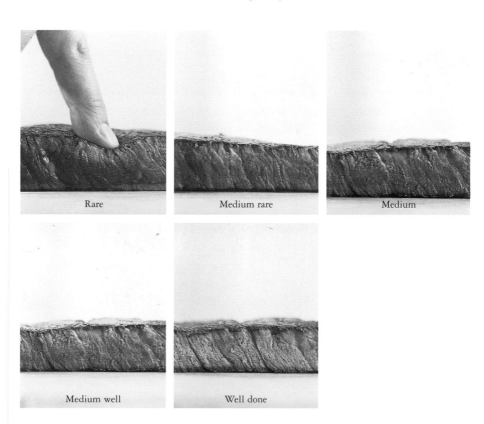

Rare

Medium rare

Medium

Medium well

Well done

- **For medium-well steak:** Cook it until the blood starts to turn brown.
- **For well-done steak:** Cook until the blood is completely brown.

Always let a steak rest for 10 minutes or so, covered loosely with aluminum foil, to let the heat continue to penetrate into the center.

HINT *If you're grilling very thick steaks, make the fire with the coals to one side of a covered grill. Grill the meat over the coals on both sides to brown it and then move it to the part of the grill with no coals. Cover the grill so that the meat continues to cook without the crust burning.*

318   How to sauté steaks and chops

Steaks and chops are all sautéed in basically the same way. In a pan just large enough to hold the steaks or chops, heat oil or clarified butter (see entry 32) over high heat until it barely begins to smoke. If the pan is too large, the juices run over to the area where there's no meat and they burn. The reason for the high heat is to make sure a savory crust forms on the outside of the meat. If the meat is too cold— take it out of the refrigerator for a few hours before sautéing—or the heat not high enough, the meat releases juices and then boils in them, which gives the meat a very unpleasant taste. Once you know the chops or steaks are browned, you can adjust the temperature according to the thickness of the chops and the kind of meat. Thin lamb chops, for example, must be sautéed over the highest possible heat and added to the pan one or two at a time to avoid cooling the pan.

Steaks

Steaks are the most challenging because everyone wants them done differently. If the steak is thick—a big porterhouse, say—you can slide a thermometer in through the side and just read the internal temperature, but thinner steaks require both an eye and a touch to judge doneness.

meat

When the inside of a thick steak reaches 110°F, it's very rare but not cold; at 115°F it's rare; at 120°F it will be medium rare (remember, it continues to get hotter inside once it's taken off the heat); at 125°F it's at the limit—more cooking will only dry it out.

HINT *The trick to making tough steak seem tender is to serve London broil or tougher cuts of meat sliced. Once the steak is done, slice it at an angle and serve the strips on warm plates.*

319 How to carve a porterhouse and other steaks

• A thick porterhouse can serve up to four people and is one of the most exciting cuts of meat because it contains the New York strip and the tenderloin at the same time. To carve a porterhouse, cut the larger loin muscle away from the bone and then cut the small tenderloin muscle. Slice each of these on the diagonal and make sure everyone gets a fair share of both muscles.

• Carving a thick strip steak or sirloin steak is simple. All you have to do is slice it into strips. If you're slicing a tougher cut of meat such as grilled flank steak or some version of London broil (which nowadays is usually chuck), slice the meat very thinly and on the diagonal. This will attenuate the toughness.

320 How to get wide slices out of thin steaks

Flank steaks, hanger steaks, and skirt steaks have become more popular than ever, but because they can be tough, they're best served sliced. To get the widest slices, slice with the knife at a 45 degree angle.

321 How to make a prime rib roast

Prime rib is one of the most satisfying and spectacular (and spectacularly expensive) roasts that you can serve at a dinner party.

To buy

The prime rib consists of the ribs lowest down the steer's back and is the same thing as a rack if you are talking about lamb or veal. It is important to keep in mind that there are two ends: the loin end, which is neater, with less fat; and the shoulder end, which contains more sinew and fat. Ask the butcher for chops from the loin end and count on one chop per two generous servings. Make sure the butcher has trimmed the chine bone so you will be able to carve the roast after it has been cooked. Have him or her leave the ribs on so they can be "Frenched" (see entry 347). This produces a stunning effect.

To roast

1. Season the prime rib to taste with kosher salt and freshly ground black pepper. Let sit at room temperature for 4 hours before roasting.

2. Preheat the oven to 500°F. If you want extra jus, spread the bottom of the roasting pan with about 1 pound of meat trimmings and aromatic vegetables (see entry 16). Preroast for 20 minutes (see entry 316).

3. Place the roast in the pan with the cooked trimmings and vegetables and roast until well browned, about 20 minutes.

meat

4. Turn down the oven to 275°F. After 30 minutes more roasting, start checking the internal temperature of the roast. Because rib roasts are so large, the temperature inside may increase as much as 10°F after removal from the oven. For rare, take the roast out of the oven when the temperature reads 110° to 115°F. For medium rare, 120° to 125°F. For medium, 130°F.

5. Let the roast rest for 30 minutes, loosely covered with aluminum foil, before carving.

To carve

There are a couple of approaches to carving. You can cut the meat away from the ribs all at once and transfer the boneless roast to a cutting board and carve it crosswise into round slices (above).

You can also separate the meat from the bone as you go, separating one rib at a time, then slicing in rounds, so you don't have to take the roast apart or lose the drama (opposite).

HINT *You can also carve the roast lengthwise—if the roast isn't too large, stand it on end and carve vertically. This method allows you to separate the more well-done meat for those who prefer it.*

322 The secrets to pot roast

We've been assaulted with so many travesties of this succulent dish that we associate it with bad cooking. When well made, pot roast is every bit as good as the finest tenderloin. Here are a couple of secrets.

• Use a cut with a lot of soluble fat in it. A chuck blade roast is best for beef, a shoulder for lamb or pork, and a shoulder clod best for veal.

• Make sure your pot roast is big enough—at least 5 pounds.

• When your pot roast is "done"—a skewer slides easily in and out of it—strain out the vegetables, skim the fat off the juices, and glaze it by baking it, uncovered, while basting. This causes the flavor of the juices to intensify and get reabsorbed by the meat.

HINT *With the roast in a pot, cover the top of the pot with aluminum foil and press the foil down slightly in the middle. In this way moisture will condense on the underside of the foil and drip down over the pot roast, basting it.*

meat

How to prepare pot roast

1. Have the butcher tie the roast or tie it lengthwise yourself. Put it into a pot just large enough to hold it, with sides high enough that you can cover the roast.

2. Preheat the oven to 400°F.

3. Surround a 5-pound roast with 2 thickly sliced carrots and 2 quartered onions. Roast in the oven until all the juices come out—you'll see them in the bottom of the pot surrounding the roast. When the juices are syrupy, be very attentive to let them caramelize without letting them burn.

4. Remove the roast from the oven and put it on the stove. Pour in enough liquid, such as broth, wine, or vinegar or a combination, to come halfway up the sides of the roast. Add a bouquet garni and bring to a gentle simmer.

5. Cover with aluminum foil and the lid (see Hint, page 269) and place it in the oven (at 350°F) or on the stove. Maintain a very gentle simmer—a bubble should rise every second.

6. After an hour or so, turn over the roast so the part that was above the liquid is now below, cover the pot again, and continue cooking in the same way.

7. When a skewer slides through the roast with no resistance, after 2 to 4 hours, transfer the roast to a smaller pot (or clean out the pot you used) and strain the braising liquid into a saucepan.

8. Put the roast in a 400°F. oven and ladle over about a fourth of the braising liquid.

9. After you've simmered the remaining braising liquid on the stove for 5 minutes and skimmed off its fat (see entry 296), pour it over the roast. Continue roasting and basting every 7 minutes or so, until the braising liquid is syrupy and the pot roast is shiny.

Should I buy a gas grill?

Gas grills are convenient—you just turn them on—and make grilled food every bit as flavorful as that made with a charcoal grill. The only problem is that most gas grills can't be used to create flavorful smoke with wood chips or sawdust. When shopping for a gas grill, look for one that will also accommodate wood for those occasions.

323 The world's best hamburger

Hamburger meat is sold according to its fat content, not according to where on the animal it comes from. Ground sirloin, in other words, just implies a lower fat content than, say, ground chuck. To be sure of what you're getting, choose a piece of meat at the butcher's and have it ground. The best meat for hamburger is chuck. For a leaner burger, ask for sirloin (round is too lean). The secret to getting the best meat for your money is to buy less expensive cuts from a good butcher rather than buying more expensive cuts from the supermarket.

When you get your hamburger home, you don't need to do anything to it except form it into patties. Don't spoil it with indifferent cheese but experiment with good cheddar, Roquefort, Comte, or Gruyère.

When the burgers are done, serve an assortment of condiments—finely sliced onions, tomatoes, lettuce, sautéed mushrooms, pickles, relish, mustard (the works)—for guests to help themselves.

324 How to light a fire for the grill

You see them in most hardware, home, and garden stores as grilling season approaches. Along with the latest in grill models, stores now sell "chimneys," one of the cleverer inventions of the late twentieth century. A chimney is essentially a metal cylinder with a few notches near the base in which to start a charcoal fire.

1. Fill the top part of the cylinder with charcoal. Stuff some newspaper in the bottom. Set the chimney in the grill base where you want the fire to be and light the newspaper with a match.

2. Leave the burning contraption alone for about 30 minutes and you'll find the charcoal all aglow.

3. Pour the charcoal coals out into the base of the grill.

325 How do I clean my caked-on, messy grill?

Those of us who don't bother to clean a grill regularly often rationalize that if it's set over the hot coals for a few minutes before food is placed on it, any bacteria on the grill will be killed. But if you want your food not to stick to the grill and don't want to look like a slob, you'll have to clean it.

1. Lay the grill on spread-out newspaper, ideally outside.

2. Spray the grill with heavy-duty oven cleaner.

3. Let sit for an hour, then scrub it with steel wool and rinse well.

4. Repeat if it is still not clean.

326 How to keep food from sticking to the grill

To ensure that your food arrives intact on the plate and not shredded on the grill:

1. Before heating, start with a perfectly clean grill and spray it with nonstick cooking spray.

2. Some foods, especially seafood, can be coated with flour (see entry 39).

3. Make sure the heat of the grill itself is very hot before you put food on the rack.

327 How to prevent flare-ups

When fat from chicken or other meat drips down on the coals, it causes them to ignite, leaving the food covered with soot. To avoid this, you can move the food around at the beginning, continually keeping it out of the flame. Chicken is best first cooked with the flesh side down so that by the time the fatty skin side is grilled, the fire is less intense and less likely to ignite. In a covered grill, the coals can be placed on one side and the food on the other.

HINT *Spray water from a plant sprayer selectively on the coals to calm them down.*

328 Smoking on a stove or grill

Many people mistake the flavor of smoke for the flavor of the grill, which should create a minimum of smoke. If you want a smoky flavor, it's better to smoke your food using wood chips or sawdust. You can smoke on the stove or in a covered grill.

When you smoke foods on the stove, you're cooking them at the same time they're smoking. You can also cook some foods using another method, and then smoke them in addition. Chicken parts, for example, can be sautéed, grilled, or roasted, and then, just as they approach doneness, be lightly smoked. Faster-cooking foods, such as boneless duck breasts, can be cooked entirely by smoking.

meat

To smoke on the stove

1. Find a round cake rack that fits in a pot or wok.

2. Place a sheet of aluminum foil in the bottom of the wok or pot and put 3 tablespoons of sawdust on top.

3. Place the cake rack, then the foods to be smoked, on top. Heat until the sawdust smokes; cover.

4. Smoke as you would steam, until the meat or seafood is cooked to the temperature you want.

To smoke with a covered grill

1. Build a fire in a grill and mound the coals to one side.

2. Place a small sheet of aluminum foil on top of the coals and ½ cup of sawdust on top of that.

3. Place the foods to be smoked on the grill rack, but not over the coals, and cover the grill.

4. Smoke the foods to the degree you want.

329 An easy stew

The secret to easy red meat stews is to skip browning the meat, which all cookbooks claim adds essential flavor and helps seal in juices, etc. In fact, it does very little. A better approach is to make what the southern French call a daube of lamb or beef.

1. Cut the meat into 2-inch cubes. Thickly slice a couple of large carrots, halve a couple of onions, and crush a few garlic cloves. Put these in a large ovenproof pot and put the meat on top.

2. Nestle in a bouquet garni and pour over enough red wine or mixtures of whatever you have around such as good broth—a chunk of meat glaze (see entry 355) is always welcome—drippings from a roast, vinegar, remains from bottles that have been sitting on the counter, and so on.

3. Bring the whole thing to the simmer on top of the stove, cover, and slide the pot into a 350°F oven. Check every 20 minutes to see how the stew is doing—a bubble should come up every second or so—and adjust the oven temperature accordingly.

4. When the meat offers no resistance when you poke it with a knife, after about 3 hours, you can serve the stew as it is or you can concentrate and/or thicken the stewing liquid.

5. If you like, sort out the cooked vegetables and add new ones such as glazed carrots or pearl onions, sautéed mushrooms, or boiled string beans. If it seems the meat is swimming in liquid, drain the meat in a colander and reduce the liquid to about ⅓ cup per serving, simmering with the pot to one side of the burner, which makes it easier to skim. If you like, thicken the liquid with a flour and butter paste (see entry 330) or a slurry of cornstarch and water.

How to improvise stews

Remember that basic stews, while the liquids used and the aromatic vegetables cooked with the meat may differ, are almost all identical, except that sometimes the meat is browned. But once the basic stew is made, and the aromatic vegetables picked out, all sorts of variations can be improvised, using glazed root vegetables, boiled green vegetables, sautéed mushrooms, little strips of bacon, and so on.

HINT *Most recipes call for browning the stew meat before adding liquid. While this may enhance the color and flavor of your stew, the effects are subtle and often not worth the trouble. To brown meat successfully, the pan must be very hot. Add only a couple of cubes at a time and wait for them to start browning before adding more. If you add too much meat at once, you'll cool the pan and cause the meat to release liquid too quickly and to boil in its own juices. When turning the meat, again, start by turning only a couple of cubes.*

330 To thicken stew

If your stew contains too much liquid or the liquid is too runny, you can strain it and simmer down the liquid to concentrate its flavor and give it a lightly syrupy consistency, which it gets because of the gelatin it contains. You can also use thickeners.

How to thicken with flour

You can make a paste of equal parts soft butter and flour, called a beurre manié.

1. With the back of a fork, work 1 tablespoon each of flour and butter per cup of liquid together into a paste.

2. Whisk this mixture into the simmering stew, a bit at a time, until it achieves the thickness you like. The stew has to simmer for the thickening to happen.

How to thicken with cornstarch and other starches

Stir together a couple tablespoons of cornstarch and an equal amount of cold water until smooth. Whisk this mixture, a little at a time, into the simmering stew. Arrowroot and potato starch can be used in the same way as cornstarch.

How to thicken with vegetable purees

Garlic puree (see entry 177) makes a great thickener. You can also puree some of the aromatic vegetables that have cooked with the stew and add some of this puree back into the stew.

HINT *The easiest way to include vegetables in a stew is to simply serve the stew with the vegetables that stewed along with the meat. To avoid cooking the vegetables too long, don't add them at the beginning of cooking. Add them instead when the stew is an hour from being done. For more refined versions, sort out the aromatic vegetables when the stew is nearly done and add other ingredients such as the pearl onions, bacon, and mushrooms used in a beef bourguignon.*

331 Using leftover stew

It's always worth making a lot of stew. It's better the next day anyway, and you can do all sorts of things with the leftovers. Here are a few ideas.

Make a pasta sauce

1. Warm the stew to separate the meat and the liquid.

2. Shred the meat, and put the shredded meat back in the liquid.

3. Simmer until the sauce has the consistency you like.

4. Add chopped fresh herbs or other flavorful ingredients if you like.

Make stuffed pasta

Separate the meat and stewing liquid and simmer down the liquid until syrupy. Shred the meat and combine it with the liquid. Flavor with herbs and form into ravioli or cannelloni with sheets of fresh pasta or boiled dried pasta.

Make a cold terrine

Check the consistency of the cold stewing liquid; it should be stiff and well gelled. If not, simmer it down to concentrate it.

1. Melt the cold stewing liquid and stew in a pot (it will turn into a liquid when just slightly warmed).

2. Take out the bits of stew meat and, if they are large, cut them into small pieces.

3. Pour a little of the stewing liquid into a porcelain terrine and let it set in the freezer.

4. Arrange a layer of meat on top of the set liquid and, if you like, sprinkle with chopped fresh herbs.

5. Pour over another layer of liquid and return as needed to the freezer until the liquid sets.

6. Add more meat.

7. Continue in this way until you've filled the terrine. Let it set for several hours in the refrigerator.

8. Just before serving, turn the terrine out of the mold onto a platter. Dip the bottom of the dish in hot water for a few seconds if the terrine won't come out.

9. Serve in slices with little pickles and mustard.

332 How to buy pork

Roasts

Most any part of a pig can be roasted, but the rack and loin sections are considered the best-tasting and best-roasting parts.

• **Ham:** A ham, of course, is a roast, and when it is cooked whole, it can easily feed twenty people. Raw hams, sometimes called leg of pork, are sometimes sold in halves—the butt end and the shank end sold separately. But beware, sometimes butchers slice out the best steaks from the center.

• **Rack:** Ask the butcher for a section of the rib part from the loin end. A whole rack will have eight ribs—the ribs that continue toward

Frenched rack of pork

Boneless pork loin with pork medallions

the shoulder become sinewy. Ask the butcher to cut off the chine bone to make carving easier; also ask him to "French" the rack or do it yourself (see entry 347).

• **Boneless loin:** This is from the rack or loin section and obviously has no bones. While easy to prepare and slice, it's less flavorful than a roast with the bones in.

Chops

There are three types of pork chops—rib chops, loin chops, and shoulder chops.

• **Rib chop:** A rib pork chop is best simply grilled or sautéed. If the butcher is cutting chops for you, ask him for those nearest the loin end; they are neater and have less sinew. If you like dramatic effect, you can trim the meat off the protruding rib.

• **Loin chop:** This is simply a cross section of the saddle (the lower back), and like miniature porterhouse steak, it includes a T-bone and two muscles—the loin and the tenderloin. Grill or sauté them to the equivalent of medium, 135°F.

• **Shoulder chop:** Messier to look at than a loin or rib chop, a shoulder chop contains sinew and fat. You can sauté or grill it, but it's best braised in a little red or white wine for a couple of hours until a knife slides easily through it. The braising liquid can be reduced to make a sauce.

333 How to brine pork to keep it juicy

Today's leaner pork is often dry. To moisten pork chops or roasts, soak them in brine. Make a brine with 2 quarts water, ¼ cup salt, and ¼ cup sugar, and if you like, 2 tablespoons Pernod. Soak the chops at room temperature for about 1 hour—experiment with times, increasing the soaking times until the chops or roasts have the desired saltiness. You can also experiment with infusing ingredients in the brine, such as crushed juniper berries, fresh fennel, thyme, bay leaf, and garlic.

334 How to sauté pork chops

Sauté pork chops over high heat, and then cook them over medium heat according to their thickness (the thicker the chop, the lower the heat, to avoid burning the outside before the heat penetrates to the inside). Pork chops are done at 135°F or when they feel firm to the touch; no less, no more.

335 How to braise shoulder chops

Because they contain sinew and fat, shoulder pork and lamb chops need a slow braise to become succulent and juicy.

1. Brown the chops in hot oil in a straight-sided pan just large enough to hold them in a single layer. Pour off the cooked oil.

2. Cook coarsely chopped aromatic vegetables such as onions, leeks, carrots, turnips, celeriac, or fennel until softened.

3. Add the chops to the pan along with enough liquid such as broth, wine, or water—alone or in combination—to come halfway up the sides of the chops and nestle in a bouquet garni. Bring the liquid to a gentle simmer, cover with aluminum foil pressed down against the top of the chops, and cover the pan.

4. Simmer gently for 2 hours, or until a knife slides easily through the middle of the chops.

5. Remove the chops from the pan and set aside.

6. Degrease and reduce the braising liquid (see entry 36), and serve as is or finish the sauce with a little cream or butter.

336 How do I barbecue ribs?

Barbecuing involves a slow baking, combined with smoking, and a final grilling phase. The slow baking is a form of braising at a heat low enough that the juices in the meat suffice as the braising liquid. If the heat gets too hot, the liquid will evaporate and the meat will dry out before it has a chance to braise. Larger pieces of meat such as beef short ribs should be braised on the stove first; then the braising liquid is simmered down to a glaze and combined with other ingredients before it's brushed on the meat while it's grilling.

To barbecue pork ribs

1. Build a fire and push the coals to one side of a covered grill.

2. Rub the ribs with kosher salt, freshly ground black pepper, spices such as cumin, star anise, and paprika, and a little sugar.

3. Grill the ribs on the side of the grill opposite the heat source. Add sawdust or wood chips to the fire from time to time to create smoke, but keep the lid on the grill.

4. Continue in this way for 2 to 3 hours, until you can pull on one of the ribs to see if it comes away easily. Brush the ribs with flavorings such as apricot preserves, orange marmalade, ketchup, mustard, vinegar, Worcestershire sauce, honey, hoisin sauce, soy sauce, or cooked-down tomatoes. Cook for 30 minutes more.

5. Just before serving, brown the ribs directly over the heat source for about 10 minutes.

To barbecue beef short ribs

1. Braise the ribs in as little broth or wine as you can—use a tight-fitting lid to minimize the liquid you need—for about 2 hours.

2. Grill as the pork ribs, but judge their doneness by sliding a skewer into one to see if it comes out with no resistance. The time needed for barbecuing will depend on the size of the ribs and how long you braised them ahead of time.

3. Simmer down the braising liquid and add it to the mixture you brush on the ribs during the last 30 minutes.

meat

281

337 What are pork "noisettes"?

The most tender cut of pork is the aptly named tenderloin. It's usually a bit more than a foot long and about two inches thick at its thickest part, and then it tapers down to a point. You can roast a tenderloin whole (brown it on the stove first) and slice it into noisettes (meaning "hazelnuts" or "little nuts"), little rounds about an inch thick. You'll get more flavor by slicing the tenderloin into noisettes first and sautéing them for about 3 minutes on each side, until firm to the touch and browned on both sides. Because tenderloins are long and thin, they are better grilled or sautéed rather than roasted.

338 How to roast a boneless pork loin

A boneless loin (see entry 332) is the loin muscle taken from the rack or the saddle. While easier to carve than a bone-in roast, which you just slice, it's less flavorful because the juices aren't held in as well by the bones.

HINT *When the roast feels firm all over when you poke it, it's done. It is also done when the internal temperature in the middle of the roast reads 135°F. It will reach 140°F as the meat rests.*

1. Ideally, soak the roast in brine (see entry 333). Bring the roast to room temperature before roasting.

2. Preheat the oven to 500°F. Season to taste with kosher salt and freshly ground black pepper and rub with olive oil. Place in a small roasting pan in the oven.

3. Roast until well browned, about 15 minutes, and turn down the heat to 250°F. Start checking for doneness after about a total of 35 minutes. Check the texture and/or temperature (see Hint).

339 How to roast a rack of pork

A boneless pork loin is a popular cut, and so is a rack of lamb. Yet most of us never think to roast a rack of pork, which is a shame, because it is a beautiful roast. Next time you think about roasting a boneless pork loin, instead ask the butcher for a rack. Request as many ribs as you need servings and tell the butcher you need them from the loin end. Ask him to "French" the roast or you can do it yourself (see entry 347). Leave a thin layer of fat on the pork, which will baste the meat as it renders and keep it from drying out.

1. Season the pork rack to taste with kosher salt and freshly ground black pepper. Let sit at room temperature for 3 hours before roasting.

2. Preheat the oven to 450°F.

3. Place the rack in a roasting pan. If you want extra jus, before you put the rack in the pan, spread coarsely chopped carrots and onions in a single layer in the roasting pan and add 1 pound of pork meat trimmings or stew meat. Put the pan with the vegetables and trimmings in the oven for 20 minutes. Then add the roast to the pan.

4. Roast until well browned, about 30 minutes. Turn down the oven to 275°F.

5. Continue to roast about 30 minutes, until the internal temperature reads 135°F.

6. When the rack is done, take it out of the oven and let it rest, loosely covered with aluminum foil, for 15 minutes before serving.

meat

7. To make a jus or gravy see entry 316.

8. Slice between the ribs to serve whole chops. As an alternative, separate meat and bones, and slice the meat.

340 How to buy veal

The structure of a calf is much like that of a pig and almost the same size, so much of what applies to pork roasts and chops also applies to veal. The main difference is that veal can be four times the price of pork. A veal roast is, indeed, a luxurious and expensive undertaking.

Roasts

Virtually every section of the calf can provide a roast.

• **Shoulder roast:** Butchers often tie up what's called the veal shoulder "clod" into a roast weighing about five pounds. It can be roasted—to an internal temperature of 135°F—but it is better braised into a pot roast (see entry 322).

• **Rack:** Much like buying prime rib, you can buy as many ribs as you like, but to qualify as a roast, a rack should contain at least four ribs. The whole rack contains eight ribs. Ask the butcher to "French" it for you or do it yourself (see entry 347).

• **Saddle:** If you're going overboard and want to serve a roast that your guests will never have encountered and that may be the most delicious they've ever eaten, you may want to invest in a whole saddle of veal. Unless you have a specialty butcher, you'll probably have to buy the whole saddle, which will weigh about thirty-five pounds. By the time you trim off the flaps, however, it will be down to about fourteen pounds, half of which is bone. A saddle will serve about twelve people generously.

• **Leg (round):** The veal leg contains many muscles, many of which are tough and need to be sliced thin. The best leg roast is the top round (ask for a top round with the cap off), which usually weighs about five pounds and costs about the same as the best beef tenderloin. Brown it on the stove and roast it in a moderate oven.

Chops and scallops

All veal roasts can be sliced into chops or, in the case of the round, into scallops (as in veal *scaloppine*). Veal, like pork and chicken, is white meat and should always be cooked to the equivalent of medium, 135°F.

* **Rib chop:** This is a chop cut from the rack, and it tends to be the most expensive. For dramatic effect, trim off any meat adhering to the ribs.

* **Loin chop:** Like a miniature porterhouse steak, simply grill or sauté it.

* **Shoulder chop:** You can sauté or grill these but they're better braised, four together as a little pot roast, or separately in a little wine for a couple of hours.

* **Scallop:** This is a thin slice from the top round that, because it is so thin, is impossible to brown properly without overcooking it. For this reason, it is best coated with flour, then beaten egg and very fine fresh bread crumbs, and then sautéed in clarified butter (see entry 32).

Braising cuts

The leg shank, left whole or cut into 1½- to 2-inch slices for ossobuco (left), can be browned and cooked as you would stew. Larger cuts such as the veal shoulder clod can be either roasted or braised as a pot roast. Cuts from the leg can be cut into cubes and gently stewed.

What's a cutlet?

A cutlet, sometimes called a scallop or scaloppine, is usually a thin slice of meat, such as veal or chicken. Some recipes suggest pounding cutlets to make them thin. Pound just enough to ensure that the cutlets, such as chicken breasts, are of even thickness.

341 How to sauté veal chops

After they brown over high heat, veal chops can be cooked more slowly because they are usually thicker and need to be cooked until they feel firm to the touch, or to an internal temperature of 135°F, the equivalent of medium.

342 How to sauté veal cutlets

The approach to sautéing depends on whether the cutlets have been floured or breaded (see entry 39) or left with no coating.

Cook very thin cutlets, with no coating or just a flour coating, over the highest possible heat, in oil or clarified butter. If the cutlets are very thin, say one-eighth inch, they should be cooked about 30 seconds on each side. If they've been pounded and are even thinner, 15 seconds on each side may be enough.

If the cutlets have been breaded, cook over medium heat until the cutlet is firm to the touch and the breading is golden brown. Because the breading will absorb the cooking fat, the best fat to use for breaded cutlets is clarified butter (see entry 32), which is delicious and won't leave specks of burned butter on the breading.

343 How to make Wiener schnitzel

Too often Wiener schnitzel—breaded veal scaloppine or cutlet—is coated with a thick layer of dried bread crumbs and then fried in oil. But when prepared with fresh bread crumbs (see entry 38) and cooked in butter, it is a treat indeed.

1. Prepare three dishes—one with flour, one with egg that's been beaten with a lot of kosher salt and freshly ground black pepper, and one with fresh bread crumbs. Dip a cutlet in the flour, pat off the excess, then dip in the egg and wipe off the excess with your

thumb and forefinger. Finally, dip in the bread crumbs, turning over so both sides are well coated.

2. Cook in a sauté pan over medium heat in clarified butter for 1 to 2 minutes, until golden brown on both sides and firm to the touch.

344 An affordable veal stew

The best veal stew meat is from the breast, but you can also use meat from the shoulder or leg.

1. Use veal stew meat about 1½ inches square. Put the meat in a pot with cold water to cover and bring it to a boil.

2. Boil for 5 minutes, drain, and rinse thoroughly (this step is important because it eliminates albumin, which will otherwise cloud the broth and make it taste soapy).

3. Put the meat in a pot with enough broth or water to cover. Add a bouquet garni, 1 large onion with a clove in one half, and a large peeled carrot cut into large sections.

4. Bring to a simmer and cook until the meat is soft, about 2 hours.

5. Strain off the liquid and measure it.

6. Meanwhile, prepare a thickener by combining equal parts flour and butter—about 2 tablespoons thickener per 1 cup liquid—in a saucepan large enough to hold the liquid. Cook over medium heat and whisk in the liquid.

7. Add 1 cup cream and season to taste with kosher salt and freshly ground black pepper.

8. Reheat the veal in the sauce and serve.

HINT *This is the simplest version of veal stew because the vegetables used for the stewing are the same vegetables that are served with the meat. For a more classic version, sort out the stewing vegetables (see Hint, page 276) and add pearl onions (simmered in a little stewing liquid) and mushrooms.*

meat

345 How to buy lamb

Roasts

Most of us are familiar with roast leg of lamb and rack of lamb, but the saddle, the cross section below the ribs, is also an elegant and undervalued roast.

- **Rack:** Except for one rib attached to the saddle, a rack is the ribs nearest the rear loin end of the animal. Be sure to have the butcher cut off the chine bone and have him "French" the rack or do it yourself by trimming away the meat that adheres to the ribs. Racks are easy to cook—about twenty-five minutes in a hot oven does the trick.
- **Leg:** This is the least expensive roast, but because of the way it's usually butchered, it can be hard to carve unless you have your butcher partially bone it.
- **Saddle:** This is the section of the lower back that the loin chops are cut from, and it makes an elegant roast.

Chops

Like pork and veal, lamb provides three kinds of chops—rib chops, loin chops, and shoulder chops.

- **Rib chop:** A rib chop is cut from the rack and is usually the most expensive chop. It looks the prettiest, especially if you trim off any meat clinging to the bones. Sauté or grill the chop over very high heat so it develops a crispy crust while remaining rare or medium rare.
- **Loin chop:** As good if not better than a rib chop, a loin chop is often less expensive. It is like a miniature T-bone steak. Cook it quickly, leaving it pink inside.
- **Shoulder chop:** The least expensive chop, it tends to be tough and sinewy if it is simply sautéed or grilled. It is best slowly braised for a couple of hours in a little red or white wine.

346 How to sauté lamb chops

Brown all three types of lamb chop over high heat and, unless very thick, cook entirely over high heat so they brown quickly. Take them out of the pan as soon as you see blood form on the surface of the chop (rare to medium rare) or when they feel firm to the touch (medium).

347 How to roast a rack of lamb

A rack of lamb may be one of the most elegant of all roasts, far better than a crown roast (see below). If you're buying racks of baby lamb from New Zealand, count on a half rack (four ribs) per person. If you're buying a rack of American lamb, count on two chops per person.

1. Preheat the oven to 450°F.

2. Season the rack to taste on both sides with kosher salt and freshly ground black pepper. Press both the right and left ends inward to get a sense of the fleshy feel of the meat when it's raw.

3. Roast in the oven until, when you push together the ends, they feel firmly in place, usually after about 25 minutes, at which point the meat will be medium rare. You can also slide an instant-read thermometer into the center of the meat: It should read about 130°F.

4. Remove the roast from the oven and let it rest, loosely covered with aluminum foil, for 10 minutes.

HINT *Have the butcher "French" the rack—that is to say, trim the meat and tissue off the ends of the bones for a decorative effect. You can also do this yourself.*

What's a crown roast?

For some reason, the idea of a crown roast has entered the popular wisdom as the most elegant of meats. In fact, it's all a bit silly, since a crown is made by tying two or more racks together, the ribs facing out,

meat

289

to form a "crown." The problem with this is that to shape the crown requires slicing between the ribs, thus exposing the meat in such a way that the juices run out and leave the roast dry. It's equally, if not more, dramatic to simply roast and serve a rack of lamb, pork, or veal.

348 How to carve a leg of lamb

1. Hold the lamb shank with one hand—use a towel if you're in the dining room—and slice the other end of the leg at an angle.

2. When you run into the bone and can no longer slice, slide the knife inward, along the top of the bone so you detach a portion of the thick section of meat—don't cut the meat completely off the bone—allowing you to continue slicing.

3. When you've removed all the meat, from the "thick" side of the legs, rotate the leg and carve the other side the same way.

349 How to braise lamb shanks

Once a forgotten part of the animal, lamb shanks have become fashionable and show up in the trendiest restaurants, and possibly your home.

1. Put the shanks in a pot or roasting pan that will hold them in a single layer. Break up 2 heads of garlic—pull off the loose paper peels—and sprinkle the unpeeled cloves over the shanks. Add 1 quartered onion per 4 shanks and 1 large carrot thickly sliced. Sprinkle with kosher salt and freshly ground black pepper to taste.

2. Roast in a 400°F oven until the juices released by the shanks caramelize on the bottom of the pot.

3. Add enough liquid such as broth, wine, vinegar, or a combination to come halfway up the sides of the shanks. Cover the shanks with aluminum foil and a lid and simmer gently on the stove or in a 350°F oven for about 90 minutes.

4. Turn over the shanks in the liquid and braise in the same way until a knife slid through one of the shanks has no resistance—the shank doesn't lift when you slide the knife out.

5. Transfer the shanks to a new pot and strain the braising liquid into a saucepan. Simmer the braising liquid and skim off the fat.

6. Pour the degreased braising liquid over the shanks and put the shanks, uncovered, in a 400°F oven, basting every 5 or 10 minutes until they're covered with a shiny glaze and the braising liquid is lightly syrupy.

HINT *To thicken the braising liquid with garlic puree, work the garlic cloves in a strainer and whisk the pulp that comes through into the braising liquid.*

350 What is offal?

As we become enamored of the more flavorful cuts of meat—long-cooked pieces such as shanks (see entry 349) and cheeks—we may very well begin to appreciate those parts of the animal that aren't really muscle, but are, well, organs. Some organs are very tasty indeed (kidneys and liver, for example), while others are as mild as barely scrambled eggs (brains). Anyone who hastily dismisses organ meats, referred to as offal, as being inedible has neither tasted them all nor ever eaten a hot dog.

Liver

Liver is delicious with Madeira sauce, made by deglazing the pan (see entry 36) with Madeira and adding a little meat glaze or broth and a bit of butter. Buy calves' liver, not beef liver, for the mildest taste.

Two secrets to sautéing liver: Make little slits around the sides to prevent curling and flour the slices to help them brown quickly. Sauté over very high heat.

Sweetbreads

There are two basic ways to cook sweetbreads. First, look for the firm round part of the sweetbread, not the raggedy long part. Blanch the sweetbreads, starting in cold water, and weight them under a cutting board until cool. At this point you can braise them—sweat some carrots and onions in a little butter, add the sweetbreads with a little broth, and braise in the oven loosely covered with parchment or foil. You can also slice the blanched and weighted sweetbreads, bread them in the same way as the chicken in entry 299, and sauté gently in butter.

Kidneys

Perhaps the least appreciated organ meat in America is veal kidneys. Brown them in oil in a small pan and roast them in a 400°F oven. One of the best-known, and most commonly served, sauces for kidneys is a mustard sauce made slightly sweet with a little port.

Brains

Brains may be the most delicate of all animal foods. They are delicious poached in vegetable broth with some vinegar or sliced, breaded or floured, and fried.

Broths, Soups, and Sauces

Simmer down a broth and you end up with a sauce; add a few vegetables or a little pasta to a broth and come up with a soup. Most fundamental to all of these is the correct preparation of broth. There's nothing tricky about it, but broth must never boil and it should be skimmed religiously as it simmers and concentrates. Sauces are more complex, but by following your nose and palate and heeding a little advice, even the best sauces are within the reach of the home cook.

351 Clear broth with great flavor and color

The secret to clear and flavorful chicken or veal broth is to cook the bones you're using before making the broth. If you're making broth from the meat of a full-grown animal, this isn't necessary, but if you're using bones or the meat from a young animal, your broth will be cloudy unless you cook the meat or bones first.

How to make white broth

1. If you're using bones of veal to make white broth, put the meat or bones in a pot and pour over enough cold water to cover. Slowly bring to the simmer.

2. Simmer for 5 minutes, drain in a colander, and rinse well. If you're using chicken to make white broth—whole pieces of chicken, not bones or cooked chicken—there's no need for this preliminary blanching.

3. Put the meat or bones in a clean pot along with aromatic vegetables and a bouquet garni. Pour over enough cold water to cover. Simmer according to the recipe.

4. Don't allow the mixture to come to a hard boil.

5. Skim off the scum and fat on the top with a ladle and discard.

HINT *There are two basic kinds of broth: "white" broth and "brown" broth, both of which are clear. White broth is useful for cream soups or sauces finished with cream— preparations that you want to stay white. Brown broth has a more robust flavor and a deeper color that makes it preferable in brown sauces, stews, and robust soups.*

How to make brown broth

1. Brown meat, bones, and aromatic vegetables in a pan in the oven until all the juices they release have caramelized on the bottom of the pan.

2. Transfer the meat and vegetables to a pot.

3. Deglaze the pan (see entry 36) with the caramelized juices by adding water.

4. Add this to the pot with the meat and vegetables. Put enough water in the pot to barely cover the meat and vegetables and add a bouquet garni. Simmer gently, according to the recipe. Never allow the liquid to come to a hard boil.

5. Skim off any fat and scum with a ladle and discard.

352 How to make affordable meat broth

Most of us don't want to spend a day's food budget on meat to make a broth and then throw the cooked meat into the trash. For this reason, most broth is made with bones. But bone broth never has the flavor of broth made with meat. The trick is to serve your family the meat that has been poached to make the broth. Try braising veal shanks (see entry 340) and serving them with a tomato sauce (see entry 374). Save the braising liquid from veal shanks for your sauces.

HINT *Serve the cooked meat for dinner with some mustard, small pickles called gherkins, and mayonnaise (see entry 367). Simmer the broth down to about one fifteenth of its volume to make the world's greatest meat glaze (see entry 355).*

How to make veal broth

1. Buy a whole veal breast, trim off any excess fat, and cut the breast apart by cutting in between the ribs.

2. Put the bones and meat in a pot with enough cold water to cover. Bring to a rapid boil. Boil for 5 minutes, drain in a colander, and rinse thoroughly.

3. Put the bones in a clean pot with aromatic vegetables, a bouquet garni, and enough water to cover. Simmer gently for 4 hours.

4. Add the meat and simmer for 3 hours more.

How to make beef broth

1. Buy an assortment of beef cuts such as shanks and a pot roast taken from the chuck in whatever quantity suits your yield.

2. Cover the meat with cold broth or water and simmer gently for 3 hours.

3. Add carrots cut into 3-inch sections, leek greens tied in a bundle, and a bouquet garni and simmer for 1 hour more.

4. Serve the meat with mustard, coarse salt, and miniature gherkins for a classic French pot-au-feu.

How to make chicken broth

1. Poach a whole chicken in broth (see entry 303).

2. When the chicken is cooked through, serve it as you would a roast chicken.

3. Save the broth in the fridge or freezer and add it to the water each time you poach a chicken. Refrigerate or freeze the broth each time. After you've poached three or four chickens, the broth will be clear and intensely flavored.

353 How to flavor weak broth

If you have a small amount of weak stock or broth that you want to use as the base for a sauce, boil down the stock or broth until it completely evaporates and forms a golden brown crust, or caramelizes, on the bottom of a saucepan. Deglaze the pan by adding more stock or water and scraping against the bottom and sides of the saucepan with a whisk to dissolve the crust. This magnifies the flavor of the stock.

HINT *One caveat: If your broth is salty, as many canned broths are, you may need to dilute it with a little water.*

354 How to prolong the life of soups and broths

If soups and broths are kept as cold as possible, well covered in the refrigerator, they will keep for at least five days.

1. After storing the broth for 5 days or more (see entry 359), bring it to the simmer and cook gently for 10 minutes.

2. Allow the broth to cool and rechill it. This will resterilize the broth so it's good for another 5 days.

3. You can, of course, also freeze broths and soups. If you're planning to freeze a cream soup, don't add the cream until you reheat the soup for serving.

355 Why make meat glaze?

In sauce recipes that call for homemade meat broth, you can save time by using meat glaze instead. Often called *glace de viande,* the glaze is essentially broth that's been simmered down (reduced) until it is syrupy when hot and has the consistency of hard rubber when cold. It keeps for months in the refrigerator and indefinitely in the freezer. While initially time-consuming to produce, meat glaze makes the most sophisticated sauces almost instantaneously.

1. Bring any kind of brown broth (see entry 351) to a simmer, skimming off any fat and scum that float to the top.

2. Reduce the broth down to about one fifteenth of its original volume.

3. Strain the glaze and store it in the refrigerator or freezer. Usually a tablespoon of meat glaze is enough to make a sauce for 4 people.

HINT *You can purchase meat glaze under the brand name More Than Gourmet at specialty markets or groceries; buy it in pint-size containers rather than the smaller sizes.*

356 How to make vegetable broth

Save extra leek greens, fennel branches, carrots, and celery in the freezer for when you want to make vegetable broth for soup or for poaching fish or poultry (see entries 278 and 303).

1. Chop equal amounts onion or leek and carrot, half as much turnip as onion, a third as much celery as onion, and some fennel branches. (If you're serving the vegetables in the broth, tie the fennel branches together with string and fish them out when the broth is done.)

2. Put the vegetables in a pot, add a bouquet garni, and pour in enough cold water to cover.

3. Simmer, covered, over medium-low heat for 20 minutes. Add wine (about a tenth the volume of the cooking liquid), and simmer, covered, for 15 minutes more.

HINT *Add wine at least 20 minutes into the cooking. If you were to add the wine at the beginning of cooking, it would prevent the vegetables from softening and releasing their flavor into the broth.*

357 How to make fish broth

The secret to avoiding fishy-tasting fish broth, other than using perfectly fresh fish heads and bones (it's best to use the bones of the fish you're cooking instead of asking the fishmonger for leftover fish bones), is to cook them for not more than 20 minutes.

1. Make sure the heads and bones are fresh, and preferably from the fish you are serving.

2. Soak them in cold water in the refrigerator for 12 hours or as long as you can. While this isn't necessary, it will make the broth clearer.

3. Break up the bones with your hands.

4. Put the bones in a pot with a chopped leek or two (or sliced onion) and just enough water to cover.

5. Add about a fourth as much white wine as water.

6. Add a bouquet garni and simmer gently for no more than 20 minutes. Strain.

358 How to make broth from shellfish

Many soup and sauce recipes call for fish broth (see entry 357). Fish broth is usually made from the fish that's going into the soup or being sauced. Bouillabaisse (see entry 289), for example, requires a broth made from the heads and bones of the fish. Today, sauces are often made with shellfish broth, which has a cleaner, more sealike flavor than fish broth.

How to make shellfish broth

The irony of shellfish such as lobster, shrimp, crayfish, and crab (all crustaceans) is that most of their flavor is in the parts we throw out—the roe and tomalley (or "mustard" in a crab) and the shells and heads. To make a shellfish broth, these are precisely what to use.

1. Save up lobster shells, shrimp heads (if you buy shrimp with the heads on them), or any other shell-fish shells or heads, in the freezer.

2. When you are ready to cook, put the shells in hot oil in a sauté pan and cook until they turn bright red.

3. Transfer to a food processor and grind (don't grind lobster claw shells, which can damage the blade).

4. Gently sweat (see entry 40) chopped onions and carrots in a pot large enough to hold the shells.

5. Add some chopped tomatoes and enough water to barely cover.

6. Simmer for 40 minutes. Strain.

HINT *To better extract the flavor and color, include a cup or two of heavy cream per quart of liquid.*

How to make broth from mussels, clams, and cockles

Unlike crustaceans such as lobster, bivalve shellfish such as mussels, clams, and cockles contain no flavor in their shells. Instead, they release flavorful briny liquid when they are steamed. Virtually any number of bivalves can be put in a pot with a little white wine and minced shallots and steamed until open. Their liquid can serve as a base for sauces and be used in seafood soups and stews.

359 A better way to store stocks

Many cookbooks and other sources recommend storing various meat stocks in ice trays in the freezer for making soups and sauces. The only problem with this method is that you need an enormous amount of freezer space.

1. Simmer down broth to about one fifteenth of its original volume, until it becomes lightly syrupy.

2. Allow this glaze to set in the refrigerator in ice trays—best of all, in ice trays that make miniature ice cubes such as those found in bars—and then snap the cubes out of the trays onto a sheet pan.

3. Spread the cubes out on the sheet pan so none are touching each other; freeze them.

4. When solidly frozen, store the cubes in resealable plastic bags in the freezer. One or two miniature cubes are enough to make sauce for 2 to 4 servings.

360 For an elegant fat-free soup

Not many of us make consommé anymore, in part because we've been fed the canned version and think making it from scratch isn't worth the effort. But if you want an elegant, nutritious, and fat-free dish that's surprisingly filling and satisfying, try clarifying a broth into consommé.

HINT *To make instant broth to use as the base for your consommé, dissolve commercial meat glaze—about 1 tablespoon per cup of soup—in water and then proceed as follows.*

1. Start with broth that is very clear to begin with, ideally refrigerated overnight so you can remove any trace of fat congealed on top.

2. Separate 3 eggs per quart of broth and save the yolks for custards, hollandaise, or sabayon sauces.

3. In a pot large enough to hold the broth, crush together the eggshells and the whites in your hands (your hands must be perfectly clean and free of grease) with 1 finely sliced leek (including the green) and a bunch of parsley and/or tarragon.

4. Add the cold broth to the egg white mixture and stir vigorously to incorporate the whites. Bring the broth to a gentle simmer and

then move the pot to one side of the heat source so the broth boils on only one side.

5. Move the pot around every few minutes so it boils on a different side each time.

6. When the broth is crystal clear except for a few specks of egg white—after about 30 minutes—gently ladle it into a strainer lined with a wet kitchen towel (first rinse the towel thoroughly to get rid of any residual soap). As the cloth gets clogged, tug on it from one side so another part of the towel covers the strainer.

7. Discard the solids. The soup will keep in the refrigerator for up to 5 days.

361   Improving vegetable soups

A basic vegetable soup such as minestrone can be as simple as tossing a collection of diced vegetables into a pot of water and simmering them until soft. If the vegetables are fresh from the garden, this is, in fact, the best treatment. The only refinement would be to add green vegetables near the end of cooking, because they cook faster than root vegetables. But since most of us don't have access to superb fresh produce on a daily basis, here are some ideas for improving a basic vegetable soup.

• **Broth:** Use brown chicken broth (see entry 351) instead of water.

• **Sweated vegetables:** Sweat the diced root vegetables (see entry 40) in some kind of tasty fat such as the fat rendered from pancetta or the outside of prosciutto.

• **Meat:** If you're sweating aromatic vegetables (see entry 16) as the first step in making the soup, include diced bacon, pancetta, or pieces of pork. If you're very fortunate and have some duck confit hiding somewhere, pull off the meat and add it to the soup.

• **Starches:** Add starchy ingredients such as fresh beans, rice, or pasta to the soup according to their cooking times. Dried beans need to be precooked in water or broth. A pressure cooker is handy for cooking dried beans, which otherwise can take well over an hour to soften.

- **Butter:** Most mixed vegetable soups benefit from a little butter being stirred in just before serving.
- **Cream:** Unless your soup is based on clear broth, a little cream, as little as a tablespoon per serving, will bring out its flavor.
- **Texture:** Give a mixed vegetable soup a little extra body by sticking an immersion blender (see entry 12) in it for a second or two to puree a few of the vegetables but leave the rest chunky.
- **Herbs and garlic:** Some ingredients, if simmered in the soup just before serving, release their flavor and do wonders. Examples of this are chopped basil, garlic puree (see entry 177), herb butters (see entry 102), and pestos (see entry 371) made with different herbs such as mint or cilantro. If the soup is a delicate one, consider whisking in very finely chopped chives, parsley, and chervil, if you can find them. Delicate tomato soups crave fresh tarragon or basil. Consider flavoring robust vegetable soups with marjoram, thyme, or oregano (be careful with oregano; its flavor can be overwhelming).
- **Dried chiles:** Dried chiles are an amazing source of complex and subtle flavors. Soak dried chiles in water to reconstitute them, then simmer them with a little cream, puree them, and add them to the soup.
- **Meat glaze:** Meat glaze (see entry 355) or any concentrated broth will add body to your soup.
- **Roasted garlic puree:** Roasting heads of garlic and working them through a food mill results in a puree that is great whisked into a vegetable soup.
- **Onions:** Sweat (see entry 40) onions until they caramelize; add them to the soup.

HINT *One of the world's great vegetable soups, pistou, is finished with a French-style pesto sauce (also called pistou). Pass the pistou at the table for your guests or family to dollop into their soup. A similar method is used to make fish soups in which the hot soup is whisked with a quarter its amount of aïoli or saffron aïoli and the soup gently heated until thickened. Extra aïoli is passed at the table.*

362 How to make any cream soup with a blender

One of the great things about learning the basics of cooking is that once you learn one thing, you can modify it to make other dishes like it. Cream soups are traditionally made by thickening milk or broth with flour, adding a little cream and chopped vegetables, and pureeing and straining the mixture.

HINT *You can use the leek and potato soup (see entry 363) as a base for any cream soup.*

1. To make 4 to 6 servings of soup, cook 1 finely chopped medium onion or the white parts of 2 leeks in 2 tablespoons butter until soft. Add 2 tablespoons all-purpose flour.

2. Cook over medium heat for 1 minute; add 3 cups milk.

3. Bring the onion-milk mixture to the simmer and add 3 cups coarsely chopped vegetables, such as onions, asparagus (just the stalks; use the tips for garnish), cauliflower, broccoli, carrots, turnips, and fennel, and simmer until the vegetables soften, 5 to 20 minutes.

4. Add as much or as little cream as you like—½ cup is usually just about right. Bring it all back to the simmer.

5. Transfer to a blender and puree. Add salt and freshly ground black pepper to taste. Serve as is. Or, to thin the soup and eliminate chunks, work it through a coarse strainer, and then again through a fine strainer, if you wish.

363 What is vichyssoise anyway?

Vichyssoise is a leek and potato soup that is pureed, thickened with cream, and served cold (although it is equally good served hot). Vichyssoise has come to mean virtually any cold cream soup that contains potato and another vegetable or vegetables. Making vichyssoise is almost as easy as opening a can.

How to make a basic leek and potato soup

1. To make about 4 to 6 servings of vichyssoise, peel and slice 2 large Yukon gold or Idaho potatoes and combine them with the sliced whites of 4 leeks and a quart of milk in a medium saucepan over medium heat.

2. Bring to the simmer and cook until the leeks and potatoes are soft, about 15 minutes.

3. With an immersion blender or a regular blender, puree the mixture and season to taste with salt and pepper.

4. Add ½ cup to 1 cup heavy cream and blend to make a warm cream soup. Strained and served cold, you have vichyssoise. Served warm and chunky, it is the French peasant soup called *potage bonne femme.*

364 How to make a quick cream soup

Leek and potato soup (see entry 363) can be converted to any cream of vegetable soup by adding a diced vegetable or vegetables such as asparagus, peas, spinach, or mushrooms to the simmering soup at the right time.

1. Make the basic leek and potato soup and add 2 cups chopped vegetables; when you do this depends on the vegetables you're using and how long they ordinarily take to cook.

2. Simmer the soup until done.

3. Puree with an immersion blender or regular blender and, if you're being meticulous, strain.

365 Are there substitutes for heavy cream?

People often ask if milk or half-and-half can be substituted for cream to make foods, especially soups and sauces, less rich. In most cases, the answer is no. Unless the soup or sauce contains starch—such as flour in a béchamel, or potato in a soup—milk and half-and-half will separate when heated. Also, cream can be boiled down (reduced) to thicken it without its separating, whereas milk or half-and-half will curdle when boiled. For cream to whip, and to boil cream down and thicken it without its curdling or separating, the cream must contain at least 30 percent butterfat (most heavy cream contains around 36 percent) to stabilize it.

366 Improving seafood soups

The simplest fish soups and stews are made by tossing fresh whole fish into a pot of boiling seawater and simmering until done. Because many of us have a hard time grappling with a whole fish in a bowl of soup, it's more convenient (at least for the diner) to fillet the fish, make the broth with the heads and bones, and then add the filleted fish, cut up or not, to the broth for the last few minutes of simmering. Obvious additions to this basic soup are onions, a bouquet garni, white wine, and maybe some potatoes or tomatoes. A dash of cream will turn it into a chowder. See also tips for improving vegetable soups (see entry 361).

• **Shellfish:** Mussels, clams, and cockles release delicious briny liquid when they cook. If you need broth for soup, you'll get much more flavor by steaming a few pounds of mussels in a little white wine and water than you will by making a fish broth (see entry 357).

• **Fish sauce:** If you're making a soup with the flavors of Southeast Asia, try 1 tablespoon or more of Thai or Vietnamese fish sauce, which always gives body to the soup. (Look for it in specialty foods stores or your supermarket.) To determine if a soup needs more fish sauce, judge its saltiness. If it needs salt, add fish sauce instead.

• **Other sauces:** Consider whisking in an aïoli, pesto, or rouille sauce (see entries 369, 370, and 371) just before serving.

• **Spices:** Saffron (see entry 95) is almost always good with seafood. Curry powder cooked in a little butter and whisked into the soup often adds dimension.

• **Fats:** Add cream or coconut milk to the soup and/or finish it with butter or herb butter (see entry 102) just before serving.

367 How to make instant mayonnaise

The secret to instant, foolproof mayonnaise is to use a little jarred mayonnaise to get started. Because the jarred mayonnaise pulls all the ingredients together with powerful emulsifiers, you simply whisk in oil and lemon juice and, if you want the color, a raw egg yolk or two. If the mayonnaise starts to get too thick, which can cause it to separate, add a tablespoon or two of water.

1. Whisk 2 cups vegetable oil or pure olive oil into ½ cup jarred mayonnaise.

2. Add water, lemon juice, or vinegar as needed to keep the mayonnaise from getting too thick.

Do I have to worry about raw egg in sauces?

The latest statistics indicate that one in twenty thousand eggs is infected with salmonella bacteria. If you're using one egg yolk to make mayonnaise for two people, it's probably worth running the risk. If you're using one thousand egg yolks to make mayonnaise for twenty thousand people, then the risk is one in twenty that you're going to make twenty thousand people sick—the risk is too high.

368 Ten instant sauces

You can use your instant mayonnaise (see entry 367) to make an assortment of sauces to use for dips for crudités or to pass at the table to dollop on grilled chicken, meats, or seafood. To serve several different flavors, divide the mayonnaise into the number of sauces you want to make.

• **Mustard:** Add mustard to taste to ¼ cup instant mayonnaise.

• **Herbs:** Add 1 tablespoon of one or more of your favorite chopped herbs to ¼ cup instant mayonnaise.

• **Mushrooms:** Combine 3 tablespoons chopped reconstituted dried mushrooms (see entry 182) with ¼ cup instant mayonnaise.

• **Garlic:** Crush 1 garlic clove into a paste and combine it with ¼ cup instant mayonnaise.

• **Saffron:** Add a pinch of saffron threads, soaked in 1 tablespoon cold water for 30 minutes, to ¼ cup instant mayonnaise—include the soaking liquid.

• **Curry:** Cook 1 tablespoon curry powder in 1 tablespoon vegetable oil over medium heat until it smells fragrant. Add it to ¼ cup instant mayonnaise.

• **Chopped grilled peppers or chiles:** Peel, seed, and chop—chunky or fine, it's up to you—1 bell pepper or poblano chile (see entry 64) and add it to ¼ cup instant mayonnaise.

• **Tomatoes:** Peel, seed, and chop 2 ripe tomatoes and cook them down until thick. Combine with ¼ cup instant mayonnaise.

• **Whipped cream:** Whip ½ cup heavy cream and fold it into ½ cup instant mayonnaise or one recipe of one of the other variations.

- **Pesto:** Add pesto (see entry 371) to taste to about ¼ cup instant mayonnaise.
- **Other possibilities** include chopped capers, chopped pickles, horseradish (great combined with applesauce). If you add more capers or pickles, the sauce will be more like a relish; add less and it will be more like a tartar sauce.

369   How to make aïoli

Make an instant mayonnaise (see entry 367) and, with the side of a knife, crush one garlic clove per cup of mayonnaise. Stir the garlic into the mayonnaise and let the mayonnaise sit for at least an hour for the flavor of the garlic to get into the sauce.

How to use aïoli

Aïoli gets another dimension when threads of saffron—a pinch soaked in 1 tablespoon of water—are added. Many may already know about using aïoli as a dip for crudités or as a sauce to dollop on grilled seafood, meats, and vegetables. However, one of the best ways is to use aïoli in seafood or vegetable soups by whisking the hot soup into about ¼ cup aïoli per cup of soup, just before serving.

370   What is rouille sauce and how do I make it?

Rouille sauce is a pasty spicy garlic sauce often served atop bouillabaisse (see entry 289) or simply spread on bread while eating the soup (or on a slice of crusty bread placed in the bowl before ladling the soup over); it's also whisked into, or spooned over, a variety of fish stews, or ends up in all three at once. Because this version of rouille has egg yolks, remember never to let it get close to the boil.

1. Stem and seed 3 dried ancho chiles (see entry 64) that have been soaked for 30 minutes in warm water.

2. Put them in a food processor or blender with 1 roasted, skinned, seeded, and chopped red bell pepper; 3 crushed garlic cloves; 2 egg yolks; ½ teaspoon saffron threads soaked with 1 tablespoon of water; 2 teaspoons red wine vinegar to taste; and kosher salt and freshly ground black pepper to taste. Include the liquid used to soak the saffron but not the chiles.

3. Turn on the processor or blender and pour in ½ cup pure olive oil in a thin steady stream. If the mixture gets too thick and stops blending, add 2 teaspoons or more water.

4. Transfer the mixture to a mixing bowl and stir in ½ cup extra virgin olive oil in a thin steady stream, until all is absorbed.

371   How to make pesto

Essentially, pesto is a puree of fresh basil leaves. Certainly the pesto from Genoa and the rest of Liguria, where pesto is said to have originated, also contains parmigiano-reggiano, plenty of garlic, olive oil, and pine nuts. Variants (including the French version, pistou) also contain chopped tomatoes. Other versions use walnuts or hazelnuts, and in the south of France, aged Gouda is used on occasion. Purists make pesto by hand, crushing leaf by leaf, in a large and very heavy mortar. The rest of us make pesto in a food processor or blender. The purists are right, pesto is better made by hand; olive oil can become bitter when beaten, and the basil loses a certain floral quality when worked in a machine. But few of us opt for the sacrifice of an afternoon of pounding and crushing and accept slightly less than perfect pesto.

In *either* case, mince the garlic and crush it to a paste with the side of a chef's knife. Toast the nuts and grind them in a food processor. Combine these and any other solid ingredients in the blender or food processor and add the oil in a steady stream with the machine on. To better retain the flavor of the best olive oil, start using pure olive oil and add it just long enough for the mixture to turn freely around and become a smooth puree. Then add extra virgin olive oil, by hand, in a bowl.

How to use pesto

Keep pesto tightly sealed in resealable bags, frozen. No air should be allowed to touch the pesto or it will turn brown. To use the pesto, just break off a chunk as needed, thaw it, and toss it with hot pasta. You can also brush pesto on grilled meats, seafood, and vegetables; toss it with cooked potatoes and serve hot or cold as a potato salad; make a ratatouille or other vegetable "stew" and fold in pesto at the last minute; whisk it into a vegetable soup just before serving; swirl it over the top of servings of seafood soup. Experiment at will.

372 Improvising pestolike sauces

Making pestolike sauces (*pesto* refers to the pestle used in a mortar) seems to be a fundamentally Mediterranean habit. There are dozens of possibilities.

• **Garlic (essential):** Mince and crush to a paste with the side of a chef's knife (see entry 25), even if you're making the sauce in a machine.

- **Egg yolks:** Yolks will make the sauce more spreadable and, used in soup, a bit creamy; they also emulsify the sauce and help carry flavor.
- **Fresh chiles and peppers:** Char peppers or chiles on a gas or electric stove (see entry 186) and remove their peel and seeds. Chop coarsely.
- **Dried chiles:** There is an amazing assortment of chiles from which you can choose to flavor your sauces. Try using different chiles and different combinations (see entry 64). Soak all dried chiles for about 30 minutes in warm water, discard the water, and seed, stem, and chop.
- **Bread:** Stretch the sauce and temper its heat or the intense flavor of garlic by soaking bread in an appropriate broth (such as the fish soup you're serving) or some of the soup or stewing liquid you're serving it with. Work in the bread with the other ingredients.
- **Potatoes:** Cook and peel a potato and work it into the sauce for bulk. Don't use waxy potatoes, which can make the sauce gluey. Ideally, use Yukon golds or yellow Finns; russets will also do in a pinch, although their texture isn't as fine.
- **Nuts:** Toasting nuts in a 350°F oven for about 15 minutes will bring out their flavor. It's a good idea to grind nuts in a food processor separately instead of just grinding them with the rest of the ingredients.
- **Herbs:** Basil is, of course, the best-known herb for pestolike sauces, but cilantro, parsley, and mint can also be used, alone or in combination.
- **Spices:** Cumin is the most popular spice in harissa, but mojos, the Canary Island cousins of moles, also use paprika or smoked paprika (pimentón), nutmeg, and cinnamon. Spices are best toasted before grinding or, if already ground, cooked for a minute in a little oil to release their flavor.
- **Fruit juices:** Boil down fruit juice; for citrus, include a strip of blanched zest (see entry 222) to reinforce its flavor.
- **Vinegar and lemon juice:** Good vinegar and lemon juice will perk up taste by making the sauce slightly more acidic.
- **Oils:** Extra virgin olive oil is the universal oil for pesto sauces, but it's worth adding nut oils—use only those made from roasted nuts (Le Blanc brand, see entry 33)—to bring out the flavor of

the nuts. If you're using extra virgin olive oil and you're using a blender or food processor, use half pure olive oil and half extra virgin. Process the pure oil into the pesto and then, in a mixing bowl by hand, work in the extra virgin oil.

How to make pestolike sauces by hand

Use the largest mortar and pestle you can find and crush the garlic to a paste, then the nuts, then the remaining solid ingredients. Work in the liquids a little at a time.

How to make pestolike sauces using a processor or blender

Combine the garlic, chiles, peppers, egg yolks, ground nuts, herbs, and spices in the machine and add pure olive oil, with the machine on, in a slow steady stream, until it is absorbed. Work in extra virgin oil and starchy ingredients such as bread and potatoes—which can get gummy in the machine—by hand.

373 How to make "green" paste for coloring sauces

Few people besides professional chefs know that it's possible to extract the chlorophyll from spinach and use it to color sauces green.

HINT *Chlorophyll is the natural dye used to color the spinach pasta you enjoy at restaurants and buy from your supermarket. If you are so moved, you can use it to color homemade fresh pasta.*

1. Pack about 10 ounces spinach leaves into a blender and add enough cold water to come halfway up the side of the blender. Puree for 1 minute.

2. Strain the spinach through a triple layer of cheesecloth and discard what doesn't go through.

3. Heat what does go through in a saucepan over low to medium heat. As soon as you see the mixture coagulate into little green clumps, strain it through cheesecloth or a fine mesh strainer.

4. What doesn't go through is the chlorophyll. It will keep in the refrigerator for a week, covered with a little olive oil.

374 How to make a basic tomato sauce

Sometimes we're stuck for a dinner idea or something to serve to unexpected guests. This quickly made tomato sauce is your answer. You can use this method to make as little or as much as you like.

1. Cook chopped onions, garlic, and carrots in pure olive oil until soft.

2. Add chopped tomatoes. Cook, covered, until soft.

3. Work the mixture through a food mill or strainer.

4. Cook down the mixture to the consistency you like.

A roasted tomato sauce

More time-consuming, but easier in its way, is to cut tomatoes in two through the equator, squeeze out the seeds, and place them flat side up in a 400°F oven until any liquid they release evaporates. Then add them to the softened aromatic vegetables in step 1 and work the mixture through a food mill for a delicious sauce. You can even use this technique for cherry tomatoes, which have more flavor, if regular tomatoes are out of season.

375 How to make ragu sauces

A ragu is a sauce with chopped or shredded meat in it. Ragus can be based on cooked-down tomatoes—in fact, what most Italians call a tomato sauce is actually also a ragu—or liquids such as wine or broth. Most ragu-style sauces are made by cooking ground meat together with aromatic vegetables (see entry 16), adding tomatoes and/or wine, and simmering. A different way, which produces a far more flavorful sauce and can be used with virtually any meat, such as duck, game, rabbit, hare, veal, or beef, is to make a stew (see entry 329), reduce the stewing liquid if necessary to make it lightly syrupy, and then shred the meat and put it back in the braising liquid. If you want your ragu sauce to be tomato based, use chopped, peeled, and seeded ripe tomatoes as part of the liquid for the stew.

376 Should I use prepackaged sauces?

In general it's best to avoid premade sauces, but certain sauce bases such as store-bought meat glazes (called *glace de viande*) and demi-glace, such as those made by More Than Gourmet, can be used to add body and flavor to your sauce. Once you have these glazes—essentially boiled-down broth—in hand, it's easy to make your own sauces. To freshen up the glazes, cook chopped onions and carrots in butter with a few sprigs of thyme and a bay leaf, add some of the packaged glaze, stir it around and caramelize it a little, and then add water. Simmer to redissolve the glaze, strain it, and simmer it back down to a glaze.

377 How to make a quick, silky butter sauce

If you've braised a fish or sautéed chicken, for instance, and you have deglazed the pan (see entry 36), simmer down the liquid to about 1½ tablespoons per serving and whisk in about ½ tablespoon butter per serving to make an emulsified butter sauce.

378 How to make a rich sauce with less butter and cream

There's no reason that we can't do at home what others do in the best restaurants. The secret to modern sauce making is to abandon the idea that the sauce has to be thick enough to cover, or mask, the food it's being served with. Now, many meat and seafood dishes are presented in soup plates that allow the sauce to be completely liquid and to surround the food instead of coating it. This means that cream and butter are needed only to enhance flavor and texture, not produce dramatic thickening.

Add 1 tablespoon butter or 2 tablespoons cream to ¼ cup flavorful liquid, such as the braising or steaming liquid, or to the wine and glaze in a deglazed sauté pan, or to a base made by caramelizing carrots and onions with a little prosciutto (as for meurette sauce; see entry 380).

If a sauce is light and very liquid, count on 4 tablespoons per serving. If the sauce is thick and rich, 3, or even 2, tablespoons are enough.

379 How to make red wine sauce

The secret to cooking with wine, especially red wine, is to cook the wine with broth, meat, or bones before reducing it for a sauce. The protein contained in these ingredients combines with the tannin in the wine and takes out some of its harshness. Avoid acidic or very tannic red wines and use wines that might otherwise be called "flabby," or too soft. When cooking with white wine, use very dry wine such as Muscadet or dry sauvignon blanc.

1. Combine 1 tablespoon glaze or 2 tablespoons demi-glace with 1 cup red wine. (If you don't have glaze, combine 1 cup red wine and 3 cups chicken or other meat broth.)

2. Simmer down the mixture until it's lightly syrupy, to about ¼ cup.

3. Whisk in 2 to 4 tablespoons of cold butter.

HINT *Demi-glace is broth that's been boiled down to a tenth its original volume and then thickened with flour. Meat glaze, called* glace de viande, *is broth boiled down to, at most, a fifteenth its original volume.*

380 How to make deeply flavored sauces

Many of us have heard of bordelaise sauce, a red wine sauce made with concentrated veal stock (see entry 352). To make a homespun version when you're out of broth or meat glaze, make a meurette sauce instead. In addition to red wine, it is traditional to use bacon, or preferably prosciutto, along with some vegetables and herbs. Prosciutto works best for this sauce, but buy the end pieces, which are far cheaper than the regular slices (and sometimes free).

HINT *Meurette sauce is best known for eggs en meurette, in which poached eggs are covered with the sauce. It is also traditionally accompanied by fried croutons.*

1. To make 1 cup of sauce, chop or dice about ¼ pound prosciutto.

2. In a large saucepan over medium heat, combine the meat with chopped carrot, onion, garlic, and celery. Add thyme, a bay leaf, and about 2 tablespoons butter.

3. Stir every couple of minutes for about 12 minutes, until the vegetables are browned and smell toasty.

4. Add 1 cup wine and boil it down until it completely evaporates.

5. Add 2 cups wine and simmer very gently for about 20 minutes.

6. Strain the mixture into a clean saucepan, bring to the simmer, and skim off any fat that floats to the top.

7. Make a smooth paste with about 2 tablespoons butter and 1 tablespoon flour (this mixture is called a beurre manié) and whisk it into the sauce with cognac, vinegar, salt and freshly ground black pepper to taste, and chopped parsley.

8. Warm the sauce and adjust the seasonings.

381 How to make simple sauces from meat trimmings

A classic meat sauce is usually based on boiled-down broth that is flavored with a vast repertoire of ingredients to give it its character. But meat sauces made in this professional way often lack the directness of sauces simply made at home with a few meat trimmings, an onion, and a carrot.

1. Brown the meat trimmings with a little onion and carrot, some thyme if you have it, and add enough broth to come about a third of the way up their sides.

2. Boil down the broth until it completely evaporates and caramelizes on the bottom of the pan.

3. Add more broth if you have it, water if you don't, and caramelize again. If your sauce contains wine, add it at one point, boil it down until it evaporates, and deglaze again with water, broth, or more wine.

4. Repeat this deglazing process as many times as you like; each caramelization will intensify the flavor of the sauce.

5. When deglazing for the final time, add a little more liquid to the pan than you need sauce, and simmer it with the meat and vegetables for about 5 minutes before straining.

382   The secret to the world's best seafood sauces

You can make the same sauces served in great French restaurants by using the steaming liquid from mussels, clams, or cockles (most cockles sold in American fish markets are from New Zealand and look like miniature clams, but they are more striated and tinted with green) as the base. A small amount of cream boiled a minute or two with the steaming liquid, and a few teaspoons of chopped fresh herbs and a few tablespoons of butter whisked in at the end, make a perfect finish. Spices such as saffron or curry, cooked a minute in a little butter, are also classic and delicious additions. You can also use the shellfish cooking liquid to braise fish and then convert it to a sauce for serving with the fish (see entry 358).

383 How to make a legendary seafood sauce

In the early twentieth century, Diamond Jim Brady took his son out of Harvard and sent him to Paris to work in a restaurant named Marguery. After two years of grunt work, the chef finally revealed to the bedraggled son the secret of Marguery sauce.

1. Braise a whole fish with mussel steaming liquid (see entry 240), or fish broth or wine and water (see entry 280).

2. Remove the fish and boil down the liquid by half.

3. Combine 1 egg yolk per ¼ cup braising liquid—whisk the liquid into the yolks, not the other way around—in a saucepan with sloping sides (see entry 30) or in a metal bowl set over a small pot of simmering water. Whisk rapidly until the mixture fluffs up and then loses a little of its fluff and stiffens.

4. Whisk in 2 tablespoons clarified butter (see entry 32) per egg yolk. For a more modern version, use half the butter or even less. Spoon the sauce over the braised fish.

384 How to make foolproof hollandaise sauce

Like mayonnaise, hollandaise sauce is an emulsion, but instead of being an emulsion of oil and egg yolk, it's made with butter. The secret to success is to use a little jarred mayonnaise as the emulsifier. If you want your sauce thin, use melted butter; for a thick sauce, use clarified butter (see entry 32). Make sure the butter is not too hot when you add it to the egg yolks or it will curdle them; the pan of butter should feel like a bracingly hot bath, but not one that would burn you.

HINT *There are many delicious sauces that are derivatives of basic hollandaise. To make béarnaise sauce, replace the lemon juice with vinegar and add minced shallots and fresh tarragon. To make a maltaise sauce, the perfect sauce for asparagus, use orange juice instead of lemon juice and a little grated orange zest. Add cooked-down strained tomatoes for a delicate tomato sauce that's delicious on fish.*

1. In a saucepan with sloping sides or a stainless steel bowl set over a pan of barely simmering water, whisk together 2 egg yolks, 1 tablespoon jarred mayonnaise, 2 tablespoons water, and 1 tablespoon lemon juice.

2. Whisk until the mixture fluffs up and stiffens slightly. Don't let it get too hot or it will curdle.

3. Whisk in 2 sticks melted or clarified unsalted butter in a steady stream.

Accomplished cooks can be stumped when it comes to making pies: The dough is too dry and it cracks, or it's too wet and it sticks,

Pies and Tarts

or it tears when you move it from work surface to pie dish. The fact is, you can do almost anything to your dough without its getting tough as long as you keep it cold. Get in the habit of moving it in and out of the refrigerator and you can bring it back together if it cracks, roll it with flour if it's too wet, or even work it with more liquid in a food processor if it's too dry.

385 How to find a good store-bought pie crust

Before you buy pie crust, check the ingredients and make sure that butter is near the top. But hydrogenated anythings are no-no's. If the package says "cholesterol free," avoid it. It will contain no butter.

386 How to make a pie dough

Basic pie and tart dough can be made by hand, with a stand-up mixer, or in a food processor, each with similar results. Keep in mind that you can make the dough sweet for dessert fillings or leave the sugar out for savory fillings.

To make pie dough by hand

1. Cut the butter lengthwise into ⅛-inch-thick slices, turn the slices on their side in a stack, slice lengthwise again, and then cut crosswise so you have perfect ⅛-inch cubes. Refrigerate if the butter has softened.

2. Combine the cold butter with the flour (include the sugar, if using) in a pile on the work surface.

3. Make a well in the middle of the pile with your fingertips and pour in the cold liquid (or eggs). Swirl them around, eroding the flour from inside the well.

4. When all the liquid has been absorbed—the dough becomes lumpy, with no loose flour—bring the dough together in front of you and, with the heel of your hand, smear it away from you, about a fifth at a time, and then bring it together.

5. Use immediately unless the dough gets warm; if so, chill it for 15 minutes.

To make pie dough in the food processor

1. To make one 10-inch pie or tart, combine 1 cup cake flour, 1 cup all-purpose flour, and ½ teaspoon salt in the food processor. (Add ½ cup sugar if making sweetened pie dough.) Process for 15 seconds.

2. Add 1½ sticks cold butter, cut into ⅓-inch cubes or slices, and about 7 tablespoons cold water or heavy cream (or 2 lightly beaten eggs). Process for 30 seconds. If the dough still looks powdery, pinch a piece. If it falls apart in your fingers, add 2 tablespoons more liquid (or 1 egg white). If it holds together, the dough has enough liquid.

3. Feel the dough with the back of a finger. If at any point it no longer feels cold, put the bowl in the refrigerator for 15 minutes.

pies and tarts

Process until the dough clumps together or clings to the sides of the food processor, 10 to 30 seconds more. If you're not using the dough right away, flatten it, wrap it in plastic, and refrigerate.

To make pie dough in a stand-up mixer

1. Mix together the dry ingredients (including the sugar, if using) on slow speed with the paddle blade for about 30 seconds.

2. Add the cold butter and combine on low to medium speed for about 1 minute.

3. Add the cold liquid or eggs and work the dough on low to medium speed for from 40 seconds to 2 minutes—the time depends on the temperature of the ingredients—until it looks like gravel. If after 2 minutes it's still powdery and looks like grated cheese, pinch a piece of the dough to see if it comes together. If it falls apart, add 2 tablespoons more liquid or 1 egg white. If it holds together in a clump, the dough has enough liquid, so continue mixing.

4. If at any point the dough no longer feels cold, put the mixer bowl in the refrigerator or freezer for 15 minutes. Work the dough on low to medium speed (not too fast or the flour will fly around) for 1 to 4 minutes, until it clumps together into a cohesive mass— you'll hear the motor straining. If you're not using the dough right away, flatten it, wrap it in plastic, and refrigerate.

5. Use the dough immediately unless it gets warm; if so, chill it for 15 minutes.

387 How can I be sure my dough will turn out right?

Cookbooks rattle off mistakes we can make with pie dough. The fact is, we can get by with a lot of little mistakes as long as we keep in mind one thing: Don't let the dough get warm. As long as it's kept cold, it can be too wet, too dry, and you can even overwork it and it will stay light and crumbly. If it's hot in the kitchen, move the dough in and out of the refrigerator.

HINT *Although most recipes direct you to let the dough rest before rolling, it's easier to roll as soon as it's made. Chilling it only makes it hard to roll. Chill the dough only if it is threatening to melt.*

388 How to make pie dough flaky

The best-tasting pie dough is made with butter, not shortening or lard. But butter makes crumbly dough, not flaky dough. There is a way, however, to bake butter-based pie dough flaky.

1. Make the dough by hand and leave the butter in relatively large chunks, about ⅓-inch cubes.

2. Chill the dough for 15 minutes and roll it out into a rectangle about 2 feet long.

3. Fold the two ends of the rectangle so they meet in the center and then fold one half of the dough over the other so you have a packet with four layers.

4. Hammer the packet with a rolling pin to flatten it somewhat and roll it into another rectangle. If it starts to become elastic and difficult to roll, don't force it.

5. Let it rest in the refrigerator for an hour and then roll it. Fold the rectangle as before, let the dough rest, and use it for pies and tarts. The crust will be very flaky.

389 How to roll out pie dough

Unless the temperature is very hot and the dough is threatening to get warm, it's best to roll it out right away (despite what most recipes suggest).

If you've refrigerated the dough and it's cold and hard, hammer it with a rolling pin to shape it into a disk about 8 inches across.

1. When the dough is soft enough to roll, position the pin one third of the way into the disk, then press and roll away from you, rolling the dough out a few inches. Give the dough a quarter turn and repeat.

2. Continue in this way until the dough is the size you want it.

To keep dough from sticking to the board and pin

The most common mistake made by both professionals and home cooks when rolling out dough is to change the direction of the rolling pin rather than changing the position of the dough. However, by keeping the rolling pin parallel to the work surface and moving the dough—not the pin—as needed, you'll keep the dough from sticking to the surface. Give the dough a quarter turn every few seconds while rolling, and continually flour the work surface by tossing a large pinch from a foot or two away from the work surface so the flour forms a cloud, lightly dusting the surface without clumping. When you move the dough around over the dusted surface, it is constantly floured from beneath, preventing sticking and tearing.

390 How to transfer rolled-out dough to a pie pan without tearing it

One of the most frustrating moments in the kitchen is when the beautifully rolled-out dough falls apart as you roll it up onto the pin to transfer it to the pie pan or ring. To avoid this, make sure the dough is cold. There are two ways to transfer dough from the work surface to the pie or tart pan:

• Fold the rolled-out dough in half or in quarters and put it in the pie pan with the fold in the middle. Unfold it.

• Roll up the dough on the pin and unroll it over the pie pan.

If the dough is falling apart and impossible to roll or fold, slide it in the freezer, and when it freezes into a hard disk, lift the disk and set it over the pie pan. When it softens, in 10 minutes or so, press it in place.

391 How to line a pie pan

First make sure the dough is cold, then transfer it to the pan (see page 390). If the dough is threatening to get warm, put it in the fridge for 15 minutes before continuing.

1. Unroll the dough over the pie pan and press it into the pan.

2. Cut around the edge of the pan with scissors, leaving an inch of dough all around.

3. Fold this excess dough under itself so you have a double thickness of dough, about ½ inch long, sticking vertically up above the rim.

4. Hold your thumb and forefinger against the inside of this extra dough and with the forefinger of your other hand, press the dough in between the thumb and forefinger of the first hand, making a crimp.

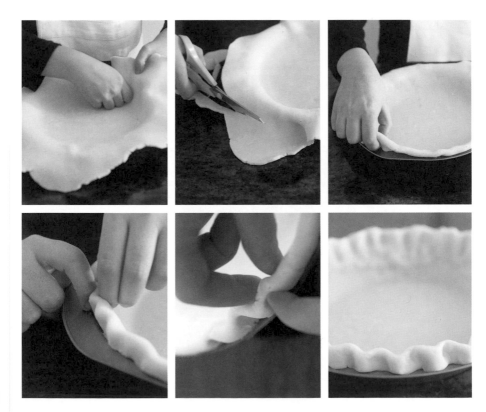

392 How to line a tart mold

Lining a tart mold is much like lining a pie pan, except that you want to form a decorative border that's higher than the rim of the tart pan.

1. Transfer the rolled-out dough to the tart pan.

2. Working around the inside of the pan, press the dough into the corners.

3. Press a small amount of the overlap down and inward to create a small lip of dough on the inside edge of the pan.

4. Press the dough against the edge to detach it and press the lip

inward. Roll this lip over the top of the tart pan to detach the excess dough and pull it away.

5. Build up borders by pressing together the lip of dough so it rises above the edge of the pan.

393   How to line tartlet rings

Bakers argue about the best way of rolling out small rounds of dough for lining tartlet molds. One choice is to roll the dough out into a large sheet and cut out rings; the other choice is the one we think is easiest.

1. Roll the dough into a sausage shape about 2 inches in diameter.

2. Slice off rounds about 1 to 1½ inches long—you'll refine the length as you work—and pound these with a rolling pin to flatten them.

3. Roll the rounds into round sheets at least 1 inch wider than the tart shell.

4. Place the dough on top of the ring and press it into the edges.

5. Push the dough that hangs outside the ring inward to form a small lip of dough inside.

6. Press the dough against the edge of the ring where you want it to cut off. Roll over the ring with the rolling pin to detach excess dough. Pinch all around the tartlet to reinforce the walls.

7. Run a knife around the edge, between the dough and the ring.

394 What to do if your dough cracks

As long as the dough isn't warm, you can bring cracked dough all together into a mound and roll it out again. Or, you can patch it by pressing pieces of dough over the cracks.

395 How to prevent soggy pie crust

If you're making a pie with a wet filling and you are prebaking the shell, it's a good idea to brush it with a thin paste of beaten egg and flour before baking. This will keep the crust from becoming soggy. Bake the crust in a moderate oven for 5 minutes to create a seal between the crust and the fruit.

396 How to make a graham cracker crust

For enough crumbs to line the bottom of a 9-inch pie or cheesecake, put 8 crackers and ½ cup melted butter in a food processor and process until smooth. Press the mixture into the bottom of a spring-form pan.

How to make a chocolate wafer crust

For enough crumbs to line the bottom of a 9-inch pie or cheesecake, put 18 chocolate wafers, sugar to taste, and about ⅓ cup melted butter in a food processor and puree until smooth. Press the mixture into the bottom of a springform pan.

397 How to make a crispy apple galette with puff pastry

One of the best possible apple desserts is this delicate tart, called a galette, made by baking thinly sliced apples on a very thin layer of puff pastry.

1. Roll a sheet of puff pastry into a rectangle ⅛ to ¹⁄₁₆ inch thick and transfer it to a sheet pan sprinkled with cold water.

2. Cover the pastry with rows of overlapping thinly sliced apples.

3. Sprinkle liberally with sugar and dot liberally with pats of butter.

4. Bake in a hot oven until crispy. If the tart puffs at some point, pop the puff with the tip of a knife.

398 Using bought puff pastry

When you are in your supermarket or grocery, check the package of puff pastry to make sure the pastry is made with butter and not margarine or some hydrogenated product. Before using, thaw it out in the refrigerator so it thaws evenly. If it comes in a very thick and hard piece, hammer it with the rolling pin before rolling it out.

399 A trick for easier puff pastry

All recipes for puff pastry emphasize the importance of not working the dough before the butter is added, in order not to toughen the dough. A better method is to replace one quarter of the water called for in the initial dough mixture with vegetable oil, and then knead the mixture for a minute in a food processor and a minute more by hand before letting it rest overnight. After it has rested, use it in the usual way.

1. Using the heel of your hand, work the butter until it is smooth and spreads evenly.

2. Roll out the dough into a long rectangle and spread the butter over half. Fold over the dough and pinch around the edges to seal in the butter. Roll out again to the same size it was before. Fold the dough in thirds like a letter.

3. Turn 90 degrees so the folds are facing you; roll again into a rectangle.

4. Repeat this 7 times, allowing the dough to rest in the refrigerator the instant it starts to resist being rolled and feels elastic.

To keep puff pastry from burning on the bottom

Because it's baked at such a high temperature, puff pastry can burn on the bottom. To avoid this, sprinkle the sheet pan with cold water before putting on the pastry dough.

How to bake puff pastry into thin sheets

Roll a thin sheet of pastry onto a parchment-lined sheet pan and poke with a fork. Cover the pastry with a sheet of parchment paper and place another sheet pan on top of it. Bake in a medium oven.

400 How to use phyllo dough

Buy these thin sheets of dough in your supermarket or grocery frozen foods section. You can use them to wrap pieces of fish or meat or line tart shells with several layers. The trick to using phyllo is to keep the sheets moist. When you've thawed out the dough, unroll it and keep the dough covered with a moist towel. Brush each sheet with melted butter as you add sheets. Three or four sheets of thickness is enough for wrapping most foods.

401 How to prebake a crust

Delicate custardlike mixtures, such as quiche fillings, need to be baked at low temperatures—temperatures too low to properly cook the pastry shell. Because of this, the shell must be baked in advance.

If you line a pie pan or tart pan with pastry and bake it, the pastry will puff up and leave no room for filling. To prevent this, you need to fill the empty shell with something to hold down the pastry.

1. Put a sheet of parchment paper over the tart or pie shell and fill it with beans or rice. Make sure the paper is larger than the shell so you have something to hold on to when you remove it.

2. Bake in a 425°F oven until the rim of the shell just begins to brown.

3. Take out the beans and continue baking until the bottom of the dough loses its sheen.

402 Using raw fruits in pies or tarts

One of the easiest approaches to making fruit tarts is simply to arrange raw fruits—berries are especially suited to this—in a prebaked shell (see entry 401). A nice touch is to spread a thin layer of lemon curd (see entry 404), crème anglaise (see entry 465), mousse, or stabilized whipped cream (see entry 420) in the shell before adding the fruit.

403 Using cooked fruits in pies or tarts

Some fruits such as pears and apricots can be roasted with sugar and butter and then arranged in a prebaked pie or tart shell. If the fruits are being baked in the tart shell, the shell should be lined with some mixture such as frangipane—a mixture of ground almonds, butter, sugar, and eggs—which will absorb the liquid released by the fruit.

404 How to make a tangy lemon curd

Anyone who has had lemon meringue pie will have enjoyed a form, albeit usually not the best one, of lemon curd. The lemon curd in most lemon meringue pies has been thickened with cornstarch, which is a definite no-no. When properly made, lemon curd is thick but not actually set, with a distinctly tangy taste. If you want the curd to be firmer or richer, add some butter to it while it's still hot.

1. Whisk together 6 egg yolks, ⅔ cup fresh lemon juice, and 1 cup sugar in a stainless steel bowl set over a pan of simmering water or in a saucepan with sloping sides. Whisk until the mixture thickens.

2. Transfer to a bowl and cover with plastic wrap touching its surface so a skin doesn't form on top. (Before covering, however, stir in butter, if using.)

3. Lemon curd can be lightened with whipped cream or fluffy frosting and used in a thin layer in cakes, in prebaked tart shells (it can then be covered with slices or wedges of fruit or berries), or in tartlets.

HINT *To make curds with other fruits, replace half the lemon juice with fruit puree. If you're using a very sour fruit puree such as passion fruit, you can replace all the lemon with puree. For other citrus flavors such as lime or grapefruit, grate in the corresponding zest and, if you like, add a little of the reduced juice. If you want a stiffer curd, add a half or whole stick of butter to the hot curd.*

405 Giving tarts "professional" sheen

Professional bakers often brush fruit desserts with *abricotage,* made from apricot preserves, to give the finished dessert a sheen. If you are glazing a hot pie or tart, brush it with the glaze as soon as it comes out of the oven.

1. Heat apricot preserves with half as much water until dissolved. Strain the mixture.

2. Brush on or over raw fruit tarts.

406 How to keep the edges of a pie or tart from browning

If the edges of the pie crust start to get too brown, especially if the shell was prebaked, cover the edges with aluminum foil.

1. Take a sheet of aluminum foil a few inches wider and longer than the pie or tart shell and fold it in half, then in quarters. Fold again as you would a paper airplane. Place the tip over the center of the tart.

2. Cut the foil with scissors an inch or so inside the outside rim of the tart. Unfold this outer section, which will form a ring you can place over the rim of the tart or pie.

407 How to make a single-crusted pie

A single-crusted pie, uncovered, is a nice way to show off in-season fruit, especially berries.

1. Line the pie pan (see entry 391) and crimp the edges with the thumb and forefinger of one hand and a finger from the other.

2. Brush the edges with a little beaten egg.

3. Cook your favorite fruit and add cornstarch dissolved in an equal amount of water, a teaspoon at a time, to the boiling fruit until it has the desired thickness.

4. Let the fruit cool before you pour it into the shell.

5. Bake at 375°F until the edges are nicely browned.

408   How to make a covered pie

The secret to a covered fruit pie—one with a double crust—is to pre-cook the filling and, if necessary, thicken it before using it to fill the pie. The exception is apples.

1. Roll out 2 sheets of dough, each a few inches wider than the pie pan.

2. Line the pan with 1 sheet of dough (see entry 391), add the filling, and put the second sheet on top.

3. Pinch together the edges and roll them up to form a rim.

4. Make six 2-inch slashes in the top sheet of the pie to allow steam to escape. Brush with beaten egg and sprinkle with sugar before baking.

409 How to make miniature tartlets

Miniature tartlet shells are great for all sorts of savory hors d'oeuvres or sweet petit fours. The only drawback is the initial investment in the molds, which are expensive. (They are available at gourmet and kitchenware stores.) The more you have, however, the more quickly you can produce these useful little shells.

1. Arrange buttered molds as close together as possible and, using a rolling pin, roll out a thin sheet of pastry.

2. Push the pastry into the molds with a little ball of pastry or with your fingers. Press on the edges to cut the pastry away from the molds.

3. Place a second set of molds on top of the first to hold the pastry in place while they bake. Bake until pale brown around the edges, remove the top molds, and bake until golden brown.

410 How to make my favorite cookie

Russian tea cookies are so delicate they seem to turn instantly to dust the moment they touch your tongue, filling your mouth with the flavor of butter and toasted pecans. This recipe is foolproof as long as the dough is kept cold at all times. When you toast and grind the pecans, chill the mixture in the freezer before combining it with the other ingredients.

1. Toast ¾ cup pecan halves in the oven until toasty smelling, about 15 minutes. Let cool and grind for 5 minutes in a food processor. Stick the workbowl, with the ground nuts, in the freezer for 15 minutes.

2. Reattach the workbowl to the base. Add ⅓ cup sugar, ½ teaspoon salt, 1 teaspoon vanilla extract, and 1 cup all-purpose flour to the nuts and process until well combined. If necessary, scrape down the ground pecans from the sides of the bowl with a rubber spatula.

3. Put the workbowl with the mixture back in the freezer for 15 minutes.

4. Preheat the oven to 325°F.

5. Cut 1¼ sticks unsalted butter into fine slices and put them in the food processor. Process until the mixture comes together into a ragged mass. Chill the mixture for 15 minutes in the refrigerator.

6. Roll the dough into 1-inch balls and arrange them on a baking

sheet. Bake until barely browned, about 25 minutes. Let cool
5 minutes and take off the baking sheet. Just before serving,
sprinkle generously with confectioners' sugar.

411 How to make biscuits

Biscuit dough replicates pie dough, but it contains baking powder
and often contains milk.

HINT *You can add a couple of tablespoons of chopped herbs
or ¼ cup grated parmigiano-reggiano or crumbled Roquefort
cheese to flavor the dough.*

1. Preheat the oven to 450°F.

2. To make about 24 biscuits, combine 1¾ cups all purpose flour with
   ½ teaspoon kosher salt and 1 tablespoon baking powder. Use a pastry cutter to chop in 6 tablespoons sliced cold butter.

3. Pour in ¾ cup milk and knead just long enough to get the dough
   to hold together. Then roll out the dough to about ⅓ inch thick
   and use a cookie cutter to cut out 1½-inch rounds.

4. Bake on baking sheets until lightly browned, about 15 minutes.

To make drop biscuits

Use 1 extra cup milk in the dough above, turning it into a batter. Use
a spoon to drop the batter onto a buttered sheet pan. Bake as above.

We're better bakers when we understand the similarities between cakes and their batters. For example, pancakes and waffles are much like

Cakes, Batters, and Custards

cakes except in how we cook them; popovers use the same batter as crepes; a cheesecake is really a custard. Beginning bakers are often surprised to discover how similar making a cake from scratch is to using a mix—sometimes just a matter of adding baking powder and salt to the flour. But if you bake from scratch, you have control over the quality of your ingredients.

412 How do I measure dry ingredients?

The best way to measure dry ingredients, especially flour, is to use a pastry scale. They have become so inexpensive and easy to use—they're all digital—that no one should hesitate to convert to the European habit of weighing ingredients for baking instead of measuring with spoons and cups. Most ingredients have consistent weights for a given volume, but if you are baking and want to weigh only one ingredient, weigh flour. Once you get used to the scale, you can dispense with all those little spoons and cups. If you prefer to use volume measurements, or if your recipe doesn't provide weights, there are two ways to go about measuring dry ingredients.

HINT *The weight of flour per given volume varies depending on how firmly packed it is and the moisture in the room.*

1. The easiest way to measure dry ingredients such as flour is to scoop into the flour with a measuring cup and level off the top by sliding the back of a knife or flat spatula over it.

2. Some recipes ask that you sift the flour first, before measuring. In this case, sift the flour, put it into the measuring cup, and level off the top. This method will give you a somewhat different amount from the first method.

413 What kind of flour should I use for cakes?

Cake flour, which has a very low protein content, is ideal for making cakes because it doesn't stiffen and thicken a mixture in a way that could make a cake dense. If you can't find cake flour, use an all-purpose flour, preferably one from the South, where flours are made softer, and one that has a low protein content, which should be marked on the package. You can also substitute all-purpose flour and use about 10 percent less than you would cake flour in the angel food cake (see entry 428) or the pound cake (see entry 426).

414 How to sift without a sifter

Some recipes say to sift ingredients because they want you to measure flour after it's been sifted, in which case you have no choice but to sift, unless the recipe also gives weights and you have a pastry scale. Sometimes sifting is called for just to combine dry ingredients such as baking powder and flour; in that case, simply stir together the ingredients in a bowl with a whisk. For sponge cakes (see entry 427), sifting is essential because the flour must be very finely broken up when it's combined with beaten eggs. You don't need a special sifter for dry ingredients; just work them through a strainer (see entry 13) with your fingers or the back of a spoon.

415 Which chocolate is which?

Chocolate comes in many forms; some kinds are best for baking, others for eating or drinking. Most chocolate comes in bars and has varying amounts of cocoa liquor, the dark flavorful component of chocolate.

Bittersweet and semisweet

These terms don't have any precise or legal meaning, but at least they imply that the chocolate contains a limited amount of sugar combined with cocoa liquor (the bitter, dark, flavorful component in chocolate) and cocoa butter (the buttery, smooth, melting but less flavorful component). Even though many American recipes call for bitter chocolate, the quality of bittersweet chocolate is usually better than that of bitter chocolate so it's better to substitute a good brand of bittersweet chocolate and cut back on some of the sugar.

Bitter

Essentially only chocolate liquor and a relatively small amount of cocoa butter, and perhaps a small amount of flavoring, bitter chocolate, as its name implies, has no sugar. Since the quality of bittersweet chocolate, which contains sugar, is generally better than most bitter chocolate, it's useful to know how to substitute it in recipes calling for bitter chocolate. Replace every ounce of bitter chocolate in the recipe with 2 ounces bittersweet chocolate and take out 2 tablespoons sugar for every 2 ounces bittersweet chocolate you use. You'll also need to take some of the butter out of the recipe to make up for the cocoa butter contained in the bittersweet chocolate—about 1 teaspoon butter per 2 ounces of bittersweet chocolate.

Milk chocolate

The exact ingredients of milk chocolate depend on the brand, but essentially milk solids and sometimes butter are added to bittersweet chocolate to make it lighter and less bitter.

White chocolate

Despite its name, white "chocolate" has little relationship to chocolate at all, since it's made with milk solids instead of dry cocoa solids, flavorings, and some kind of hydrogenated fat. However, good-quality white chocolate is made with cocoa butter and has some of the subtle flavor and aroma of the best chocolate.

Cocoa

Since chocolate is composed mostly of cocoa butter and a mixture of flavonoids and other compounds called cocoa liquor, the variations in the best chocolates have to do with the proportions or percentages of each of these compounds. Cocoa has the highest percentage of cocoa liquor and hence can be powdered and be made somewhat dry because it contains so little fat. Most of the best European cocoa has been chemically treated with an alkali intended to take away some of its sharp acidity and harshness. Cocoa that has been processed this way is Dutch-process cocoa. Without this treatment cocoa is said to be natural.

Couverture

You're likely to run into this term in European recipes, and if you buy couverture, or covering, chocolate from a good European maker, it will be made with a high percentage (32 percent) of cocoa butter, which makes it useful for covering candies or other sweets that require a thin coating. In Europe, standards dictate that couverture chocolate have a high cocoa butter content. In America today, much of the chocolate we can buy for eating and cooking meets that cocoa butter standard and is technically couverture.

Compound chocolate

This is chocolate in which the cocoa butter has been replaced with hydrogenated vegetable oil. Many people are fond of this chocolate because it reminds them of candy bars from their youth.

416 How to melt chocolate

If you're melting chocolate with cream or other hot liquids, there's no need to melt it separately—just add the chopped chocolate to the hot liquid and let it sit a minute before stirring until smooth. To melt chocolate alone:

1. Chop the chocolate with a heavy knife.

2. Put the chocolate in a bowl set over a saucepan of barely simmering water.

3. Stir gently with a rubber spatula, scraping down the sides of the bowl as you stir.

Note: In candymaking, the temperature of the chocolate needs to be closely monitored with a candy thermometer (see entry 43).

HINT *While chocolate can be melted with liquids such as cream or milk or even water, keep in mind that if only a little liquid is added to melted chocolate, the chocolate will congeal. Therefore, if you're adding liquid to chocolate, count on adding at least 1 tablespoon per ounce of chocolate.*

417 Can I substitute cocoa for chocolate in recipes?

To convert a cake recipe calling for bittersweet or semisweet chocolate to one using cocoa powder, replace every ounce of bittersweet or semisweet chocolate with 5 tablespoons cocoa, 1 tablespoon sugar, and 2 teaspoons butter. The cake won't be as moist, but if you're brushing it with simple syrup (see entry 215), this won't matter.

HINT *In some cases, such as when making foam cakes in which melted chocolate is being folded with an airy mixture, you can fold in half as much cocoa powder instead of the melted chocolate.*

418 How to get the flavor out of a vanilla bean

Professional bakers sometimes call the vanilla bean "the pastry chef's truffle" because of its deep exotic flavor. But most of us use pure vanilla extract, made by soaking vanilla beans in alcohol, which has a much less complex and beguiling flavor than the whole bean. If you're using a vanilla bean in a hot liquid, just split it in two lengthwise so the tiny seeds, where the flavor is concentrated, can disperse in the liquid. If you're adding vanilla to a dry mixture, split the vanilla bean in half lengthwise and scrape out the seeds with a knife; add the seeds to the dry ingredients.

How to make vanilla sugar

Keep used vanilla bean halves in a container of granulated or confectioners' sugar to infuse and scent the sugar.

419 How to whip cream

We all love whipped cream, but we sometimes resort to a can for fear of making a mess in the kitchen or making butter in the bowl. With a few guidelines, you'll never make a mess again.

• Put the cream in the bowl you're beating it in (along with the whisk you'll be using if you are beating the cream by hand) and stick it in the freezer for 5 minutes. Cream for beating must be very cold.

• When you remove the cream from the freezer, begin to beat it immediately.

• Remember, when cream is cold, it beats very quickly. It will take about 1 minute by hand, less with a stand-up mixer, more with a hand mixer. The exact time depends on how stiff you like your cream whipped—to soft, medium, or stiff peaks.

Whipped cream stages

• **Soft peaks:** The cream gets fluffy but runs off the whisk or beaters when you lift them.

• **Medium peaks:** The cream clings to the whisk or beaters but sags.

• **Stiff peaks:** The cream sticks straight out when you hold the whisk sideways or lift up the beaters.

Whipped cream flavorings

• **Vanilla:** Add 1 teaspoon vanilla extract to every 1 cup heavy cream.

• **Chocolate:** Add 1 tablespoon cocoa, worked to a smooth paste with a little of the cream, to each 1 cup heavy cream.

• **Spirits:** Add 1 tablespoon spirits such as cognac, rum, bourbon, or kirsch to 1 cup heavy cream.

• **Orange, lemon, and lime:** Grate 1 teaspoon citrus zest into 1 cup heavy cream.

420   If your whipped cream weeps

A lot of us would use whipped cream to frost cakes, but we've seen that after a few hours, it loses its shape and leaves the cake a soggy mess. The secret to foolproof whipped cream frosting is to work a little gelatin (see entry 105) into it to stabilize it.

1. From 1 cup heavy cream, combine 2 tablespoons of the cream with 1½ teaspoons (½ packet) gelatin in a small bowl set over a pan of simmering water.

2. Whisk gently until the gelatin dissolves. Take the bowl off the heat.

3. Whip the rest of the cream just until it is a little less stiff than you want the final cream to be. Whisk or beat the gelatin mixture into the cream.

4. Whisk or beat briefly, until the cream has the consistency you desire. Use the cream right away to frost a cake. Keep the cake in the refrigerator until you serve it; it will stay for several days without the cream breaking down.

421   What is soft-ball syrup?

Pastry chefs and candy makers often cook sugar with water into hot, concentrated syrups. This syrup, cooked to the soft-ball stage, is used for making buttercream frostings, white fluffy frostings, and certain types of ice cream.

HINT *If a syrup is allowed to firm beyond the soft-ball stage, it is called hard-crack and then, eventually, caramel (see entry 464).*

1. Combine 1 part water with 2 parts sugar in a saucepan. Bring to the boil.

2. Dip a spoon handle into the boiling syrup and then immediately into a glass of cold (not ice) tap water.

3. As the syrup concentrates, it first forms threads. As the threads firm and start to look a lot like chewed gum, the syrup achieves the soft-ball stage, which is the stage most often called for in recipes.

422 How do I choose a cake pan?

Most round or square cake pans come in standard sizes of 8, 9, and 10 inches across and at least 1 inch deep. While most layer cake recipes will do fine in any of these sizes, the material any pan is made of will make a difference. Aluminum or another very conductive metal is the best choice because it encourages heat penetration, while pans made of shiny metal, such as stainless steel, reflect heat and discourage conductivity.

Nonstick cake pans are now available and they are the best choice. When baking in a nonstick cake pan, butter and flour the pan anyway because the butter and flour form a delicate buttery crust that adds to the cake's flavor.

Volume of baking pans

Round pans

8 × 2 inches = 7 cups
9 × 2 inches = 8 cups
10 × 2 inches = 10 cups

Square pans

8 × 8 × 2 inches = 8 cups
9 × 9 × 2 inches = 8 cups

Springform pans

9 × 2½ inches = 10 cups
10 × 2¾ inches = 15 cups

Loaf pans

8½ × 4½ × 2½ inches = 6 cups
9 × 5 × 3 inches = 8 cups

Half sheet pans

13 × 17 × 1 inch = 6 cups

Tube pans

10 inches = 12 cups

423 What's the best cake pan?

A springform pan eliminates any worry about the cake sticking to the pan, since you can run a knife around the sides and along the bottom just over the base to detach and lift out the cake. You can also frost the cake by first placing it on the base of the springform pan and then holding it level from the bottom. Or you can assemble the cake in layers in the springform pan so the cake ends up with perfectly smooth and even sides.

cakes, batters, and custards

424 How much batter to make

A recipe designed to make one 9-inch round cake can be spread into a half sheet pan (13 by 17 inches) to make a thin cake suitable for layering or rolling. To make a thicker sheet cake, suitable for serving right out of the sheet pan, double the recipe.

425 How to fold heavy mixtures with airy mixtures

Recipes often call for folding heavy ingredients or mixtures such as melted chocolate or thick béchamel sauce with airy mixtures such as beaten egg whites.

HINT *If you've folded a mixture such as chocolate mousse and find at the end that it has lumps, these can be hard to eliminate. If your mousse has lumps or little bits of chocolate in it, disguise them by adding coarsely chopped walnuts or other nuts. No one will notice the lumps.*

1. Beat about a fourth of the light mixture into the heavy mixture to lighten it.

2. Pour this mixture over the egg whites. Cut into it with a rubber spatula and literally fold it into itself.

3. Invariably the heavy mixture will try to hide on the bottom of the bowl, but you'll remember to slide the spatula along the bottom of the bowl and keep lifting it and folding.

426 How to make a pound cake

The simplest butter cake is a pound cake, made by beating together sugar and butter for a very long time (this is important to do and is often ignored) to incorporate air into the butter. Eggs are added to the mixture, beaten for a while, and then flour is worked in just long enough to incorporate it.

1. Preheat the oven to 325°F. Butter and flour two 8 x 4 x 3-inch loaf pans.

2. To make 2 loaves, beat 2 sticks softened unsalted butter with 1½ cups sugar until light and creamy for 5 minutes.

3. Beat in 5 eggs, one by one.

4. Flavor with pure vanilla extract or lemon zest.

5. Work in 2 cups all-purpose flour just until smooth.

6. Bake until a skewer or cake tester comes out clean, about 1 hour.

What if your pound cake looks raw in the center or is heavy?

If your pound cake has a glossy, raw-looking patch in the center of each slice, no matter how long you cook it, or your butter cake is inexplicably dense, you're not beating the sugar and butter together long enough at the beginning. Always beat for 5 minutes on medium to high speed in a stand-up mixer until the mixture is very light and fluffy.

427 How to make a sponge cake

Sometimes called a génoise, a sponge cake is made by beating eggs with sugar until frothy and light and then folding in flour and melted butter. It's lighter than pound cake and useful for making layer cakes or rolled cakes.

1. Preheat the oven to 350°F. Butter and flour one 9- to 10-inch round cake pan.

2. Combine 4 warmed eggs (see Hint) with ½ cup plus 2 tablespoons sugar.

3. Beat until tripled in volume and somewhat stiff.

4. Sift over ½ cup cake flour while folding.

5. Fold in 3 tablespoons melted unsalted butter (optional).

6. Pour the batter into the cake pan. Bake until the center bounces back to the touch, about 25 minutes.

HINT *To warm eggs, put whole, unbroken eggs in a bowl of hot tap water. This is easier than warming them after they've been cracked.*

Tips for sponge cake

• Sometimes the butter is left out to make the cake lighter; sometimes more than the usual small amount of butter is added to make the cake more flexible so it can be rolled.

• Hot heavy cream is also sometimes added to make a sponge cake moist and flexible—perfect for rolling.

• A chocolate génoise includes cocoa powder added at the same time as the flour.

428 How to make an angel food cake

Angel food cake is essentially meringue (sweetened beaten egg whites; see entry 430) that has had flour folded into it and then baked. Angel food cake has a lovely spongy texture, really more spongelike and "bouncy" than a so-called sponge cake (see entry 427). Angel food cake also contains no fat, making it a healthy and "safe" dessert option.

1. Preheat the oven to 350°F.

2. Combine ½ cup sugar, 1 cup cake flour, and ¼ teaspoon salt in a bowl and set aside.

3. In a mixing bowl, beat 16 egg whites to medium peaks.

4. Add 1¼ cups sugar and beat to stiff peaks.

5. Fold the flour mixture into the egg whites.

6. Fill one 10-inch ungreased tube pan with the batter and bake for about 1 hour.

429 How to make a dump cake

This is an easy, foolproof cake that can be made in a sheet or in rounds. It's also known as a high-ratio cake—the ratio of sugar to other ingredients is high.

1. Preheat the oven to 350°F. Butter and flour the cake pan(s).

2. Combine 2 sticks cold, sliced, unsalted butter with 1½ cups sugar and 2 cups all-purpose flour, using a stand-up mixer set on medium speed. Beat until the batter breaks up into pieces the size of baby peas.

3. Add 5 eggs and pure vanilla extract or lemon zest all at once and beat just long enough to make a smooth batter.

4. Bake for about 1 hour, until a skewer or cake tester comes out clean.

430 What's a meringue?

Meringue is made with sugar and beaten egg whites. The simplest technique is to beat the sugar into the whites. This meringue can be piped out into cookies on a parchment-lined sheet pan and slowly baked. The rounds of meringue can then be stacked like the layers of a cake. The fluffy frosting in entry 439 is essentially an Italian meringue.

Nut meringue

Also called dacquoise, this cake is made by folding chopped roasted hazelnuts or almonds into beaten egg whites before the mixture is piped onto a parchment-lined sheet pan and baked slowly.

431 How to make a cheesecake

There is some question as to whether a cheesecake is a cake at all, because it's essentially a custard held together with eggs as all custards are. An example is the Jewish-style cheesecake, a simple custard of cream cheese and sour cream, flavored with vanilla and set with eggs.

1. Preheat the oven to 300°F. Butter a 9-inch springform pan.

2. Beat two 8-ounce packages cream cheese with 1 cup sugar, 4 eggs, and 1 teaspoon pure vanilla extract. When smooth, beat in 3 cups sour cream.

3. Pour the mixture into the pan and set it in a roasting pan filled with enough very hot tap water to come halfway up the sides.

4. Bake until set.

5. Leave the cake in the oven, turn off the heat, and let cool with the oven door open.

How to know when custard cakes are set

Rather than risk spoiling the look of your cake by poking at it with a knife, gently move the pan holding the cake back and forth while watching the surface of the cake. When uncooked, the surface will form waves and move back and forth in the dish. As the mixture cooks, the sides will remain stiff and only the center will move. When the center forms no waves and stays still, the cake is ready. (Use the same method to determine when a custard is set.)

432 How to make molten chocolate cakes

The secret to preparing a molten chocolate cake so it is gooey and runny in the middle and at the same time cakelike on the outside is to freeze the custard, in the dishes, before baking. The advantage of this is obvious—you can freeze the cakes up to 5 days ahead of time (just make sure they're well covered with plastic wrap) and bake them while your guests or family finish dinner.

1. To make 6 servings, butter six 5- or 6-ounce ramekins with 1 tablespoon softened butter. Coat the insides with cocoa powder.

2. Slice 8 tablespoons (1 stick) butter and put it in a metal bowl with 8 ounces bittersweet chocolate, coarsely chopped. Set the bowl over a pan of simmering water and stir until the chocolate melts.

cakes, batters, and custards

361

3. Beat 4 large room-temperature eggs and ⅓ cup sugar on high speed in a stand-up mixer until the mixture quadruples in volume.

4. Pour the chocolate mixture into the egg mixture. Fold in while sprinkling over 3 tablespoons all-purpose flour.

5. Pour the mixture into the molds, cover with plastic wrap, and freeze.

6. When you're ready to serve, bake in a 450°F oven until the cakes have risen by about half their original height, about 15 minutes.

7. Remove from the oven, sprinkle with confectioners' sugar, and serve.

433 How to make baba au rhum

Baba and savarin are essentially breads that are soaked in a light simple syrup (see entry 215) flavored with rum or another spirit. They have the sweetness of a cake and the moistness of a custard. A baba traditionally is shaped like a cylinder and has a domed top. A savarin is made with the same batter, but it's baked in a large ring mold.

1. Soak ½ teaspoon active dry yeast in 2 teaspoons barely warm water for 5 minutes.

2. In the mixing bowl of a stand-up mixer, combine the yeast with 2 cups all-purpose flour, ½ teaspoon salt, 1 tablespoon sugar, 2 eggs, and ¾ cup warm milk. Work the dough with the paddle blade on medium speed until the dough pulls away from the sides and clings to the blade, about 8 minutes.

3. Add 1 stick sliced butter and continue beating until it disappears, 3 to 5 minutes.

4. Put the dough in a bowl and cover it with plastic wrap; the plastic should touch the dough's surface (or else a crust will form), but it should not be tucked under the dough. Put the dough in a slightly warm place.

5. When the dough has about doubled in size (this should take about 90 minutes), press down on it with your fist to flatten it. Butter twelve 4-ounce baba molds and fill them halfway with dough. Cover the molds loosely with plastic wrap and let rise in a warm place for 30 minutes, or until the dough comes almost to the top of the molds.

6. Preheat the oven to 350°F.

7. Bake until the babas are golden brown and have risen up out of the molds, about 30 minutes. Let the cakes cool in the molds for 5 minutes before turning them out.

8. While the babas cool, combine 2 cups sugar with 2 cups hot tap water and stir until the sugar dissolves. Let the syrup cool to just slightly warm and add ½ cup (or to taste) dark rum, kirsch, or cognac. Transfer the syrup to a mixing bowl.

9. Press the babas down in the syrup for a minute until they are well soaked. Whip 1 cup heavy cream with 1 tablespoon confectioners' sugar and 1 teaspoon vanilla extract until stiff peaks form.

10. To finish the babas, slice them vertically in half and pipe or spoon the whipped cream over the insides.

11. To finish the savarin, pipe or spoon whipped cream into the middle of the ring.

434 How to make a rolled cake

A rolled cake is a thin sheet of cake that you spread with a filling and then roll up. Use any cake recipe, such as a foam cake with extra butter or cream in it, designed to be especially moist; you won't want it to crack when you roll it.

1. In a parchment-lined half sheet pan, bake the same amount of cake batter as for a standard 10-inch cake pan.

2. Set the oven 50 degrees hotter than if you were baking a standard

round cake—about 400°F instead of 350°F—and bake until the center of the cake bounces back to the touch, about 15 minutes.

3. Sprinkle a second sheet of parchment paper with confectioners' sugar, turn the cake over onto it, and peel off the parchment.

4. If the cake seems dry, lightly brush it with a simple syrup (see entry 215), which will keep it from cracking when you roll it.

5. Spread over the filling. Stand at one end of the cake and pinch the end together into a round. Keep rolling tightly to hold the cake together, lifting the parchment that supports the cake as you go.

435 How to stop cakes from sticking

If a cake pan is well buttered and floured, the cake rarely sticks. Before baking, brush the bottom and sides of the pan liberally with softened butter—be careful not to leave any patches ungreased—and coat them with flour by rotating a handful of flour in the pan so it adheres to the sides and bottom. Tap the pan against the work surface to shake out any excess flour. As a further precaution, you can bake your layer cake in a springform pan or you can cut out a round of parchment paper or wax paper the exact size of the bottom of the cake pan. After you brush the pan with butter, put in the parchment round and brush it with butter. Butter the sides of the pan and flour the sides and the parchment as above.

How to work with sheet cakes

Instead of turning a sheet cake onto a cake rack to let it cool, which in turn will cause it to stick, cut a sheet of parchment paper the same size as the cake, dust the paper with confectioners' sugar, and turn the sheet cake out onto the paper. If you lined your pan with parchment paper before baking, peel it off before the cake cools. This leaves the cake with the bottom up, which is usually good since the edges and corners are more even.

436 Telling when a cake is done

Professionals know when a cake is done by gently touching the surface. When the cake feels firm and bounces back to the touch and the finger leaves no imprint, it's ready. Some cooks slide a knife or toothpick into the center of a cake, and when it comes out clean—with no batter or crumbs clinging to it—the cake is ready. Another sign that a cake is done is that a finished cake will pull away from the sides of the pan. However, keep in mind that cheesecake is an exception to this (see entry 431).

How to store cakes

To store cakes in the freezer, wrap them tightly in two layers of plastic wrap and a layer of aluminum foil. They will keep in the freezer for up to 3 months.

437 Frosting a cake on a cake stand

By placing the cake in the center of a revolving cake stand, available at baking supply stores, you can spin the cake around while you apply the frosting. A lazy Susan will also work.

1. Spread the frosting over the top of the cake so that the excess comes down the sides.

2. While holding the spatula vertically against the side of the cake, spin the revolving stand and spread the frosting evenly over the sides.

3. Smooth the top by holding the spatula flat against the rotating cake stand.

HINT *A revolving cake stand makes giving a cake a smooth finish remarkably easy. It is heavy, and the best brands are rather expensive, but it allows you to spin the cake while you are holding a metal pastry spatula—the long, thin kind— against the surface. This is much easier than moving the spatula around the cake if it is on a plate, platter, or decorative but stationary cake stand. If you love to frost and decorate, or if you frost a lot of cakes, you may want to have this kind of professional cake stand. Buy the heaviest cake stand you can afford; the heavier the stand, the better it will stay in place as you work.*

438 Frosting a layer cake on a cardboard round

Generally, home bakers frost their layer cakes on a platter, which makes it very hard to frost evenly. You'll get better results on a cardboard round.

To assemble the layers

Assemble and frost the cake layers on a round of cardboard at least ¼ inch wider all around than the cake, which gives you room to frost the sides. Hold the cake by its cardboard base with one hand, so you can use the other hand and a straight spatula to apply frosting to the sides while rotating the cake as needed. This also allows you to hold the cake at eye level, making even application of the frosting easier.

To frost

1. Put the frosting all at once on top of the cake.

2. Spread the frosting over the top of the cake, working from the center outward, so that extra frosting hangs over the edges; use this to coat the sides and smooth them with a bench scraper or spatula.

3. Smooth the top of the cake, leaving you with more frosting hanging over the edge of the cake to spread along the sides. Alternate between smoothing off the sides and the top of the cake until it is evenly and completely covered.

4. Freeze the cake for 15 minutes to firm up the frosting. Reapply a thin layer of frosting by heating a metal spatula that's at least as long as the cake is wide by dipping it in hot water or waving it over a hot flame. If you've dipped the spatula in water, wipe off the water with a towel. Smooth the cake with the warm spatula.

Using a cake ring or springform pan

You can also construct the layers of a cake in a cake ring or springform pan. Spread the frosting over the layers all the way to the ring or pan so that the sides of the cake will remain perfectly even.

439 How to make fluffy frosting and silky buttercream

If you want a light and fat-free frosting, make a classic Italian meringue by beating soft-ball sugar into beaten egg whites. This recipe makes 10 cups, enough to frost two 4-layer cakes or 3 sheet cakes. However, don't try cutting the recipe in half—the mixture won't get as foamy. When you beat butter into this frosting, it loses volume, so that in fact you'll end up with only just a little over 5 cups.

1. Combine 2 cups sugar and 1 cup water in a saucepan and bring to the boil.

2. Beat 6 egg whites to medium peaks, then reduce the mixer speed to low while the sugar is cooking.

3. When the sugar reaches the soft-ball stage (see entry 421), turn the mixer on high and pour the syrup into the egg whites in a steady stream. Make sure the syrup doesn't touch the beater or the sides of the bowl or it immediately hardens and forms lumps that stay in the meringue.

4. Beat until it stiffens and cools to room temperature.

5. To make silky white buttercream, beat 4 sticks of butter, broken into chunks, into the white fluffy frosting. Beat until stiff and fluffy, about 10 minutes.

440 How to make royal icing

1. Add about 1 cup confectioners' sugar to 1 egg white. Stir with a fork until smooth to make an icing that forms strands when you lift it with the fork.

2. Color the icing with sifted cocoa powder or food coloring, or leave it white.

HINT *One of the easiest, most playful ways to decorate a cake or other dessert is to fill a paper cone (see entry 446) or other piping tool with different colors of royal icing, and then wave the cone over the cake as you squeeze, forming lines and curves reminiscent of Jackson Pollock's "drip" style of abstract expressionism.*

441 How to make crème fraîche

Crème fraîche, double cream, and clotted cream are delicious with berries or other fruits and can be dolloped on scones, galettes, blinis, and pancakes.

When cream is skimmed off the top of fresh milk, it contains native bacteria that, when left to their own devices, especially in a warm place, ferment the milk slightly and turn some of its lactose, a sugar, into lactic acid. The acidity of lactic acid causes the cream to thicken and gives it a tangy flavor. Nowadays most cream is pasteurized so the native bacteria are killed. Fortunately, some brands of sour cream and buttermilk contain the kind of bacteria needed to ferment cream in this way.

If you combine ½ cup of buttermilk or sour cream with a quart of heavy cream and store the mixture in a bowl, covered with plastic wrap, in a warm place for twenty-four hours, the cream will thicken into crème fraîche. If after twenty-two hours the cream shows no sign of thickening, don't despair; it often thickens suddenly just when you're about to give up.

HINT *If after twenty-four hours it doesn't thicken, it may not be warm enough. It should feel just slightly warm when you touch it with one of your knuckles.*

What is double cream?

Besides providing the pleasure of extra richness, double cream can be used to thicken sauces because of the extra butterfat it contains.

1. To make double cream, start out with crème fraîche.

2. Line a wide strainer with a clean kitchen towel and place it over a bowl.

3. Add the crème fraîche, cover with plastic wrap, and let drain for 12 to 24 hours in the refrigerator.

What is clotted cream?

Particularly popular in Great Britain, clotted cream is the part of the cream that floats to the top and congeals. Spooned off the surface, it's jarred and then sold at high prices. Literally, it's the crème de la crème!

442 Whipped cream chocolate frosting

This frosting, which the French call *crème d'or,* or "golden cream," has the same ingredients in the same amounts as ganache (see entry 444), but it is made differently and the result is lighter. Like ganache, it makes an excellent frosting for cakes. For a firmer texture, melt some butter with the chocolate.

1. Melt 8 ounces bittersweet chocolate in a metal bowl set over a saucepan of simmering water.

2. Beat 1 cup heavy cream to medium peaks. When the chocolate is melted, fold it into the cream. Use as a frosting.

443 5-minute buttercream

Buttercream is hard not to love, but it needs to be served at the right temperature. Recipes for professional buttercream call for cooking egg yolks with soft-ball syrup (see entry 421), but an easier way is simply to beat together confectioners' sugar and butter.

Beat 3 sticks butter with 2 cups confectioners' sugar and a flavoring such as melted chocolate, very strong coffee, pure vanilla extract, orange zest, or reduced fruit purees.

A cake coated and filled with buttercream must be at cool room temperature, because in the refrigerator the butter congeals and in a warm room it melts.

How to keep crumbs out of your frosting

When using a spatula to frost a cake, be sure to wipe it on a wet towel each time before you put it back into the frosting. This easy step keeps the spatula from transferring crumbs to the frosting and eventually back to the cake.

A three-layer cake gets filled and frosted with buttercream

444 How to make a ganache

One of the most versatile, quickest, and most useful dessert mixtures is ganache, a word you often see or hear in fine French pastry shops. Usually equal parts melted bittersweet chocolate and heavy cream, ganache can be a sauce to pour over ice cream, a shiny glaze to finish a cake, or a fluffy frosting. Ganache is almost foolproof, but if you're using chocolate with a high cocoa-liquor content, it can sometimes separate. To bring it back together, beat the ganache into a little hot heavy cream. It is as simple as this.

To make sauce

1. In a small saucepan over medium-high heat, bring 1 cup heavy cream to a boil. Remove the pan from the heat.

2. Add 8 ounces coarsely broken pieces of bittersweet chocolate to the pan. Let sit for 5 minutes, then stir with a whisk until smooth.

3. Pour the hot mixture over ice cream or other warm or cold desserts.

To make glaze

Make the sauce as directed in steps 1 and 2 above. Pour the chocolate mixture over the top of a cake and let it drip down all the sides. For a perfect covering, chill the cake and then pour over a second coating. The chocolate will coat the sides smoothly.

To make frosting

Make the sauce as directed in steps 1 and 2 above. Chill the chocolate mixture briefly. Beat the mixture in a stand-up mixer with the whisk attachment until the sauce turns fluffy and pale, about 5 minutes.

445 How to make a paper cone

Professional bakers often use a homemade paper cone for detailed decoration. You can fill a paper cone with different colors of icings to write with or decorate cakes with, or, if don't have an artist within to channel, just wave the cone over the cake and create an abstract effect.

1. Cut out a square of parchment paper and cut it in half on the diagonal.

2. Take one end of the diagonal and turn it inward so that it forms a fold—eventually the tip—in the middle of the longest side of the triangle.

3. Twist the triangle of paper around and fold the paper inward to hold the cone in place.

4. Cut off the tip with scissors or a knife to create an opening.

HINT *If you can't figure out how to make a paper cone or would rather not (and you would not be alone), cut off one corner of a reclosable plastic bag, fill the bag with the icing, close it up, and you are ready to frost.*

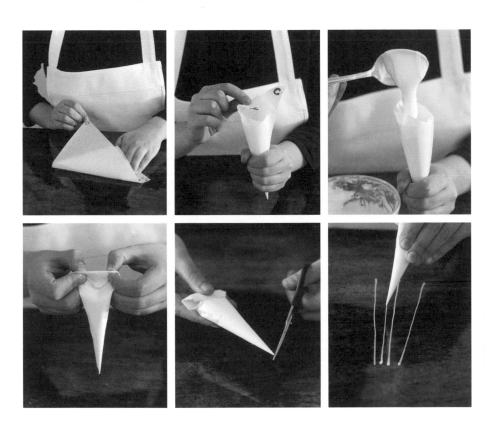

446 How to fill a pastry bag

At first glance, a pastry bag may appear to be a little intimidating, but once you get used to it, you'll find it convenient for many baking tasks, such as decorating cakes or filling pastries such as éclairs.

1. Select the tip you want to use and put it in the end of the bag.

2. Push some of the bag material into the back of the tip with your thumb to clog the hole and keep the filling from leaking out.

3. Fold up from the bottom of the bag about 4 inches to make a sleeve.

4. Hold the bag with one hand by spreading your hand under the sleeve. Fill the bag three-quarters full using a rubber spatula or plastic pastry scraper.

Using a pastry bag to add fillings to a cake

It's sometimes neater and easier to pipe filling onto a cake round than it is to spread it with a spatula.

1. Position the pastry bag tip directly over the middle of the cake.

2. Squeeze gently while working toward the outside in a spiral pattern.

447 Cake decorating tricks

There are any number of methods and little tricks you can use to give a frosted cake a finished, even professional look.

Serrated knife

Use your hands to hold each end of a serrated knife with the blade against the surface of the cake. Bring the knife toward you while gently moving it from side to side, creating a wavelike pattern on the surface of the cake.

Chocolate curls

Chocolate curls clinging to a frosted cake give it a professional look. For small curls, scrape a block of chocolate with the wide end of a pastry bag tip, which is sharp and curved. For larger curls, use a vegetable peeler. If the chocolate is too brittle and doesn't curl, heat it for a few seconds in the microwave. If the curls are too soft and don't hold their shape, let the chocolate cool, or stick it in the refrigerator for a few minutes before you start curling again.

Burned sugar

This simple decorating technique can change an everyday-looking dessert into something special. Sprinkle the cake or pastry liberally with confectioners' sugar. Heat a metal skewer until almost red hot on the stove and burn in lines or a crisscross pattern.

Chopped nuts or cake crumbs

It's often hard to make the sides of cakes look perfectly smooth or appealing. To hide rough or unfinished-looking sides, press roasted chopped, slivered, or coarsely ground nuts against the sides of the cake with your hands. Cake crumbs—made by working cake that's several days old through a strainer or drum sieve—hugging the sides of the cake are a pretty addition and conceal any number of flaws.

Fluffy frosting

You can create a dramatic effect with fluffy frosting (see entry 439) using a spoon after applying the frosting with a spatula. Spread fluffy frosting over the top of the cake. Use the back of a spoon, and with a quick motion, make a shallow indentation in the frosting while pulling the spoon out so that the frosting is pulled up and away from the cake. Do this all over, and the top will look light and fluffy. To add to the effect, put the cake in a very hot oven for a minute or two to brown the edges.

Berries

If you have fresh berries, use them on your cakes. Pipe little rosettes of frosting around the top and bottom edges of the cake. Place colorful fresh berries—raspberries, blueberries, and strawberries are obvious but delicious choices—in the center of each rosette.

HINT *For a really over-the-top finish to your cake, warm fruit jelly and fruit puree in a pan, add gelatin (see entry 105), and pour the mixture over the top of the cake. To hold the topping in place while it sets, ring the top of the cake with a strip of aluminum foil (remove it when the fruit is set). For instance, strawberry jam and strawberry puree will create a beautiful shiny red topping for your cake.*

448 How to give assembled cakes a professional look

Many of us have great success at baking a cake, but when it comes to slicing and layering the cake with frosting, it comes out looking uneven and amateurish. To give your finished cake a professional look, assemble the cake in a springform pan or cake ring lined with plastic wrap. In this way you can use different fillings—even runny liquid fillings such as Bavarian cream, which will be held in place by the cake ring while they're allowed to set. When it's time to unmold the cake, soak a towel in hot tap water, wring it out, and wrap it around the cake ring or springform pan. Hold it for 30 seconds and push the cake out from the bottom. You can also use a blow torch along the sides, taking about 30 seconds to go around the cake. Push from the bottom and watch it emerge.

449 How to make crepes

One of the great things about crepes is that they can be made ahead of time—just separate them with a sheet of wax paper to keep them from sticking, wrap them tightly in plastic wrap, and refrigerate or freeze until needed, a week in the fridge, a couple of months in the freezer. While the ideal pan is a flat nonstick crepe pan, any nonstick sauté pan will work. Electric crepe makers are available at gourmet stores.

To make the batter

1. To make about a dozen 7-inch crepes, add enough eggs to a cup of flour—usually about 5—to allow you to make a stiff but smooth paste.

2. Add enough milk, a little more than a cup, and whisk to give the batter the consistency of heavy cream. Add 3 tablespoons melted butter.

3. If the batter is still lumpy, strain it.

To cook the crepes

1. Heat 1 to 2 teaspoons butter in a nonstick pan over medium heat.

2. Ladle in just enough batter to cover the pan with a thin layer.

3. Cook until crispy on the edges and pale brown on the bottom.

4. Pinch the far edge of the crepe, lift it, and flip it over. Cook for 1 minute more on the second side.

Crepe fillings

Sweet fillings can be as simple as a little sugar and butter, jam, Nutella (found in most supermarkets), Grand Marnier or other liqueur, or ice cream. Savory fillings can include creamed turkey or chicken, cheese, ham, or mushrooms.

450 How to make a clafouti

A clafouti is a kind of crustless tart, made by baking berries or other fruits—cherries are traditional—in crepe batter. Bake clafoutis in a porcelain or glass tart or quiche dish, not in a metal tart pan with a removable bottom, which would let the batter leak out.

HINT *Some fruits such as pears, apricots, and peaches are best preroasted with sugar and butter. You can add the liquid left in the bottom of the pan to the crepe batter.*

1. Sweeten a crepe batter with a little confectioners' sugar.

2. Arrange the fruit in a tart dish and pour over the batter.

3. Bake at 350°F until the clafouti sets and is golden brown, about 40 minutes.

A quick and easy batter for crepes and clafoutis

To make a cup of crepe batter, combine ½ cup flour with 2 large eggs and stir until smooth. Add ½ cup of milk or enough so the batter has the consistency of heavy cream. Add 3 tablespoons melted butter.

451 How to make blinis

For a special brunch or even dinner, consider the elegant pancakes known as blinis. Blinis are yeast-leavened pancakes, traditionally made with buckwheat flour and served with caviar or smoked salmon. Refined recipes call for folding the leavened batter with beaten egg whites, but this isn't really necessary.

1. Make the crepe batter in entry 449, but use warm milk and add ½ teaspoon dried yeast to it.

2. Leave in a warm place until the batter bubbles up and rises by at least 50 percent.

3. Cook like pancakes.

452 Pancakes without a mix

Pancake batter is almost identical to crepe batter except that it contains baking powder. Baking powder produces carbon dioxide when it is moistened, which is what makes pancakes rise. If you find yourself without a mix, make your own.

The batter

To make enough batter for about a dozen small pancakes, make the crepe batter in entry 449 but include ¾ teaspoon baking powder in the flour and add only enough milk to give the batter a thick but spreadable consistency.

To cook the pancakes

1. Heat 1 tablespoon butter in a nonstick pan or griddle, over medium heat, until melted and frothy.

2. Ladle in the pancake batter according to the size pancakes you like.

3. Cook over medium heat until bubbles form and begin to break. Turn over the pancakes.

4. Cook until golden brown on the second side.

453 Waffles without a mix

The secret to light, airy waffles is to separate the eggs, beat the whites, and fold them with the rest of the ingredients just before cooking. To make enough batter for 4 large waffles, stir together 2 cups flour, ½ teaspoon baking powder, and ¼ teaspoon salt. Separate 4 eggs, add the yolks to the flour mixture (don't stir yet), and beat the whites to stiff peaks. Melt 8 tablespoons (1 stick) of butter and add it to the flour mixture with 1 cup milk. Stir the batter until smooth and add another ½ cup milk. Fold with the beaten egg whites. Brush the waffle iron with melted butter before cooking the waffles.

cakes, batters, and custards

383

To cook the waffles

1. Preheat the waffle iron according to the manufacturer's instructions.

2. Brush the waffle iron with melted butter.

3. Ladle in enough batter to cover the bottom and come within ½ inch of the sides.

4. Close the waffle iron. Cook until you no longer see any steam escaping from the iron. If the waffle threatens to stick when you open the iron, it's not quite done. Give it another minute or two of cooking.

454 How to make popovers

Cooks are often mystified (and amazed) by popovers because there's no air in the batter. There's really no great skill required to make them. Serve popovers for breakfast as soon as they come out of the oven. Pass jam, maple syrup, butter, or honey to spread over the hot pastries.

1. Preheat the oven to 450°F. Put the popover pan in the oven to warm it. When it's hot, oil the pan.

2. Using the crepe batter from entry 449, fill the pan about half full. Immediately close the oven door and bake until the pastry is puffed and golden brown, about 12 minutes.

3. Turn the oven down to 300°F. Bake for 10 more minutes.

4. Serve piping hot from the oven.

HINT *Use the heaviest popover pan you can find so it can deliver a lot of heat as soon as you add the batter. If you don't have a heavy popover pan, you can use nonstick muffin tins,*

*preferably a few of them. Ideally, stack several tins, one fitting
in the other, in order to thicken them. This way there's more
hot metal surrounding the batter at the moment you pour it in
the pan.*

455 How to make cream puffs

Everyone likes cream puffs, especially when they are made just hours
before serving.

1. To make 12 large cream puffs, combine 2 cups water, 16 tablespoons (2 sticks) unsalted butter, and 1 teaspoon kosher salt in a
   saucepan over medium heat.

2. When the butter has melted, add 2 cups all-purpose flour. Stir
   with a wooden spoon over high heat until the mixture comes
   together, about 2 minutes.

3. Transfer to a mixing bowl and, one by one, work in 9 eggs, until
   when you drag a wooden spoon through the batter, the sides of the
   indentation close in and touch. If they don't, work in an egg white,
   or more if needed.

4. Preheat the oven to 400°F.

5. Line 2 sheet pans with parchment paper held in place in the corners with a little of the batter. Pipe out mounds about 3½ inches
   across and 1½ inches high in the middle with at least 4 inches
   between each mound.

6. Beat 1 egg with 1 teaspoon salt and brush the tops of the mounds,
   at the same time smoothing them.

7. Bake until golden and puffed, 15 to 20 minutes.

8. Turn down the oven to 275°F. Bake for 30 minutes more to cook
   them through.

9. Let cool for 30 minutes.

For the cream in the "cream" puff

Beat 2 cups heavy cream with 2 tablespoons sugar and 1 teaspoon pure vanilla extract to stiff peaks (see entry 419). Cut the cream puffs horizontally in half, fill the bottoms with whipped cream, and replace the tops.

456 How to make muffins

Muffin batter is a kind of thick crepe batter that's, of course, baked in muffin tins.

HINT *Add roasted chopped nuts, fresh berries, chopped fresh or dried fruit, or a mixture to the batter before baking.*

1. Preheat the oven to 400°F.

2. To make about 24 muffins, combine 1¾ cups flour with ½ teaspoon salt and 2 teaspoons baking powder.

3. Whisk together 2 eggs, ½ cup melted butter, and ¾ cup milk.

4. Quickly whisk together the two mixtures and fill greased muffin tins or tins lined with muffin cups about two-thirds full with batter.

5. Bake until puffed and lightly browned, 12 to 15 minutes.

457 Custards—sweet, savory, and versatile

A custard is a mixture that usually contains milk or cream, is combined with eggs or egg yolks, and gently cooked until it sets.
- Quiche fillings (see entry 128) are savory custards.
- Crème brûlée (see entry 461) and pot de crème are custards made with cream and egg yolks.

- Panna cotta is a light custard containing gelatin (see entry 105).
- Crème caramel (see entry 464) is a custard made with whole eggs.
- Crème anglaise (see entry 465) is a custard made with milk, sugar, egg yolks, and vanilla and stirred on the stove until it thickens into a silky sauce.

To make up your own custards

Remember that a whole egg or two egg yolks set ¾ cup liquid.

1. To make 1 quart custard, combine 3 cups liquid with 4 whole eggs or 8 egg yolks and flavorful ingredients such as cheese for savory custards, or chocolate, coffee, vanilla, or fruit purees for sweet custards (see entry 459).

2. Bake in a slow oven in custard cups or ramekins placed in a baking dish containing enough hot water to come halfway up the cups (see entry 458). The custards are set when they no longer make little waves on top when you shake them gently.

458 What is a water bath?

A water bath, or bain-marie, prevents sudden changes in temperature, which would have dire results when baking custards, soufflés, and other delicate mixtures. You can use a high-sided baking dish or a roasting pan as a water bath. Fill it with enough hot water—usually the hottest tap water is good—to come halfway up the sides of the dish(es) of whatever is being baked.

459 How to flavor a sweet custard

Instead of relying on recipes or exact amounts for flavoring custards, it's more reliable to flavor to taste.

• **Chocolate custard:** Beat cocoa powder with the eggs and sugar or melt chocolate directly in the milk or cream.

• **Coffee custard:** Infuse ground dark-roast coffee in the hot milk or cream and then strain it out.

• **Vanilla custard:** Use a whole vanilla bean, cut in half lengthwise, to infuse the milk.

• **Fruit custards:** Add strained fruit puree directly to the hot milk or cream.

• **Ginger custard:** Whisk powdered ginger with the egg yolks or whole eggs or grate fresh ginger into the mixture and strain it out before baking.

• **Kirsch custard:** Add the kirsch as late as possible so the aroma doesn't cook off. When flavoring crème anglaise, make sure the sauce is completely cold before adding spirits.

460 How do I know when a custard is done?

To check doneness, jiggle the custard back and forth and watch the surface. When the custard is barely cooked, the surface will move back and forth. As the custard cooks, the edges of the surface will stiffen but the center will still move. When the center stops moving, the custard is done. If you're baking a tray of custards, check several because they can cook at different rates in different parts of the oven.

461 How to make crème brûlée

1. Make a custard with heavy cream, egg yolks, and sugar and flavor it with vanilla, chocolate, coffee, or fruit.

2. Bake it gently in individual shallow dishes so it ends up in a layer no thicker than an inch. Let cool.

3. Sprinkle granulated sugar over the top of the set and cooled custard to form a thin even layer.

4. Melt the sugar with a blow torch or under the broiler until it browns and turns shiny.

462 How to make dulce de leche

1. Take one (or more) can of Eagle brand condensed milk and put it, unopened, in a pot of water. Bring the water to a boil.

2. Boil gently for 3 hours, adding more water to the pot as necessary.

3. If you're serving dulce de leche as a sauce, open the can and pour its contents into a bowl. If you're layering it into another preparation, use it while it's still hot.

4. To serve dulce de leche on its own as a creamy dessert, chill the can in the refrigerator, cut off the ends, and push the now firm dulce de leche through the can onto a platter. Slice it and serve it on plates with a dollop of whipped cream.

What are condensed and evaporated milk?

Don't confuse these two; they are not substitutes for each other. Evaporated milk is milk that has been, in essence, partially dried out—half its water content has been processed out and no sugar has been added. Sweetened condensed milk is milk that has half the water boiled away and has had sugar added to it. South Americans like to add condensed milk to their coffee, but the best use for it is dulce de leche. This butterscotchlike, rich, sweet dessert or sauce (it can be either, depending on its temperature) doesn't contain eggs but behaves, especially when cold, as though it does. When the dish is made by hand, the process is long and laborious, but the preceding method is as easy as boiling water.

463   How to make caramel

Caramel is simply sugar that's been melted and cooked until it turns deep reddish brown and acquires its distinctive flavor. Homemade caramel is easy to make and much tastier than anything you can buy in bags from the supermarket. Most recipes for caramel call for combining sugar and water, but this is unnecessary because, for the sugar to caramelize, the water has to evaporate.

1. Put sugar—at least ½ cup—into a small heavy-bottom saucepan with a shiny, not dark, bottom (so you can see the color of the caramel) and stir it with a wooden spoon over medium to high heat until the sugar melts.

2. When the sugar turns dark red-brown and has no more lumps, stop the cooking by dipping the bottom of the saucepan in a bowl of water for 1 second—longer and the caramel will congeal.

To make caramel syrup

To make 1½ cups caramel syrup, melt 2 cups sugar in a saucepan and cook as directed in step 1 above. When it reaches the caramel stage, don't dip the bottom of the saucepan in water. Stand back and add 1 cup water, a little at a time to avoid spattering, to the hot caramel. Bring the syrup to a boil and stir constantly until the mixture is smooth.

To make caramel sauce

Follow the directions for caramel syrup, using heavy cream instead of water.

How to make butterscotch

Butterscotch is similar to caramel except that it also contains butter that has been caramelized. It's great over ice cream or with roasted fruits such as apple and pear. When serving apple or pear sections with butterscotch, roast the fruit with the sugar and butter called for here and when it browns, add the cream.

To make 1½ cups butterscotch sauce, caramelize 1 cup sugar and add ½ cup water. Boil until evenly dissolved into a caramel syrup. Add 8 tablespoons (1 stick) butter and boil until the mixture is frothy and deep brown, and it has a distinct nutty aroma, about 5 minutes. Add ½ cup cream—stand back, it spatters—and boil just a second, until you get a smooth sauce.

464 How to make crème caramel

Crème caramel is a delightful and much less rich alternative to crème brûlée. Making the caramel and using it to line the bottoms (the eventual tops of the custards) of the ramekins is both the key and the trick.

1. Pour enough caramel (see entry 463) into 5-inch ramekins to form a thin layer on the bottom.

2. Make a custard mixture by pouring hot milk into eggs beaten with sugar (see entry 457).

3. Pour this into the molds and bake in a water bath (see entry 458).

465 How to make crème anglaise

Crème anglaise makes a magnificent sauce for fruit desserts and cakes. It is also used as the base for more elaborate preparations such as Bavarian creams, which are essentially crème anglaise and whipped cream set with gelatin. Crème anglaise, basically liquid custard, is scary to make because if it gets too hot, it turns into scrambled eggs, and determining when it's done is a little tricky. But don't be deterred. Instead, remember that the worst that can happen is that you ruin a batch. If you make it several times and you study it carefully, you'll recognize when it's done. Crème anglaise is kept liquid by being stirred instead of being allowed to set.

1. To make 1 quart of sauce, bring 3 cups milk with a split vanilla bean or other flavoring to a simmer. Whisk 8 yolks with ⅔ cup sugar until pale.

2. Pour half the boiling milk into the yolk mixture, stir well, and pour the yolk mixture into the saucepan.

3. Cook over medium heat, stirring constantly with a wooden spoon, until it thickens—sometimes within seconds.

4. Continue stirring for a couple of minutes off the heat so the heat retained in the pan doesn't overcook it.

5. Allow the crème anglaise to cool at room temperature for about an hour. Then either refrigerate it or chill it in a bowl of ice.

How to tell when crème anglaise is done

Crème anglaise is just custard (see entry 457) that's kept liquid by being stirred instead of being allowed to set. There are two methods for telling if the crème anglaise is ready.

WOODEN SPOON METHOD

Most recipes recommend dipping a wooden spoon into the hot crème anglaise and then drawing a line with your finger across the spoon. If the line stays in place, the custard is ready. Usually what happens is the crème anglaise boils over while you study the spoon.

RIPPLES METHOD

A more reliable method is to watch the ripples that form on the surface of the crème anglaise while you stir it with a wooden spoon or spatula. At first there will be lots of fine ripples; when these turn into smooth, silky waves, the crème anglaise is done. Continue stirring for a couple of minutes off the heat so the heat retained in the pan doesn't overcook the sauce.

466 How do I make chocolate pudding?

Pudding is made like crème anglaise—by thickening milk with egg yolks on the stove—but it also includes cornstarch, which helps it stiffen when it cools.

1. Prepare crème anglaise (see entry 465), but whisk 3 heaping table-spoons unsweetened cocoa powder and 3 level tablespoons corn-starch into the egg yolks before adding the milk.

2. Pour the hot pudding mixture into individual serving dishes and let cool at room temperature. Refrigerate before serving.

467 How to make a simple frozen soufflé

A frozen soufflé isn't really a soufflé in the sense that it's baked and puffed up from the heat of the oven. Instead, it is made by filling paper-lined soufflé dishes with a mixture of fluffy frosting and strained cooked-down fruit puree. For individual servings, prepare in small ramekins, as described below.

1. Make fluffy frosting (see entry 439). Fold in 1½ cups strained fruit puree.

2. Fold a strip of wax paper so the strip is about 4 times the width of the ramekin and about twice its height. Wrap it around the ramekin and attach with a paper clip or rubber band. Prepare 5 more ramekins this way.

3. Fill the ramekins with the fruity meringue; the mixture will come about an inch over the edge of the ramekin. Freeze for at least 3 hours or up to a couple of weeks. If freezing for longer than a few hours, remove the collars after the mixture has hardened in the freezer and wrap tightly in plastic wrap before putting back in the freezer.

4. Sprinkle with confectioners' sugar and pull off the paper before serving on dessert plates.

Food would be dull indeed if we had nothing to drink with it. A simple pitcher of lemonade or ice tea or an old Burgundy, each has its place. Mildly alcoholic aperitifs such as

Beverages

lightly sweet wines from Germany, sherry, Campari, or, of course, champagne, are nice before dinner, leaving room for plenty of wine during the meal. After dinner, people serve heavy rich wines such as Port or Sauternes or highly alcoholic digestives such as kirsch, framboise, grappa, or brandy. Liqueurs are a bit sweet for modern tastes, but good to have on hand, along with plenty of water—ideally, sparkling and still.

468 Types of wineglasses

Nowadays, at least in less formal situations, we can get by with one or two sizes of all-purpose wineglasses. If you go this route, opt for larger sizes—a glass is rarely too large for a wine—and avoid glasses with ugly rims. If you like the ritual of an assortment of glasses, here are some choices:

• **Small short glasses for sherry or champagne:** Most connoisseurs of fine champagne prefer to drink it in a wineglass rather than a flute so the aroma of the wine is captured in the glass. These glasses are also good for sherry, Madeira, or semisweet wines served as aperitifs or with cheese.

• **Bowl-shaped glasses:** Large bowl-shaped glasses are traditionally used to serve Burgundy. If your guests are so attuned, you can tantalize them by setting out glasses that hint at the upcoming wines.

• **Small tulip glasses:** These are usually associated with Alsatian wines, Rhine wines, or Moselles. In less formal settings, the classic green-tinted glasses lend a festive note, even if they do distract from the color of the wine.

• **Chimney glasses:** While not associated with any particular kind of wine, these glasses concentrate the aromas of wine and are good all-purpose glasses for fine red wines.

Bottle colors and shapes

If your host is teasing you and trying to make you guess the wine, take a hint from the bottle. Bordeaux, cabernet, and merlot are bottled in straight-sided bottles that come to a sharp shoulder. Burgundies, Rhone wines, Beaujolais, pinot, chardonnay, and chenin blanc bottles have rounded shoulders. Rieslings from the Alsace and Moselle regions come in green bottles, while Rhine wines—fuller-bodied, usually slightly sweet—are in brown bottles.

469   How to chill wine fast

Fill a bucket with ice and add a couple of handfuls of kosher salt to it. Move the bottle around in the ice water every few minutes and give it a twirl. Rinse off the salt water before serving.

470   The secret to a perfect mixed drink

Keep mixed drinks like martinis and manhattans from becoming watery by chilling the liquor in the fridge for at least a couple of hours before mixing the drink. The cool liquor melts the ice more slowly and so dilutes the drink less quickly. Having your freezer on the coldest setting, so the ice cubes are well below freezing, will also help your drinks.

471   How to pour champagne

The most genteel way to serve champagne to guests who are standing is to set the glasses before them (on a table or tray) and pour the champagne. Don't wait for the bubbles to settle down to pour more into the glass. Instead, pour just a little champagne into each of the glasses. By the time you return to the first glass, the champagne will have settled down so you can pour in the rest of the champagne, which will bubble up less because you're pouring it onto a base of champagne instead of directly into glass.

472 What if I don't have champagne glasses?

All the better! Much of the nuance of a fine glass of champagne is lost when the champagne is served in a flute or, even worse, a coupe glass. Serve your best champagne in a white wineglass large enough for you to fit your nose in. You'll appreciate much more of the aroma and complexity of the wine.

473 Why should I drink beer from a glass?

Many of us just naturally grab a bottle of beer from the fridge or from a bartender and swig it right out of the bottle. However, if you put the beer in a glass first, it will have much more flavor because of the effect of its aroma. You don't have to make a big deal about it, as though you were tasting fine wine. You'll notice it without even trying.

474 Pouring glass to glass without spilling

Be bold. Pour quickly and decisively. If you hesitate, the liquid will run down the side of the glass you're pouring from.

475 How do I make clear ice cubes?

Use hot water. The cloudiness comes from air in the water. Heating the water drives the air out.

476 The world's best eggnog

The secret to eggnog is to make a crème anglaise (see entry 465). This cooks the egg yolks and gives the eggnog a delightful silkiness.

1. For every 2 cups crème anglaise, beat 1 cup cream to medium peaks (see entry 419).

2. Fold the whipped cream into the cold crème anglaise.

3. Flavor to taste with brandy, whiskey, or rum. Grate a little nutmeg over each serving.

477 What liquor to freeze

Eau de vie—clear fruit brandy made from virtually any fruit (kirsch, made from cherries, is the best known)—should be served frozen.

478 How to enjoy coffee

It wasn't so long ago that coffee was served during the meal. This is still sometimes the case at a diner or corner café, but most of us now like wine or water with our meal instead and coffee after. Nowadays serving strong coffee—perhaps espresso, black, with no accompaniments and in demitasses after dinner—after a long series of wines is always welcome, perking up the guests and giving everyone a break from drinking. If you don't have an espresso machine, you can make strong after-dinner coffee with a simple plastic filter and paper filters; use 1 heaping tablespoon of ground coffee per small cup, or more to taste. When making strong coffee, use well-roasted beans, such as French roast, Italian roast, or roasts labeled for espresso. American roast, which is a lighter roast, becomes too acidic when it's made strong. And don't hesitate to serve cream and sugar.

479 How to enjoy tea

Americans are drinking more tea than ever before. It's especially welcome in the afternoon, perhaps accompanied by a little sweet pastry, but for many it's the hot beverage of choice throughout the day.

Tea bags are ubiquitous, but newcomers to tea should realize that the tea in these bags is of a lesser quality. It's better to buy loose tea, which comes in a seemingly infinite variety of grades and styles. Start with a kind you like—then experiment with others!

To make tea from loose tea leaves, you have several choices. You can dump the leaves in the tea pot and then fill it with boiling water; to serve, put a small strainer over the cup and pour through the strainer. Or you can buy a tea ball, in which the leaves are placed, and put that in the tea pot—this avoids having to strain the tea leaves out of the hot brew. Alternatively, smaller tea balls (some in the shape of covered spoons) are available when you just want to make a single cup.

In any case, let the tea leaves steep in the hot water for about 5 minutes. Be careful not to oversteep the leaves, which can result in tea that's too bitter.

480 How to enjoy lemonade

European cafés don't actually make lemonade but instead serve a squeezed lemon in a glass with ice and sugar and water (sometimes sparkling water) on the side This allows everyone to adjust the sweetness to his or her own taste. But if you want to make traditional lemonade, combine the juice of 6 lemons with ¼ cup sugar and enough water to make a quart.

For a more lemony version, peel the zests away from the lemons, blanch them for a minute in boiling water and then cook them with the sugar and half the water at a gentle simmer for 30 minutes. Strain, let cool, and add the rest of the water and lemon juice.

beverages

While many of the old-fashioned rules of etiquette are ignored in our fast-paced society, there are still times in restaurants or in other's

Etiquette

homes when a few guidelines can help us come off as polite and sophisticated. Helping someone with a chair or a coat or holding open a door may not seem like a big deal, but at the right moment such touches can make an enormous impression. Try sending a thank-you card after a party and you'll never be forgotten. Here are some guidelines for dining out or hosting a formal dinner party that will keep you looking your best.

481 How to eat in a 4-star restaurant

Although many of the finer points of restaurant etiquette that once prevailed are ignored these days, there are still a few hints that make getting by in a restaurant a little easier.

• When you've decided what you're going to order, put the menus together to the side of the table to signal the waiter that you're ready to order.

• If you get up from the table or you're taking a pause and you don't want the waiter to clear your plate, arrange your fork and knife in the middle of the plate, with the fork turned up in the eight o'clock position and the knife in the four o'clock position. When you've finished eating, arrange both the fork and knife in the four o'clock position with the fork on the left, turned down, and the cutting edge of the knife facing the fork.

If you're still dining   If you're done

• If you get up from the table to go to the bathroom, don't put your napkin on the table; put it on the chair. Otherwise the waiter may think you've left.

• If you're at a large table and plates are being passed, pass from left to right.

482 How to order wine in a restaurant

Ordering wine in a "fancy" restaurant can be intimidating. The best approach is to be honest about what you know and don't know. If you do know something about wine, a good approach is to zero in on two or three wines (or more if there are lots of people and lots of courses), tell the sommelier what you're thinking, and ask what he or she thinks is best. This signals to the sommelier how much you want to spend, so he or she can recommend accordingly, and also says something about your tastes. If you know little about wine, think about wines you've had that stood out. Maybe you were once struck by the fruitiness of a German Riesling or the minerallike quality of a good Chablis. Perhaps you have a preference for New World wines or Old World wines. New World wines tend to have more forward fruit and are usually meant to be drunk young, while Old World wines may be more austere and subtle but may have more identity. To someone used to drinking California white wines, French white wines such as Muscadet, Sancerre, or Chablis may taste acidic and austere. One approach is to tell the sommelier that you want to learn about certain wines. Perhaps you've never tasted wines from Alsace or the Loire valley or a Nebbiolo from Italy.

If there are a lot of people at your table, you have the opportunity to taste several wines. You can ask the waiter or sommelier to serve two similar wines at the same time so your guests can compare. If there are fewer of you at the table, say just two, look for half bottles rather than wines by the glass. Two half bottles instead of one full bottle will give you more opportunity to try new wines, and wines in half bottles will be in better shape than wines by the glass.

About the whole cork thing—the way the sommelier puts the cork religiously next to you on the table—I think it's really quite ridiculous because a cork always smells like a cork. If you're ordering old wine and the cork is crumbling, that might be a signal that the wine has gone bad, but otherwise just leave the cork there. Don't bother with sniffing the wine when ordering champagne: Just have the waiter serve it.

When it comes time to sniff the wine, there are two main things to look for: corked and madeirized wine. Sometimes with wine that is corked (this happens about every twentieth bottle with Old World wines), the wine smells like the cork, a kind of old woody smell that will obscure the fruit of the wine. If you think the wine is corked (or know it's corked), be modest and tell the sommelier you think the wine is corked but you're not sure and what's his/her opinion. Madeirized wine, the second common problem, happens with white wines. First notice the color of the wine. If a white wine (other than a sweet wine) shows signs of browning, it may have madeirized. Such wine is oxidized and smells and tastes a little like sherry and will almost always be slightly brown. If you suspect this, approach the sommelier in the same respectful way.

Wine rarely turns to vinegar, but if you're ordering an old wine, you'll probably be paying a lot of money and you'll want to make sure it is good. When the waiter or sommelier presents the bottle, notice the space between the bottom of the cork and the top of the wine (this is called the ullage). If there's more than the usual space, the wine may be bad. Look at the wine in the glass and notice its color. White wines should be green, gold, or yellow, but not brown; old red wines should be brick-colored, not brown. If the wine is old and brown, it may in fact have oxidized into vinegar or lost all its flavor. If it tastes sour and is brown and thin, send it back, but if it's purple or red and not full of flavor, it may just be "closed in"; if you're in a fine restaurant, ask the waiter to decant the wine to help it "open up."

Many fine restaurants will automatically decant certain wines, which is to say carefully pour them into a decanter. This leaves any sediment in the bottom of the bottle (sediment is normal and even desirable, since it indicates the wine wasn't overly filtered) and helps the wine release its aromas. While traditionally only old wines were decanted, it's perfectly acceptable in a fine restaurant to ask the waiter to decant a young wine to help it develop flavor.

The best advice is to be modest but enthusiastic and involve the restaurant staff in your meal. Let them know you care about wines and want to learn about them (however much you know, there's always something to learn). Don't show off. Be yourself.

483 Which glass goes where?

It's always fun to make an impressive show of an assortment of glasses at each place so your guests get to anticipate an assortment of wines. While you may just have to put the glasses where they fit, traditionally the water glass goes about an inch out from the tip of the main knife. Wineglasses, in the order they're going to be used, are arranged in an arc, to the right of the water glass. A typical order of wineglass would be: dry white wine, Alsatian or German white wine, Burgundy w(balloon), champagne, red wine, and Port or Madeira.

484 How to eat bread

Don't serve yourself directly from the bread basket or plate; put a piece of bread on your butter plate. Tear off bite-size pieces. The same goes for the butter: Don't butter your bread straight from the dish in the center of the table. Transfer a piece of butter to your butter plate and then serve yourself, again a bite at a time, from your own butter plate.

Acknowledgments

The amount of work needed to transform a manuscript into a readable book—even, if I may flatter myself, a relatively clean manuscript—is unimaginable. While I'm able to write quickly, I rely on others to pick up the many loose ends and to clarify the ambiguities that inevitably pop up during such a lengthy project. I've witnessed Ann Bramson and Trent Duffy leaning over the manuscript, pencils in hand, for days at a time, spotting missing details as well as the odd, more or less blatant inconsistency. Debbie Weiss Geline also spent many days, sometimes with me, sometimes alone, pointing out contradictions, uncertainties, and weaknesses, forever at me to refine and verify. Anna Berns was forever at our sides, good humored when good humor wasn't always at hand, providing the missing document, image, or note. Others at Artisan who deserve my thanks include Nick Caruso, Danielle Costa, Jan Derevjanik, Jaime Harder, and Nancy Murray.

On the home front have been Alice Piacenza, who painstakingly identified photos, and Laurie Knoop, who kept the burgeoning chaos of the office, referred to as the "vortex," under some semblance of control. Zelik Mintz, as always, provided love and support.

Index

index